Gerhard Brunzema

His Work and His Influence

Edited by
Thomas Donahue

The Scarecrow Press, Inc.
Lanham, Md., & London
1998

SCARECROW PRESS, INC.

Published in the United States of America
by Scarecrow Press, Inc.
4720 Boston Way
Lanham, Maryland 20706

British Library Cataloguing in Publication Information Available

Library of Congress Cataloging-in-Publication Data

Gerhard Brunzema : his work and his influence / edited by
   Thomas Donahue.
         p.   cm.
   Partly excerpts from previously published works.
   Discography: p.
   Includes bibliographical references (p.) and index.
   ISBN 0-8108-3366-2 (cloth : alk. paper)
      1. Brunzema, Gerhard, 1927–1992.   2. Organ-builders—Germany.
   3.   Organ-builders—Canada.   4. Organ—Construction.   5. Organs.
   I. Donahue, Thomas, 1953-   .
   ML424.B84G47   1998
   786.5'1923'092—dc21   97-25565
   [B]   CIP
                                                                    MN

ISBN 0-8108-3366-2 (cloth : alk. paper)

♾ ™The paper used in this publication meets the minimum requirements
of American National Standard for Information Sciences—Permanence of
Paper for Printed Library Materials, ANSI Z39.48-1984.
Manufactured in the United States of America.

Contents

PART II: THE ORGANS

Figures

Figures 23 through 38 are photographs.
All other figures are line drawings.

BRUNZEMA ORGANS

BRUNZEMA ORGANS OPUS 12

SELECTED PIPE SHADE DESIGNS

Stoplists

AHREND & BRUNZEMA: RESTORATIONS

AHREND & BRUNZEMA: NEW ORGANS

BRUNZEMA ORGANS

Foreword

Gerhard Brunzema left a mark on two continents. In his early days, together with Jürgen Ahrend, he led organ-making in Europe to levels unheard of. In Canada he lifted a major firm with new impulses to remarkable achievements, before being able to take things in his own hands again, endearing himself to numerous sensitive players and countless grateful listeners.

His works will continue to sound his praise—also, I believe, to sound His praise.

Gustav Leonhardt

Preface

From 1954 to 1992, Gerhard Brunzema was involved with the design, construction, and restoration of 431 pipe organs. Of this total, 204 were new mechanical-action instruments, his preferred style. His approach to building new organs was distinctive; that he formulated this approach so early in his career and it proved to be musically successful is a tribute to his judgment. That he was doing exceptional work at a time when there were other prominent builders producing noteworthy organs is a tribute to his skill. In addition, since the question of how to design an organ is one that is immediately met with an abundance of wildly different opinions from builders and non-builders alike, the fact that Gerhard Brunzema maintained his convictions about organbuilding over the years is a tribute to his fortitude.

The purpose of this book is to honor the achievements of Gerhard Brunzema as an important part of twentieth-century organbuilding. Part I is a collection of diverse essays that reveal his approach to organbuilding and how he and his instruments proved to be an inspiration to many people. Part II documents the organs he was involved with during his career. It includes listings of all the organs, information on 68 selected instruments, numerous photographs and line drawings, and the complete technical documentation of one specific organ. Additional material includes: writings and organ proposals by Brunzema himself; a selection of representative designs; listings of sound recordings, video recordings, and photographs; and indices that cross-reference his instruments by location and size.

I wish to offer thanks to Ruth Brunzema for allowing me access to her husband's papers and photographs; to Friedrich Brunzema, for doing translations and providing innumerable details about his father's work; and to Leslie Smith, who worked for many years with Gerhard Brunzema in the Fergus workshop, for contributing considerable insight. For the preparation of several of the photographs, I am grateful to Seal's Camera Store, Auburn, New York. The writing of this book was made possible through a grant from the San Francisco Chapter of the American Guild of Organists. I also note with appreciation the generosity of Davis Folkerts.

The following persons provided additional information: Henry Karl Baker (the Organ Literature Foundation, Braintree, Massachusetts), Jeannette Campbell (Newton, Iowa), Truth Cavanagh (Saint Andrew's United Church, Wolfville, Nova Scotia), John Corrie (Church of Saint Mary the Virgin, Falmouth, Maine), Charles Crutchfield (Saint John's Episcopal Church, Charlotte, North Carolina), Pierre Dionne (Casavant Frères Limitée, St-Hyacinthe, Québec), Thomas Erickson (Red Wing, Minnesota), Marnie Giesbrecht (University of Alberta, Edmonton, Alberta), Carroll Hanson (Iowa City, Iowa), Larry Hoey (Saint Peter's Cathedral, Scranton, Pennsylvania), Mary Alice Kubovy (Omaha, Nebraska), James McNeil (Glace Bay, Nova Scotia), Lawrence Moe (Alameda, California), Stephen Pinel (the American Organ Archives of the Organ Historical Society, Princeton, New Jersey), Joan Ringerwole (Dordt College, Sioux Center, Iowa), Barbara Ritchie (Cedar Rapids, Iowa), Stanley Scheer (Casavant Frères Limitée, St-Hyacinthe, Québec), Shirley Wildeman (Winnipeg, Manitoba), and Rudolf Zuiderveld (Illinois College, Jacksonville, Illinois).

The following allowed access to organs: Ruth Brunzema (Brunzema Organs Opus 23 and Opus 41); Edward Wagner (Brunzema Organs Opus 26); Blessed Sacrament Parish, Kitchener, Ontario (Brunzema Organs Opus 12); Holy Family Church, Toronto, Ontario (Brunzema Organs Opus 27); Saint John's Episcopal Church, Charlotte, North Carolina (Brunzema Organs Opus 28); Williamsburg Presbyterian Church, Williamsburg, Virginia (Casavant Frères Opus 3275); Church of Saint Mary the Virgin, Falmouth, Maine (Casavant Frères Opus 3384); and Saint Peter's Cathedral, Scranton, Pennsylvania (Casavant Frères Opus 3414).

The following material was used for this book:
"Orgelkanon" by Gerhard Krapf. Copyright ©1994 by Gerhard Krapf. Used by permission. Notated using NoteWorthy Composer™, NoteWorthy ArtWare, Inc.
"The Work of Gerhard Brunzema" by Friedrich Brunzema. Used by permission.
Excerpt from "Jürgen Ahrend and Gerhard Brunzema" by Uwe Pape, *The Organ Yearbook* 3 (1972): 24-35. Copyright ©1972 by Laaber-Verlag, Laaber, Germany. Reprinted by permission.
Excerpt from "An Interview with Harald Vogel" by Douglas Reed, *The Diapason* 77 (March 1986): 10-13. Copyright ©1986 by *The Diapason*. Reprinted by permission.
"Apropos New Organs and Restorations" by Peter Williams, *The Organ Yearbook* 5 (1974): 111-114. Copyright ©1974 by Laaber-Verlag, Laaber, Germany. Reprinted by permission.
Excerpts from *The Organ* by Peter Williams and Barbara Owen, from The New Grove® Musical Instrument Series (New York: W.W. Norton, 1988), p. 195. Copyright ©1980, 1984, 1988 by Macmillan Publishers, Ltd. Reprinted by permission.
"Gerhard Brunzema" by Jürgen Ahrend. Used by permission. Translation by Friedrich Brunzema.
Excerpt from "Jürgen Ahrend: An Appreciation" by Fritz Noack in James L. Wallmann and Lawrence H. Moe, editors, *Jürgen Ahrend, Organbuilder: Celebrating Forty Years of His Career (1954-1994)*. Copyright ©1995 by the American Organ Academy. Reprinted by permission.
"In Memoriam Gerhard Brunzema" by Carroll Hanson, *The Diapason* 83 (Aug. 1992): 12. Copyright ©1992 by *The Diapason*. Reprinted by permission.
"Remembrance" by Christoph Linde. Used by permission.
Excerpt from "Gerhard Brunzema: Instrument Builder and Businessman" by Matthew Redsell. Copyright ©1982 by Matthew Redsell. Reprinted by permission.
"Brunzema Organs, Incorporated" by Jan Overduin, *The Organ Yearbook* 15 (1984): 124-129. Copyright ©1984 by Laaber-Verlag, Laaber, Germany. Reprinted by permission.
"In Memoriam Gerhard Brunzema" by Davis Folkerts, *The Diapason* 83 (Aug. 1992): 12. Copyright ©1992 by *The Diapason*. Reprinted by permission.

"Organum Plenum" by Hans Zbinden. Used by permission. "'And the Breath Came into Them, and They Lived': The John Melbye Wagner Memorial House Organ" by Edward Wagner. Used by permission. "An Interview with Gerhard Brunzema" by Craig Cramer, *The American Organist* 19 (January 1985): 12. Copyright ©1989 by the American Guild of Organists. Reprinted by permission of *The American Organist* magazine.

"Castles of the Soul: The Organs of Gerhard Brunzema." A Rogers Community 20 Production. Copyright ©1991, Kitchener, Ontario. Transcript used by permission.

"Chorale Prelude on *Schmücke dich, O liebe Seele*" by Barrie Cabena. Copyright ©1992 by Barrie Cabena. Used by permission. Notated using NoteWorthy Composer™, NoteWorthy Art-Ware, Inc.

Excerpt from *The European Organ, 1450-1850* by Peter Williams. Copyright ©1966 by B. T. Batsford, Ltd. Reprinted by permission.

"The Baldachin Chamber Organ at Schloss Churburg, Schluderns, Italy" by Egon Krauss. Copyright ©1971 by Laaber-Verlag, Laaber, Germany. Reprinted by permission.

"The Covering of Organ Pipes with Pure Tin Foil by Using Epoxy Resin Cement" by Gerhard Brunzema, *ISO Information* 1 (1969): 55-56. Copyright ©1969 by *ISO Information*, D 74348 Lauffen/Germany. Reprinted by permission of Orgelbau-Fachverlag Rensch, D 74348 Lauffen/Germany.

"Unit Organs?" (letter to the editor) by Gerhard Brunzema, *The American Organist* 19 (Jan. 1985): 12. Copyright ©1985 by the American Guild of Organists. Reprinted by permission of *The American Organist* magazine.

"Karl Schuke: A Tribute" by Gerhard Brunzema, *The Diapason* 77 (March 1986): 10-13. Copyright ©1987 by *The Diapason*. Reprinted by permission.

The following supplied photographs and drawings:

The photograph of the Brunzema organ at Pella, copyright ©1982, by Barbara Ashton. Used by permission.

The photographs of the Brunzema organs at Winnipeg and Edmonton, copyright ©1982, by Everett Roseborough. Used by permission.

The photograph of the Edward Wagner house organ, copyright ©1986, by Karen Bussolini. Used by permission. The photograph of the William Humphries house organ, copyright ©1987, by Michael Belenky. Used by permission. All other photographs of Brunzema organs and the portrait of Gerhard Brunzema are from the Brunzema Archives. Used by permission of Ruth Brunzema.

The drawings of Casavant Frères organs are by Jean-Claude Gauthier, from the Casavant Frères Archives. Used by permission of Stanley Scheer.

The drawing of Blessed Sacrament Parish, Kitchener, Ontario, by Leslie Smith. Used by permission.

The drawings of Ahrend & Brunzema organs and pipe shade designs are renderings by the editor, based on material in *40 Jahre Orgelbau Jürgen Ahrend, 1954-1994* and the Brunzema Archives.

The drawings of the Kitchener organ are redrawn by the editor from the originals in the Brunzema Archives.

Gerhard Brunzema
Chronology

1927:	July 6, born in Emden, Germany
1948–1952:	Apprentice and journeyman with Paul Ott, Göttingen, Germany
1953–1954:	Technical high school in Brunswick (Braunschweig), Germany; laboratory work with Dr. Werner Lottermoser
1954:	Partnership with Jürgen Ahrend in Leer, East Friesland, Germany
1955:	Master's degree (Orgelbaumeister)
1960:	Married Ruth Engelhardt
1962:	Lower Saxony State Prize for Craftsmanship; daughter Meta born
1963:	Son Friedrich born
1972:	Tonal director, Casavant Frères, St-Hyacinthe, Québec, Canada
1980:	Formation of Brunzema Organs, Inc., Fergus, Ontario, Canada
1992:	April 7, died in Toronto, Ontario, Canada

Member
Rotary International, 1972–1992
The Presbyterian Church, 1927–1992
Royal Canadian College of Organists, 1972–1992
International Society of Organbuilders, 1960–1992

Part I
THE WRITINGS

✛ 1

Orgelkanon
in memory of Gerhard Brunzema

Text from Psalm 150   *Gerhard Krapf*

Lau - da - te, lau - da - te

Do - mi - num in sanc - to.

Lau -da - te e - um in cor -dis et

or - ga - no. Om - ne, om - ne quod

spi - rat lau - da - te De - um.

❖ 2

The Work of Gerhard Brunzema, I: Germany

Friedrich Brunzema

My father, Gerhard Brunzema, was born in Emden in Eastern Friesland in an area that has a rich and somewhat unique culture. Around Emden, stretching as far as the Dutch province of Groningen, are a large number of historic organs scattered about in smaller villages. Most of the churches in Eastern Friesland are reformed churches; they have very plain white interiors, lacking pictures and ornamentation of any kind. Some of the organs in this area, such as the one in Rysum, date back to the late fifteenth century, and a large number of instruments from the seventeenth and eighteenth centuries have been well preserved.

After serving a very short period as a radar operator for the navy in World War II, Gerhard Brunzema returned to Emden, where an organbuilder was installing a new instrument in his home church. This sparked an interest and a passion for this wonderful instrument that prompted him to build and to restore many organs that bear testimony to his search for excellence.

It is somewhat coincidental that my father and I both did our apprenticeship in organbuilding in Göttingen, where Paul Ott had set up shop. Paul Ott started to build mechanical pipe organs before 1940, which was at the time quite revolutionary. The *Orgelbewegung* or "Organ Reform Movement"—in effect a return to the roots of the organbuilding tradition as developed in the Middle Ages—was something new, as most builders at the time were using some form of electromechanical, pneumatic, or electropneumatic action. Of course the *Orgelbewegung* also brought with itself new ideas as to how the organ should sound. The ideas of the second half of the nineteenth century advocated a warm, mellow sound, and a disposition consisting of many 8′ registers with flutes and strings while keeping mixtures, quintes, and reeds to a bare minimum. The *Orgelbewegung* brought with it a desire to interpret music from the eighteenth century and earlier, which changed the way organs were built. The disposition of the organ changed, becoming similar to organs that were built around Bach's time. People discovered that the historic organs that had slider windchests with one channel per note sounded different from instruments that had a windchest designed in such a way that there was one channel per stop. Mechanical key action was rediscovered: "tracker" organs provided a tactile feedback to the organist that pneumatic or electropneumatic instruments could not give. Mechanical key action often demanded a keyboard that was integrated with the instrument, as long distances posed friction and other mechanical engineering problems that were (and are) difficult to solve. One advantage of the integrated "console" was rapid feedback: one could repeat keys very quickly. Both mechanical key and stop action imposed constraints on the builder that changed the way the instrument was designed and how the instrument looked.

After the war, Germany was rebuilding and many new pipe organs were needed to replace either aging and error-prone electromechanical instruments, or those that had been destroyed in the war. After his apprenticeship, my father became a master organbuilder and set up a shop with Jürgen Ahrend, who had also apprenticed with Paul Ott. The first shop was located in Leer in Eastern Friesland. After a year or so, larger facilities were needed and they moved to Loga near Leer, where a new shop was constructed.

In the next two decades, the firm of Ahrend and Brunzema, as it was called, did some amazing restoration work of historical organs in Eastern Friesland. This restoration work was a good teacher for both my father and Jürgen Ahrend, as both the mechanics of constructing an organ and the tonal ideas could be studied. It was a time of learning, discussion, and experimentation: What was the effect of using different alloys in metal pipes? Could one hear the difference between hammered lead and normal lead? How was one to construct a wind supply to achieve flexible or "live" wind in the instrument?

During this time, my father also began to be interested in the scientific study of organs; in particular, how changes in scaling and construction of pipes could be modeled mathematically. This interest in the acoustics of the pipe organ had already been present when he studied with Professor Werner Lottermoser at the *Technische Hochschule* in Brunswick (Braunschweig).

❖ 3

Excerpt from "Jürgen Ahrend and Gerhard Brunzema"

Uwe Pape

Ahrend and Brunzema are amongst the few builders who have been able to realize a systematic method of work right from the beginning of their activities. All the work done by hand closely follows historical traditions, in such things as the making of chests and pipes, the mechanical systems and the case itself. It is for them obvious to build only slider chest organs with mechanical key and stop-action. Chests are made of solid oak; metal pipes of various tin/lead alloys, often with a high lead content when softer, rounder voicing is called for. Case pipes are generally plated with pure tin foil. . . . Stopped pipes have soldered caps and are given beards for fine voicing.

When possible, pipes stand directly on the chest and receive direct wind. Normally there is no nicking. Jürgen Ahrend's voicing is clear, round and powerful with the Principals, soft and

restrained with Gedackts and flutes; Mixtures, often based on the
1' rank are bright and brilliant. Reeds, prepared and made by the
same firm, are strong, imitating the orchestral trumpet in strength
of tone and in many organs too strong for the plenum. This is especially so, of course, with the horizontal reeds *en chamade*. Heard
as an entity, the organ-sound is balanced and warm, though bright
and powerful; the smaller organs have now and then a more sterile
effect, being poor in mutation ranks. The builders regard a complete 8.4.2. Mixture Principal chorus as the most important part of
the specification, basing it on 8' Principal even in small organs
(though the pipes are stopped in the bass). Next is the strongly
marked flute chorus which, especially on the second manual, has
its own distinct and careful functions; in many cases the "crown" is
provided by Oktav 1'. Mutations are uncommon, both the Quints
and the Tierce—hence the organs' array of fine reed stops.

Most consoles are open and unclosable. Compass is usually
C-f'-f''' . . . and the stopknobs (with their names handwritten on
some thin material) large and manageable. Those of the Rückpositiv are not with the others but, as in old organs, protrude
from the back of the Rückpositiv (Scheveningen, Aurich,
Bremen-Oberneuland). . . . Portable regals and chamber organs
have narrower compass. The keys are plated with ivory and
ebony, occasionally with bone. . . . The action is easy and exact to the touch; trackers and wires of familiar type, rollers usually of wood. The builders find that metal rollers have no advantages over wooden. Brustwerk chests are generally closed.
In Leer (Lutheran Church at Loga) the doors were later sealed
up with wood, on the strength of a comparable Brustwerk by
Christian Vater, while at Haarlem (Baptist Church) the Brustwerk is completely closed and opened only for tuning.

The cases are built on an oak frame and showed at first strong
tendencies toward the Gothic and Renaissance types. Simple forms
with square-angle towers and pipe-flats are countered by oblique
and in-turning curves, especially in churches suitable for such features of design. More recently the cases have been more independent, tending to the straight, square and massive with proportions
achieving elegance, as at Bremen-Oberneuland. The earlier characteristics of strongly profiled cornices, firm lines and case-sides (as
at Veldhausen and Farge) have more recently become less con-
spicuous (Groningen-Helpman, Bremen-Oberneuland, Haarlem).
The cases are very shallow, often only 60 to 80 cm [24 to 32

inches] deep, as at Veldhausen, Leer-Heisfelde, Scheveningen, Aurich, Leer-Loga and elsewhere. This aids the directness of sound, as does the frequently separate pedal-cases (behind the organ at Farge and Aurich, in free towers at Bingum). All the visible parts of the case are ornamented with motifs of fauna and flora (Farge, Scheveningen), although where possible and practical historic cases have been taken over.

Ahrend and Brunzema restore organs only with complete respect for the original instrument and its builder. Probably the most important in recent years are the organs at Marienhafe (East Friesland) and Innsbruck. . . .

On the occasion of the award of the State Prize for Craftsmanship (Lower Saxony, 1962), the firm was described in the citation as follows:

The master organ-builders Jürgen Ahrend and Gerhard Brunzema of Loga have—after learning together at the same time—developed their workshop since 1954, from the smallest beginnings to an efficient concern, whose products are distinguished by respect for the elements of modern organization and by the best practices of the trade.

Because of the rarity of this profession, the Jury found evaluation particularly difficult, not least since a judgment of the visual effects would have been insufficient; the Jury accordingly relied for its recommendation also on the opinions of native and foreign professional experts. It found their evaluations confirmed on visits to the workshop and to organs already built, and by the aural impression of the organs' outstanding tone qualities. The way that applied techniques of the craft lean on the ancient art of organbuilding is shown to have particular advantage in pipe-making; using solid wood for the casework also makes towards full expansion of sound; while exact knowledge of things relevant to the mechanism of old organs and the insight acquired therefrom are a further reason why the playing-action of these organs is held as ideal.

Both young master organ-builders have their work recognized not only by contracts for new organs but also for restoration of valuable old instruments, here and abroad. It must also be emphasized that their economic considerations are defined, without compromise, by the standard of quality.

The Jury recommends that this exemplary mutual accomplishment be distinguished by the award of the State Prize for Craftsmanship, Lower Saxony.

(Chapter reprinted from Pape 1972, 24, 26, 28)

❖ 4

Excerpt from "An Interview with Harald Vogel"

Douglas Reed

The idea of restoring the historical instruments back to their original condition is a twentieth-century idea. . . . And we have the privilege to have very capable organbuilders in our region [East Friesland], among them Jürgen Ahrend, who restored the three Schnitger organs we used for the organ competition [at the third Dollard Festival, 1985]. Jürgen Ahrend has been the pioneer, in the first years together with Gerhard Brunzema, who is now working in Canada. [In 1955], for instance, the organ in Westerhusen has been restored back to its original condition of the first half of the seventeenth century, including the meantone tuning and so on. That's the first time they ever heard a meantone organ. . . . This was unusual back then and has served as the model for the restoration practice for other parts of Germany and Holland. And finally, I think the ideas of *faithful* restoration have been used all over Europe and also the United States, and it all started here [in 1955].

(Chapter reprinted from Reed, 10)

❖ 5

Excerpt from "Apropos New Organs and Restorations"

Peter Williams

Where, for instance, direct restoration is involved, particularly instructive are the recent two-manual works of the former Ahrend & Brunzema at Innsbruck (Hofkirche, Ebert c1550) and Marienhafe, Ostfriesland (Gerhard von Holy [1710]). The Innsbruck organ . . . shows many attempts to return to as "old" a sound as possible, not only in the strong, breathy voicing but in pitch (a' = 445 Hz), compass (C–a", short), small wind-trunk (about 25 cm square cross-section), action etc. The keyboard has been much altered and looks seventeenth-century; it goes without saying that the "original" specification has been reconstructed, including the Hornli Mixtures. Clearly several features must always remain subject to enlightened guesswork, as was the case with the earlier restoration of Marienhafe (1969). The specification there shows several interesting details:

HW   16.8.8.4.4.2⅔.2.2.V-VI.II.III.8
RP   8.4.4.2.1⅓.2.II.8
Ped   pulldowns only
Tremulant (main trunk), 4 bellows, HW/RP (*Schiebekoppel*),
W.P. 63mm
Compass CDEFGA–c′–c‴, pitch almost semitone above a′ = 440 Hz

Both organs have the striking quality of tone first heard at Westerhusen (single-manual, seventeenth century) . . . ; both incorpo-
rate new pipes, sometimes when the original were missing, sometimes when they were thought inadequate. . . . A more healthy
sign of the truthfulness aimed at by such builders as Ahrend &
Brunzema is the avoidance of false over-decoration in the casework itself, [and the avoidance] of dazzling consoles and tidy
stop-knobs.

(Chapter reprinted from Williams 1974, 111)

❖ 6

Excerpt from *The Organ*

Peter Williams and Barbara Owen

From the early 1950s Beckerath of Hamburg and the two Schuke firms of Berlin (East and West) produced organs of strong character, often influenced by old instruments they had rebuilt. . . . Ahrend and his former partner Brunzema (pupils of Paul Ott) continued the trend toward strong-toned organs, omitting mutations and relying on highly coloured flue and reed stops (usually made of hammered metal); old instruments restored by the firm (e.g., at Westerhusen) have a natural, unforced but startlingly powerful, breathy tone. The organ at Westerhusen . . . is a revelation of the musical colour open to a seventeenth-century organist of Friesland and Groningen. The stop-lists seem nondescript; an example by Ahrend & Brunzema (Bremen-Oberneuland, 1966) is

Hauptwerk	16.8.8.4.4.2.Mixtur.8
Rückpositiv	8.4.4.2.1⅓.II.Scharf.8
Pedal	16.8.4.16.8.2

But the sound is far from nondescript, and the idiosyncratic tone of such instruments is well removed from the neo-Baroque anonymity typical of so many organs of the 1950s.

(Chapter reprinted from Williams and Owen, 195)

17

❖ 7

Gerhard Brunzema

Jürgen Ahrend (Translated by Friedrich Brunzema)

The first of April 1946 marked the start of my organbuilding apprenticeship with Paul Ott in Göttingen. At that time, there was only one apprentice in a shop that numbered approximately twelve employees. About a year later, a sympathetic young man with a friendly smile joined us: it was Gerhard Brunzema from Emden. At the time he was barely 20 years old, had been drafted for military service after his senior matriculation, and had been (for very few days) a prisoner of war with the Russian army after the end of the war. He told me that he escaped from drunken and sleeping Russian troops, somehow managed to go westward, and then arrived later in his bombed-out hometown of Emden.

With the goal of taking up some sort of technical profession (engineering or something similar), at first he had started an apprenticeship at the *Nordseewerke,* a shipbuilding wharf, in Emden. The erection of a new Paul Ott organ in the New Reformed

Church in Emden, where he lent a helping hand, led him on another path: that is, to our organbuilding shop in Göttingen.

At Paul Ott's workshop, the training consisted entirely of a craftsman's apprenticeship, during which knowledge of materials as well as the entire rich palette of the craftsmen's fabrication techniques were transmitted to us. We gained theoretical background by attending the trade school once a week together with the cabinetmakers.

In the shop, Gerhard Brunzema did not have it as easy as myself: he was three years older than I, and was therefore no longer in the ordinary apprentice age range. The journeymen were noticeably more reluctant to share their knowledge with him. But one could not hinder his desire to learn more in his own way: his eyes were everywhere, and he stood around many workbenches to gain new knowledge, even if this curiosity was disliked by some.

From the onset, we had a lot in common: exchanging ideas in the shop and also privately. For example, he had a talent for continuo playing. At my parents' house, he accompanied me on the harpsichord while I was playing the flute. From time to time, we also went to the theater together in Göttingen and listened to concerts (mostly organ music). While working for Paul Ott, we often tuned the reeds of the organs in the city together.

Within half a year, we both completed our journeyman's examination, and then often installed new organs together. After I had bought a motorcycle in 1951, we felt more free and organized trips to visit organs and organbuilders. These excursions led us to Denmark, Sweden, the Netherlands, and Switzerland. We got to know many interesting organs, but also important people: Sybrand Zachariassen with important coworkers such as Poul Gerhard Andersen, Weding, and Christensen, or the organists Finn Viderø in Copenhagen and Gotthard Arner in Växjö. In the Netherlands we also saw many interesting organs and organists. Especially important for later times was the meeting of Cor Edskes from Groningen (more about that later). In Switzerland, there were many interesting people, especially the Metzler brothers organbuilders, with their still-active father.

The way that Gerhard Brunzema mastered problems—and I joined him voluntarily in this—can be demonstrated by the following little anecdote. During our summer vacation of 1952, we reached, as almost always unannounced, the organbuilding shop of Metzler in Zürich-Dietikon. It was morning when we arrived; the brothers were friendly and asked us to return at the end of the work day because they were busy. We then visited the organ in the Grossmünster church and searched for an appropriate place to set up our tent for the night. Then we returned to the Metzlers' shop. After a tour of the shop, the evening together became interesting. There was a lot of shop talk and laughter, and we left around midnight. Because there was still a lot to talk about, we decided to meet again at 6 a.m. before work! We only had six hours to erect our tent, sleep, pack, and be on our way again. A breakfast together with bread, cheese, and lots of milk, prepared by the Metzlers' mother, was a friendly farewell after a somewhat strenuous visiting program.

At that time, plans also matured to start our own independent organbuilding shop together. It was especially Gerhard that was convinced that our talents complemented each other well. I was content to be led by his ideas, which were innumerable. In those years we almost always talked about organs and organbuilding, from dawn to dusk.

During the spring of 1953, we came to the decision to start a business. If one knows the saying that East Friesians (and Gerhard was a true East Friesian) only reluctantly leave their homeland for more than a day, then one can understand that East Friesland was the only choice for the location of our shop. There were other important reasons. In East Friesland and in the neighboring Netherlands, there is an enormous quantity of historic organs of the most interesting kind, and consequently a rich area for organ studies and restorations.

In the meantime, I had gotten to know Gerhard's family a little bit, but got very close to his sister Emma, who was married to the young theologian Theo Immer. At the time, they lived in Göttingen. This way, I met especially dear people from East Friesland.

We got closer to our goal when Gerhard left Paul Ott's shop in the fall of 1953 to study one semester in Brunswick. At the *Physikalisch Technische Bundesanstalt* (Physical Technical State Institute) he was able to work with Dr. Werner Lottermoser on acoustical research projects involving pipe organ sound. During this time, I prepared myself for my master's examination.

In the early summer of 1954, Gerhard Brunzema and I started our own organbuilding shop in the small East Friesian town of Leer. In addition to our modest savings, we received some unexpected help: an organ-playing lawyer from Canada, who had liked us for a few years, gave us his new Volkswagen Beetle. Payment for this was expected at some undetermined time later. This was very generous, and for us a big help. With this car we were mobile and also able to transport tools and materials.

We started in a small shop that we rented in the *Großstrasse* in Leer. Gerhard was careful in acquiring the most important tools and the needed materials. Using his self-taught six-finger typing method, he did our correspondence on a typewriter. The logo for the letterhead was designed by his brother, the architect Daniel Brunzema.

I got to know the entire Brunzema family as very caring and helpful people. On many weekends, we rested from the weekly work in Gerhard's parents' house in Emden, where I was always cordially welcome. We often attended the Saturday evening concerts in the New Church, or the church services there. Later when Emma and Theo moved to the village of Hinte near Emden, we went often to their church as well. There, the organ was still pneumatic. It had a case dating from the late Baroque era, and sounded very rough.

Gerhard's family sometimes recalled the catastrophic times experienced during the Nazi era. I learned that Gerhard's father, Dr. Friedrich Brunzema, was one of the few physicians that dared treat Jewish patients. They came secretly at night to see him. This was admirable because it was extremely dangerous. Both parents were true Christians and also led their children on this path. I also learned that many reformed Christians did good deeds during Germany's evil era and refrained from becoming Nazis. I believe and know that Gerhard's father refused to let his children take part in Hitler Youth demonstrations, etc., during Church Service. He was under the real threat of an "examination" testing his "loyalty to the state," a common sanction for those instances. No matter what the outcome of events might be, all of this was extremely dangerous. This spirit, and also a dependable truthfulness, belonged to Gerhard's personality. I have never witnessed him withholding a single penny of taxes from the State, or even paying or receiving anything "under the table."

How did Gerhard Brunzema and I live and manage financially in the first years when money was extremely tight? To strengthen our business was especially difficult, because the little capital available to us was spent on materials and setting up the shop. The depressed prices for organs did not even pay for organbuilding of lower quality. Colleagues around us tried to increase sales by purchasing organ parts or by expanding their facilities. Our idea from the start was completely different: We wanted higher quality. True musical instruments were to be created, sounding as good as historical instruments, and possibly better built. This was the goal that we tried to attain, and it was at first our Dutch neighbors that noticed the change in organbuilding in the small town of Leer. Our work got some exposure thanks to the knowledgeable organ expert Cor Edskes from Groningen. Right from the beginning, we made excursions to many organs with him. He showed and demonstrated where in his opinion sound quality could be found. We kept our ears open, but also saw and measured a lot. This took time, but we were modest and therefore it did not cost a lot of money.

Only after a few years did the prices for instruments improve. We did not use much money privately, bought no clothes, and lived in a simple house, sharing a common room in the attic. Each of us had his bed under the sloping rafters. Water for washing was available from a faucet on the exterior wall of the house, and during wintertime from the basement of the landlord. Often, water would freeze in its bowl in our upstairs room.

In 1955 we traveled to Spain to study the pipe organs of that country, and we brought back two *botijos* or drinking vessels that were introduced to us by a Spaniard in a village. When he recognized how thirsty we were, he led us into his cool clay hut. From a pit in the floor, in a corner of the room, he took a clay vessel with two openings and showed us right away how to drink from it. One holds one of the openings at a distance above the open mouth to drink. This wonderfully cool water was just one of the many lessons that Gerhard and I took back from this country with rich, old traditions. From then on, we always had fresh drinking water during our trip and then in our attic. For years, we ate Friesian black bread with honey, sometimes also with butter. At lunch time, however, we treated ourselves to a warm meal in a nearby inn, which was available at a low price on a weekly basis.

At that time we were often called "A and B," and some Dutch organists gave us the title of "apple juice organbuilders," since we did not care much for alcohol.

Gerhard's dislike of arguments, especially with architects and organists, was evident. Sometimes, however, when he thought that he or we were right, a heated argument could arise and he made his point clearly. In all other cases, he left it up to me to resolve tensions or to get "burned" in a verbal dispute.

In his youth, Gerhard had taken piano lessons. Practice, as he said, happened before school with his mother sitting at his side. This was difficult, because from what I know, most of the six children played piano. His basic knowledge was then supplemented by organ lessons, where he must also have learned harmonization. He could improvise in a very beautiful way, which is most important for organ playing. I recall that my mother once said, "Someone who can play the organ as well as Gerhard must be a good person."

Our business flourished because we produced good results. After three years, we hired two other employees to make pipes in our own pipe shop. Two cabinetmakers, one of which was my own brother, were already helping us.

Gerhard and I worked mostly together, or talked about how we were going to do things. Oftentimes, we had long discussions focused on the topic at hand. I cannot recall any dogmatism at all. After we hired a few people, Gerhard's work included the direction of the office and creating drawings. I was responsible for the planning of the scales and voicing of the pipes. Many things were done together. In addition to this there were many larger and smaller things including travel, excursions, and conferences. Gerhard's opinion on conferences was: "Being part of it is everything." Because I thought differently, I often let him take advantage of these opportunities by himself. I knew that my interests were "in his good hands," be it at symposiums, conferences, or at the State Church business offices.

Gerhard was made for this: He had a sharp mind and possessed maturity and dignity so that people were interested in his views. Details such as clothing were important to him. He was almost always seen in the shop wearing a suit.

My marriage in September of 1957 led to changes in our lifestyles. My wife (to whom, incidentally, Gerhard was distantly related) and I moved to an apartment in the *Kirchstrasse,* where Gerhard was a welcome and frequent guest. It was during this time that we received our first large commissions: Scheveningen, Aurich, and Bremen-Martini.

As a consequence of the many commissions, the year 1958 brought another big and important change: We built a new shop in Loga on the *Mühlenweg.* Even with low construction costs during that time, it was a big risk, because we did not have our own capital. We had some adventurous plans regarding the new building. Near Emden, in Wybelsum, we bought barracks made from wood that could be screwed together. Our plans were to erect a building from this material on a stone foundation. A smart man at the building department gave us all kinds of reasons not to go ahead with these plans. As a consequence, we built a brick building about 30 meters long and 10 meters wide (33 × 98 feet). Our barracks were sold plank by plank to the carpenters. A wooden barn that we also purchased gave us material for a wood shed, which became our first building. The first of July, after three months of construction, we moved into our new premises.

In 1959, the three-manual organ for the Zorgvlietkerk in Scheveningen, Netherlands—then our most important project—was the first instrument constructed in the new shop. During this time Gerhard was engaged to Ruth Engelhardt, who came from the Sauerland region. Ruth's mother was the daughter of a businessman from Gütersloh and was a capable and generous woman of happy disposition, characteristics that Ruth had inherited as well.

To understand how the partnership between Gerhard Brunzema and Jürgen Ahrend split up after 17 years of good collaboration, one has to understand Gerhard's philosophy regarding organbuilding at the end of the 1960s. The sound of our organs should strive to emulate the standards of historic instruments. They should be built using mechanical action, yet taking advantage of modern technology. The casework should be of contemporary and modern design. This meant a lack of ornamental trim and carved pipe shades. This is how the well-known Ahrend and Brunzema organs with geometric pipe shades by other designers came about. Since I leaned more and more to an understanding of the organ as a historical musical instrument, going our separate ways was the best solution for both of us and for the growth of the organbuilding shop in Loga. Both of us were free to develop our own styles.

In all of this, Gerhard remained true to his own convictions. He contributed greatly to raising the standards of organbuilding, and this not only in Germany. Subsequently, we saw and talked with one another at a conference about once a year, until the death of Helmut Winter in 1982.

Gerhard Brunzema's premature death shocked us all very much. A man departed from us that had been an organbuilder with his entire soul, and one who greatly influenced this cultural area for a generation.

I gratefully remember our years together.

❖ 8

Excerpt from "Jürgen Ahrend: An Appreciation"

Fritz Noack

I remember asking a well-known organist what he thought about trying to work for A & B [Ahrend and Brunzema] for a while before leaving for America. I will never forget his reply: "They are, of course, the best organ craftsmen in Germany, and have done a lot of looking at the insides of old organs—they even went to Spain on a motorcycle—but they are so arrogant." It was meant as a warning. . . . They do not follow the standard neo-Baroque catechism, and they do not accept mediocrity. . . . They do not go by the "as everybody knows" rules, but bother to find out specifics, even if that means uncomfortable travel, crawling around in dirty old organs and—if necessary—being a bit obnoxious to get access to the knowledge everybody else took for granted.

This was, of course, the strongest possible endorsement. . . . The decision to allow me to work for them for a short time [in the summer of 1959], as were apparently all decisions in those days of the early Ahrend & Brunzema firm, was made by both partners

in unison. Even though they were people of almost opposite temperaments, I felt a strong kinship with both Gerhard and Jürgen
because they were both essentially incurable individualists. Both
had strong opinions (fortunately mostly correct ones) and a deep
love for old organs. . . .

Organs like Westerhusen and Uttum had not only regained
their original lustre, but I was also impressed by the overall quality of the work. . . . The restored organ was musically on a par
with the original and technically probably better.

(Chapter reprinted from Noack, 13–14)

The Work of Gerhard Brunzema, II: Québec

Friedrich Brunzema

In 1972 my father accepted an offer to become tonal director at the well-established Canadian firm Casavant Frères Limitée, located in Saint-Hyacinthe near Montréal. At that time, the firm had over 200 employees and was producing pipe organs at the rate of one instrument per week for the Canadian and United States markets. Although initially the Casavant brothers had constructed mechanical pipe organs, the firm had built very few mechanical instruments. Mechanical pipe organs had been a money-losing proposition for Casavant, which was something my father changed very quickly. When he left the company in 1979, one-half of the production was mechanical instruments. The following data details Casavant's mechanical-action organs from 1973 to 1979.

Year	Organs with mechanical action	Stops on mechanical-action organs
1973	4/30 (13%)	94/635 (15%)
1974	12/52 (23%)	119/930 (13%)
1975	11/45 (24%)	164/797 (21%)
1976	11/38 (29%)	118/731 (16%)
1977	11/32 (34%)	106/578 (18%)
1978	21/39 (54%)	317/686 (46%)
1979	24/47 (51%)	232/681 (34%)

The work at Casavant gave my father an incredible opportunity to develop his mathematical modeling of the pipe scales. With the advent of the programmable calculator, numbers could now be crunched with ease, and the sheer volume of instruments provided excellent empirical data. In most instruments, my father was involved in the disposition, the external features of the instrument, and the scaling. He gave guidelines for the voicing of the organ, and often traveled to the site before the construction began and after the instrument was finished. Also, Casavant had equipment that allowed measurement of reverberation times and other acoustical properties of the room where the new instrument was to be installed.

❖ 10

In Memoriam
Gerhard Brunzema

Carroll Hanson

In 1972 the organ culture of North America was awash in the various manifestations of the Organ Reform Movement (*Orgelbewegung*) as its exponents and practitioners envisioned them: low pressures, nickless voicing, open toes, slider chests whenever possible, and encasements. However, at that time there were fundamentally different developments and perspectives on the horizon that arose from actual experiences with historically important European and American organs and their adept restorations. It is from this latter environment that Gerhard Brunzema reached our continent and began to exert his influence more directly. He honed Casavant's already developed mechanical action capabilities and brought to this shop a palette reflecting his admiration for the tonal precedents of his homeland. Moreover, I recall, in an early interesting aside, Gerhard's remark that it was too bad that North America did not fully appreciate how much in common there was between its best nineteenth-century instruments and those an ocean and one or two centuries distant.

Though Gerhard worked throughout the country in his Casavant days, there seemed to exist a special mutual embrace between him and the Midwest. My colleague to the north, Tom Erickson, and I had the good fortune to work with him on a number of projects including two for which his collaborations at Casavant are probably most widely known: The Maternity of Mary Church in St. Paul, Minnesota, and Dordt College in Sioux Center, Iowa. A devoted and devout man, Gerhard seemed to resonate with the beliefs and aspirations of the people who helped to underwrite the costs of the instruments for their houses of worship.

Gerhard Brunzema was a man of his time. The organs were grounded in historic precedent but gave witness to the time in which they were built. He did not join the lockstep, retrograde procession into visual/architectural historicism. There were two points that I recall he kept firmly in his mind (and in ours): (1) Do not exceed the level of ornamentation of the room in which you are going to work, and (2) Remember that this is not the eighteenth century. In what strikes me as a sad irony, Gerhard could not seem to merit the full approbation of some of his contemporaries who were influenced by his pioneering work with Jürgen Ahrend because he remained contemporary in his visual design. I suspect future organ historians will find it refreshing to study someone who was unapologetic about reflecting his productive years in the latter half of the twentieth century. His efforts stand as an estimable legacy.

(Chapter reprinted from Hanson, 12)

✦ 11

Remembrance

Christoph Linde

I believe I was sixteen years old when I heard one of the first small organs that Gerhard Brunzema was involved with. My father, pastor of our church community in Germany, had helped choose a positive organ with four registers from the workshop of Ahrend and Brunzema [Iserlohn, Opus 6]. This instrument was soon integrated into choir concerts, of which I was an active member as a young tenor.

Almost twenty years passed before we had a chance to meet in Canada. At that time my family and I lived there. As a young organbuilder I had been to North America on various occasions, while Gerhard and his family first came to Québec after his separation from Ahrend.

We both worked for Québec firms that occasionally competed for the same contracts for mechanical-action organs. However, family contacts outweighed professional contacts when we first got to know each other. Our wives are both extroverted and spontaneous and brought together both families, including the children. The relationship between both families became a source for mutual admiration and was strengthened by an ethically similar world view, as it turned out.

With the passing of time, it becomes increasingly easier for me to write about Gerhard's personality than it would have been earlier. Throughout the years and on those occasions we would meet, I sometimes felt that I did not have full access to him as a person. In terms of his career, Gerhard was highly analytical in all points concerning our shared profession, as can be discerned from his upbringing and his development. Instruments built under his influence, including those at Casavant, were visually and tonally marked in a far-reaching manner by his understanding of the instrument in regard to the liturgy of the era following the Reformation up to the early Baroque.

I think that, in conjunction with this, I am able to say something about our friendship, which developed with time. I am twelve years younger than Gerhard and more impulsive than he was. In his own peculiar way, some of his thoughts he kept to himself. With perseverance and critical reflection, one would succeed in getting concentrated comments from him which were highly constructive for the matter itself. He furthermore applied his mind to my own intentions in regard to organbuilding, provoking me with equally critical analysis. I think we both profited from our discourses. As born Europeans, we frequently spoke of our professional destinations and what we were to do and accomplish in North America. Despite our (at times) contrasting views in this respect, we became closer over time, with healthy differences.

Many instruments designed by Gerhard Brunzema between 1972 and 1977 I understand very well; others I find rooted too closely in a continental European tradition within their given immediate environment. This, however, had been Gerhard's intention, as he confirmed to me. This I explain with the importance the Reformation had on him, in a way, as a person. I was a youngster when I began to travel overseas and was able to see organs of the nineteenth and early twentieth centuries with tracker and electropneumatic actions. Many aspects of the "American" organ unknowingly may have influenced me in the long run, and this might not have been the case with Gerhard. He analyzed my positions with a rational approach; I, rather, have matters work with me, sift them out, and put them into action. Above all, Gerhard's instruments showed an extremely high degree of coherence in physical design and tonal form and shape. Both aspects represent many of his ethnic views.

The period of his own workshop in Fergus, Ontario, followed. It was pure fun and enjoyment when I and my wife, Gabriele, saw Gerhard and Ruth's shop growing: Needless to say, they had their share of difficulties in making it grow. There has been an admirable partnership between them. The workshop's layout and overall concept expressed so well Gerhard's profound understanding of organbuilding. Gerhard's remaining time in this shop with the numerous small and cleverly thought-out details was spent with co-workers who were professionally and personally committed to him.

Gerhard was capable of accomplishing something else: Because of his solid and convincing views toward organbuilding, his wife became an organbuilder herself. This has not happened without severity for Ruth, as Gabriele and I know. Seldom have I seen so nicely handcrafted and voiced wood pipes as Ruth built them . . . and they sound so well, too.

❖ 12

Excerpt from "Gerhard Brunzema: Instrument Builder and Businessman"

Matthew Redsell

The choice of shop location [in Fergus] is excellent; it is in an industrial park with lots of open space, and, as Mr. Brunzema pointed out, "the vacant field beside the main building is for possible expansion." Once inside the building you realize immediately that an efficient, carefully planned operation had been provided for. There are two large rooms, each the size of small concert halls (the right shape, too); one for assembly, the other for heavy and presumably noisier machinery. Careful attention has been paid to the needs of the builders. There are very fine cabinetmaker's benches near windows on wooden floors, which are easier to do standing work on. Large windows at each end of the shop make fine work easier to see. The drill press, which is mounted on the wall, allows a piece of wood of large dimensions to have a hole made in its center, and has all the drill bits and attachments mounted on swinging doors right at arm's length. The tool cabinets are easily moved from one place to another by a simple attachment to the wall. Even waxed paper dispensers are carefully placed.

Another ingenious feature is an area built into the wall for storing plans. Each rolled-up plan is enclosed in a short section of cardboard mailing tube with an outside cover and handle attached to it. If this cover is placed so that the handle is vertical, the plan is not there and must be in the shop. If the handle is horizontal, then the plan is in storage.

It is obvious that Mr. Brunzema has spent much more money on this building and machinery than most of us younger builders could ever hope to scrape together, but equally obvious is the fact that this has not been a "spur of the moment" decision; it was all carefully planned. His experience has been gained over many years. . . .

Mr. Brunzema has an air of confidence and a fine sense of humor which permeates his conversation. The most significant exchanges between us during my visit in November 1981 are set out below.

I very carefully picked the place [Fergus]. I wanted to be in a quiet place where neighbors, friends, and acquaintances lead less complicated lives than those of the city. I wanted to be fairly near a major market (the United States), near a major airport, and in an area where woodworking is done. It is not a curiosity here. Toronto was not the place. I didn't need most of its advantages and we were near enough for important things. . . .

I came that September [1979] with plans in my pocket. I had gone to a friend who is an architect in Québec, but we couldn't begin that year because of the cold. We had to wait. We started in April 1980, and three and a half months later, one week later than we had planned, we moved in. Our official opening was the twenty-third of July. . . .

I was born and brought up in northern Germany, and I suppose the traditions of the music in the churches there will always be with me. This tradition should appeal to those Canadians and Americans whose language background is generally speaking "Germanic" in flavor. I am trying to reinforce very simple, good-sounding, high-quality, basic organs, with only one manual. People do tend to refuse the simple type, the basic type at first. But I follow my own experience and inclination toward the simple basic instrument to the extent that I can. . . .

I feel I have a moral and social responsibility to "stay afloat," to keep my building business in such shape that society can depend on it, for being there, for employment, for its products, for the quality of those products. The profit I take I enjoy, but it is a byproduct of my first commitment—to my community. A steady business is also important to one's well-being; and communication with musicians and sponsors is necessary as well as communication with builders.

(Chapter reprinted from Redsell, 9–13)

❖ 13

Excerpt from "Brunzema Organs, Incorporated"

Jan Overduin

As motto, Brunzema has adopted Wisdom 11:20: "You ordered all things by measure, number, and weight." In practice this means that he relies not just on his wealth of experience as an organ-builder, but uses also his skills as a mathematician. Carefully and in detail he assesses and analyzes each acoustical condition, in accordance with which he plans the location, size, and tonal structure of the organ. The acoustic analysis of the building is made from recorded clusters (if the church already has a pipe organ) and/or balloon explosions (if the church has no pipe organ). From the building's reactions to this spectrum of sound, Brunzema, by means of some rather complicated mathematical formulae, is able to calculate, "weigh and measure" with considerable accuracy the details of the organ's construction so that it can be designed to greatest advantage. Generally speaking, the plenum of a Brunzema organ is rich and vibrant, reeds, when present, adding dramatic power to the tutti without destroying the blend. Even small organs tend to be based on an 8′ Principal. The organs are not copies of historic instruments; neither do they follow any particular national style, despite Brunzema's familiarity with the best examples, worldwide.

Acoustical considerations lead to certain unique features, such as the use of two 8′ Principals. The second Principal or *Schwebung* in the Italian *Voce umana* tradition is tuned slightly sharp. There is also an 8′ Gedackt. . . . Cases, including the back walls, are made of solid oak. The firm makes its own mechanisms and keyboards in order to keep construction simple and allow for an absolute minimum of maintenance. Pedalboards are ordinarily of the straight and parallel type. . . . Pipes, except for the wooden ones, are imported from Germany, although the firm hopes to make all its pipes soon. Open pipes are cone-tuned; stopped and chimney pipes have soldered caps. Without moving canisters, the pipes can be made of softer material, allowing for improved tone. Tuning of these pipes is done by adjusting the pipe's ears.

Consoles are open, and compass is C–g‴, except for the Kisten Orgel, which is [CD–d‴]. The action, so far of the suspended kind only [for Opus 1–Opus 14], is firm as well as comfortable to the touch. Rollers and trackers are of wood. Cases tend to be simple and without fancy ornaments. Larger pedal pipes are located at the back outside the case, allowing the cases to be shallower, and a better projector of the sound.

The flexibility and vitality of sound is aided by a slightly unstable winding system. To attempt to build organs "well-adapted for human hearing" . . . is based on the theory that the human ear has functioned for millions of years mainly as a warning device, developing extreme sensitivity to minute variations of sound and tiny levels of contrast. Utmost stability and rigidity of sound, indeed any kind of steadiness or same-ness, causes lack of interest and boredom in the listener. Thus Brunzema organs are winded by reservoirs without regulating systems such as schwimmers. (The Kisten Orgel is an exception, and does use a regulator.)

Brunzema prefers to stay away from transposable keyboards, because of the implication of equal temperament. He prefers to tune in a modified temperament, which although not noticeable enough generally for church officials to have been informed, nevertheless does not sound well up or down one semitone. There is greater historical precedent for organs with *whole-tone* transposable keyboards, for which, however, there is no demand at present.

(Chapter reprinted from Overduin, 125–126)

❖ 14

The Work of Gerhard Brunzema, III: Ontario

Friedrich Brunzema

After having found a site in Fergus, Ontario—a location closer to the main market for pipe organs, the United States—my father proceeded to design a workshop where high-quality mechanical instruments were to be designed and built.

In 1980 the factory was completed, consisting essentially of two large spaces: a machine room and an assembly room. The building was designed to accommodate the construction of large instruments. (It was possible to build wooden 16′ resonators in the given space). The design had included an erection room with a ceiling height of 12 meters (39 feet), a room to set up a pipe shop, and some office space. Unfortunately, due to financial constraints, this part was never built. As with his organs, great attention was paid to details, especially in the setup of the machines. My father wanted to provide facilities where the machines and tools were well-ordered and quickly found. Since the largest cost in a pipe organ is the cost of labor, he always strove to improve the facilities.

Gerhard Brunzema had some clear ideas on what he considered to be desirable in an organ. These ideas were firmly rooted in the organbuilding tradition of northern Germany and are related to its cultural history. This is the reason why he was not interested in building copies of historic French, English, Spanish, or Italian instruments as many contemporary American builders are currently doing. As an organbuilder, he viewed himself somewhat as an artist. After the work has been commissioned, artists are usually free to decide how to execute the details. He longed for similar freedom, since the instruments were going to bear his name.

He was a firm believer in building instruments in the contemporary style. Previous generations of master organbuilders had always built instruments according to the accepted styles of the day: One can easily guess the age of a historic instrument just by looking at its external features. Most of the casework in my father's instruments was simple and straight-lined, usually lacking trim, moldings, and other ornamentation, except perhaps the pipe shades. He believed in making the entire case out of oak, which was sometimes (often in the house organs) painted or stained. He favored flat/parallel pedalboards over concave/radiating pedalboards because of historic reasons and because of space requirements. Front pipes were normally made with 70 percent tin, and usually there would be pipe shades. He disliked combination actions in mechanical pipe organs because the motors required space within the instrument and because he considered the electronics in the combination action unreliable in comparison to the expected lifetime of the instrument. Wind systems usually had wedge-shaped bellows and "flexible" winding.

As with most builders today, the process of building an organ began with a request from a client. Usually the client provided a drawing of the room that was to house the instrument and other details such as size, budget, and so on. From this information he usually devised a stoplist, and a preliminary drawing would be made that showed the façade of the instrument. He then invoked his own computer program that could estimate the price of the organ. This program took into account the internal parameters for the organ, such as the number of keyboards, stops, windchests, and divisions. Also, it considered the location of the client, computing travel time and other costs incidental to the setup of the instrument. Moreover, it gave a very accurate prediction of the weights of individual divisions and parts of the instrument as well as the organ's total weight.

After an agreement had been signed, my father got a recording of air-balloon explosions for reverberation analysis. After this, he designed the scales for the instrument using a computer spreadsheet. The spreadsheet included all the necessary construction details to be able to build the stop, as well as information related to voicing. For the "C" notes in the organ, the spreadsheet calculated the predicted loudness, air consumption rate, and other relevant parameters. After having determined the scales and knowing the diameters of the pipes in the instrument, the windchests were laid out.

After the initial windchest design, detailed construction drawings would be made for the case, the stop action, the layout of the key action including the couplers, and the wind system. At this point, we would start constructing the individual parts of the instrument. We carefully documented how to make most parts: with drawings and/or photographs, which jigs to use, how to use them, and where necessary tools could be found within the shop. The goal of this was to reduce the amount of time spent to produce a specific part.

Windchests were constructed using quartersawn poplar for the note-channel grid and the toeboards. After making the grid, it was planed smooth. A "sandwich" consisting of the grid, the sliders, and the toeboard was put together. Hole centers for the pipes would be transferred from the windchest drawing, and the holes were bored. After this, bottom layers of plywood were glued to the grid using a large press. On the bottom of the grid, grooves were cut with a router for the pallet openings. A pallet box was fitted to the bottom of the windchest grid that had holes for the pulldowns. On the top, spacers made from maple were glued to the top of the windchest. Toeboards would be finished by drilling and sometimes channeling the boards as required. The sizes of the holes on the windchest as well as those within the toeboards were taken from my father's calculation list. Rackboards were made when the pipes had arrived from our supplier.

The case, bench, and pedalboard were usually made from quartersawn white oak. Construction of the case would start with a bottom frame; the sides of the instrument were made with frame and panels. This would lead to the tranverse impost, where the

Hauptwerk windchest or windchests were located. With large instruments, such as those in Pella, Charlotte, or Seoul, the impost was close to the ceiling of the assembly room. With the windchests installed, the stop action would be built. At this time we would install the other parts belonging to the lower half of the instrument: a Brustwerk windchest, the keyboards, rollerboards, and the key action including coupler mechanism. All those parts were constructed in our shop as well. Given enough space, my father tended to favor wooden rollers for the key action. After the stop action was complete, we would make the stopknobs and engrave them.

The impost would be taken down to allow the construction of the top part of the case. Removable panels would be made and fitted in the back of the case. While on the floor, the front pipes were installed and the pipe shades were made and fitted. The design of the pipe shades was always something tricky that involved trial and error; often the client was also involved. The windchests were mounted on the impost and all the pipes were properly racked. Stays were made for long reeds and other longer pipes needing support within the case. After this, the pipes and the top part of the case were removed and the impost was reinstalled on the lower section of the organ. The key action, blower, and wind system were then connected.

Next, we would establish the mouth heights or cut-ups for the flue pipes and do some pre-voicing, usually for all the C notes, and the middle C, C#, and D notes for all the stops. The cut-ups would be done according to my father's spreadsheet information. With the functioning organ in this state, my father would take a sound level meter and analyze the actual sound level produced in the shop. After this test was passed, all the flue pipes were cut up to the specification and pre-voiced so that they were speaking. With the samples, it was possible to determine the lengths of the pipes. All flue pipes would be cut to length in the shop, based on a geometric progression of the known pipes. Gedackts and other stopped pipes were cut to length, voiced, and then the caps were soldered on.

After this step, all pipes were repackaged. The instrument was taken apart piece by piece, a process that usually went very quickly compared to the time it had taken to set things up initially. Once packaged, the organ was shipped. For a larger-size organ, it took a few days to unpack the instrument and to get it technically ready. After this, it was time for the voicing. My father was usually involved with either voicing the pipes himself or listening at the keyboard to the sounds produced by the pipes. On average, voicing proceeded at a bit more than one stop per day. At the end of the day, near the completion of the instrument, my father would improvise and make some music with the organ.

To this day I am persuaded that there is something magical in the way a great pipe organ makes music happen.

❖ 15

In Memoriam
Gerhard Brunzema

Davis Folkerts

Central College in Pella, Iowa, is blessed with two organs by Gerhard Brunzema. In the college chapel is a 1981 two-manual and pedal instrument of 18 registers, and there is also a Kisten Orgel, Brunzema's Opus 9, used everywhere from a teaching studio to a 660-seat performing arts auditorium. In the town of Pella, the Second Reformed Church has an organ which was rebuilt in 1974 with substantial additions and replacements designed by Mr. Brunzema, then through the Casavant firm.

My first acquaintance with Mr. Brunzema was at an American Guild of Organists national convention many years ago when I chanced to share a seat on a bus returning from a concert an hour's ride from the convention center. I discovered that he was a man of few and well-chosen words conveying a wealth of thought. That first impression proved to be on target as I got to know him better.

When we began negotiations for the chapel organ at Central College, I had some rather definite specification ideas. Mr. Brunzema challenged those ideas, and I needed some time to bend to his concepts. In all our conversations he was always gentle but firm. He knew precisely why his scheme was better—it would take me some time to learn that. Indeed, I am still learning, and I am sure this instrument has much more yet to teach. As a designer, Mr. Brunzema was a great artist. Balance, blend, sensitivity, color, and versatility characterize his instruments.

When the organ was delivered and assembled, my esteem for Mr. Brunzema soared further. His supreme workmanship was the result of limitless patience and of relentless standards of perfection. In voicing, no recalcitrant pipe or stubborn reed ever exasperated him. The most I ever saw was a slight shake of the head as he patiently pulled out the pipe, adjusted it, and replaced it for who knows how many times.

Some six or seven years after the installation of the chapel organ and the acquisition of the Kisten Orgel, I put Gerhard Brunzema's patience and understanding to a test I never intended. I had done some touch-up tuning, trying to take the last degree of care, but alas, I had slipped and the result was somewhere between a mess and a disaster for the top of that pipe. As I rather apprehensively explained what I had done, expecting some justified chiding, I got instead, with a decided twinkle in his eye, this gentle response: "I made the organ—I can fix it." In almost no time the top of the pipe looked and behaved like new, and then I got the short course in cone tuning!

Personally and professionally I will miss Gerhard Brunzema very much. The world has lost a great artist. No tribute can compare to the legacy he has himself left us through the love, skill, care, and artistry with which he created many very beautiful organs.

(Chapter reprinted from Hanson, 12)

Organum Plenum

Hans Zbinden

The prelude sounds, the service starts.
  The worship now begins.
A faithful flock has gathered here.
  To God arise the prayers and hymns.

From ancient times we worshipped God
  With prayers and hymns and rite.
The people and their priest did sing,
  In worship they did unite.

Worship then was liturgy,
  The "work" of God and man.
Voices only filled the church
  Without the voice of Pan.

Then slowly came this other voice
  And aided worship now.
The priest and choir heard a tone
  To make the worship flow.

To give the priest his starting note
   The pipe now had its rôle.
An "intonation," clear and firm,
   Did give the pipe a goal.

More and more the pipes were heard
   "In alternatim" did they sing;
Back and forth the voices flew,
   In worship they did ring.

And slowly grew this instrument.
   Organum was its name.
Its pipes and voices mingled now,
   The mass was not the same.

The pipes now sounded evermore,
   Their rôle began to grow.
These solemn sounds were needed now
   To make the worship flow.

The bishop comes with earnest step,
   The pipes give festive sounds.
He moves, processes with his peers,
   Solemnity abounds.

The mass has ended, the celebrants leave.
   A recessional takes place.
Again the pipes give forth their voice
   And music gives its grace.

As time went on the organ grew,
   More music did the pipes impart.
The prelude came in Luther's mass,
   Thus did the worship start.

A new group now is added as
   The priest and choir sing.
New songs are heard: the people's voice,
   And mighty hymns now ring.

The keepers of this awesome task:
   Musicians with great skill.
They move the service, lead the voices
   With strong, determined will.

And many are the masters who
   Have guided worship there.
Old names emerge from distant past,
   Each one a skillful player.

From northern climes and distant times
   A Buxtehude sat to play.
Then Bruhns and Lübeck offered up
   Their preludes to the day.

And other masters did we hear
   From far and wide as well:
Clérambault and Couperin
   Made their music swell.

More recent times have brought new tones:
   Flor Peeters and Max Drischner.
Then add to them Heinz Zimmermann
   As well as Hermann Schroeder.

Such masters were my mentors true,
   These and so many more.
For now the task did fall on me
   To make the music soar.

I take my place each Sunday now
   And seek to carry on
As others did before my time
   With music in the morn.

The liturgy, the back and forth
   Of versicle and response,
All lift to God with organ tones
   Our many needs and wants.

To these are added, week by week,
   The hymns and anthems bright.
A prelude sets the tone to start,
   The organ sounds with might.

Yet every week the task renews
   Fresh music to prepare.
The masters, anthems, hymns indeed
   Must all be played with flair.

The dream arose, it was a wish
  To make a special place,
To practice in one's music room
  And so avoid the hectic pace

Of running off to church at night
  Through weather thick and thin
To practice music, oh! so late,
  And mastery to win.

A dream it was until one day
  Another master came.
A builder true from distant shores:
  Gerhard Brunzema was his name.

I learned of him and made the call,
  To Canada it went.
A fervent prayer? A wish? A hope?
  A dream is what I sent.

Before too long we met and talked
  And he listened to my notion.
He seemed to know my very dream
  And sense my strong emotion!

To know the man, to know his work,
  Required a visit north.
To Fergus in Ontario
  My wife and I went forth.

And there we met him, Meister Gerhard,
  And met his wife as well.
The two of them, Gerhard and Ruth,
  Were there to show and tell

Us of the organs, great and small,
  Which came from the Master's hands.
The sights and sounds convinced me soon:
  He was the man for me,
    He from Canada's lands!

That evening we were all together
  To share a simple meal.
A blessing came on food and dream,
  The dream would soon be real.

Komm, Herr Jesus,
  Sei Unser Gast,
Und segne was Du
  *Uns bescheret hast.**

Luther's grace, how oft' have we said
  And prayed those lovely words?
They now became a blessing true
  To guide this special work.

The Master went to work at once
  To craft an instrument
From woods like ebony and rose
  And oak for the cabinet.

The pipes arose, aligned on chests
  In rows so straight and true,
In front there stood the Praestant 4′
  So shiny and so new.

Now other voices stood behind
  The Praestant, short and tall.
Meister Gerhard knows his craft:
  They blended, one and all.

And now it stands, this wondrous work
  Almost beyond belief.
Again the German says it best:
  "Der Fachmann staunt, der Laie wundert sich!"†

---

*Come Lord Jesus, Be Thou our guest, Let this Thy gift to us be blest.
†The expert is astounded, the layman stands there puzzled.

I look at it. Such a sight and sound!
  From what heritage did it grow?
In Friesian lands such organs stood
  In times of long ago.

The case work rises, the pipes, aligned,
  All stand within their frame.
The Golden Mean is evident
  A harmony of form.

The sounds I hear, are they the same
  The masters heard of yore?
I play their works, I hear these sounds
  And then I long for more.

I draw my Sweelinck from the shelf.
  An Echo Fantasie
Comes forth in tones so bright and true,
  For me: reality.

I draw my reed. Regal its name!
  A fiery, awesome sound.
Was this the sound the Spaniards heard
  When reeds their playing crowned?

And then I draw Organum Plenum,
  A massive sound, both firm and clear.
Prelude and fugue now issue forth.
  Is this the sound that Bach did hear?

This treasure stands before me now,
  Such richness overwhelms me.
It reaches back to masters old.
  In trance, I now can see

And hear them playing on this keyboard,
  Delighting in its sound
And touch, their fingers moving smoothly.
  Their praise would then abound.

Our Meister Gerhard built this work,
  Created it with love and skill.
A tribute to his heritage
  And to his gentle will.

Organum Plenum is the sound
  Which fills our worship now.
To Meister Gerhard goes our praise,
  To him our hearts do bow,
That he has captured through his craft
  These sounds of great renown!

❖ 17

"And the Breath Came into Them, and They Lived": The John Melbye Wagner Memorial House Organ

Edward Wagner

Ever since I took my first organ lessons at age 14, I have always loved what happens when we switch an organ on: the sounds of wind filling bellows, windways, pipechests. What was inert, an artifact, now is full of breath, full of life. Each time we start the blower a kind of resurrection happens, the organist's revelation of what Ezekiel saw in the Valley of Dry Bones. When we touch the organ's keys and the breath leaps into the pipes and makes them sing, we become the instruments of that wonderful Hebrew word *ruach* which means it all: wind, breath, spirit.

Ruach has taken on special significance for me. In September 1984 my younger brother John died at age 36 of brain cancer, and my mother and I began to talk of a suitable memorial. At about the same time, after almost twenty years as a church musician, my ministry was showing signs of taking a path more typical of ordained people. So nearly at once the dream of a distinctive, lasting, and appropriate memorial for John coalesced with my need to continue playing the organ when access to church instruments might no longer be as easy. As my mother, Beatrice, my wife, Daphne Ross, and I continued to talk, the notion of a house organ for Daphne's and my West Hartford home developed into a firm decision.

We were clear about the fundamentals. The organ must be honestly and sturdily designed and made, and must visually and tonally fit comfortably into our 15 ft. by 25 ft. living room. Money was an object: The house organ might cost as much as our Steinway model M piano, but not much more. These were the parameters; it was up to me to engage a builder and draw up the specifications.

John and I were raised in Canada on Georgian Bay. Bea, who is widowed, still lives near our hometown of Owen Sound, and John, who was an officer for Canada Steamship Lines and a lifelong bachelor, lived with her during the winter tie-ups that occur annually when the Great Lakes freeze over, and for the final eighteen months of his life. Gerhard Brunzema had established himself in Fergus, Ontario, which is about a ninety-minute drive from Owen Sound. It made sense to try a Canadian organ builder from the same area in which John had lived. Brunzema Organs was therefore the first company I called, and as it turned out, the only one.

I knew long before I called that Gerhard was a master builder. What we were blessed to discover—first myself, then Daphne and Bea—was that he and his family were warm, deeply caring, and pious people. Human qualities are fundamentally important to us, and we have come to believe that art and its maker's character are inseparable. The difference between even superb craftsmanship and art—what mysteriously causes an object to become alive, and so to surprise, enlighten, disturb, delight, and heal—seems to us to have everything to do with *who* its maker *is*.

Spirit, person, and *character* are words with related meanings. All of them can be used to describe Brunzema Organs Opus 26, our house organ. To me and to the many who have now seen, heard, and played it, it is a work of art. Visually and mechanically it seems to arouse not only admiration but contemplation. Tonally it is a sober yet winsome conversationalist, speaking forthrightly and plainly but with grace, charm, sweetness, and wit. There is something else, too, for which our family is particularly grateful. We think of it as the organ's overall modesty, a sort of "positive humility." Our family values independence at the same time it rejects "prima-behavior." Distinctive as it is, our organ in no way demands to be the center of attention. In fact, a few first-time visitors to the house have actually only gradually become aware of it: "Oh! Is that an *organ* in your living room?"

I find the organ's basic character reminds me of John's. I tell my son Graeme, who was only one year old in August 1986 when it was installed and who now likes to play it when he gets tired of piano practice, that when he plays this organ he learns something about his uncle John, whom both he and the Brunzemas never knew. The pastor in me warns that I am probably projecting memories of my brother into the sounds of the organ. Still, whatever the psychic processes involved, those memories refresh our connection and can sometimes produce feelings that are powerfully healing.

This is what happened at the dedicatory recital, which I played during the week after All Saints' Day, 1986. Bea and Daphne had prepared exceptional food; friends, many of them church folk who had supported us during John's long dying, crowded the room; my musical colleagues Susan Casper and Barbara Riihimaki sang and assisted at the piano; and we had the pleasure of welcoming among us Gerhard, Ruth, and Meta Brunzema. I wanted to say something about the special significance of the organ we were about to dedicate and I found myself referring to the verses of two hymns that had been engraved on the organ, hymns that we later sang as part of the recital. Both are largely the work of John Mason Neale. One, "The Return Home", is a funeral hymn with an arresting first verse:

Safe home, safe home in port!
  Rent cordage, shattered deck,
Torn sails, provisions short,
  And only not a wreck!

The other, "They Whose Course on Earth Is O'er," has in it these
lines:

> Yet in sacrament and prayer
>   Each with other hath a share;
> Saints departed even thus
>   Hold communion still with us.

I talked about *ruach* as breath, wind, and spirit, about the resurrection that occurs when the wind fills an organ with life, about
the song that comes from the pipes, and about how that living
music can be a communion between the saints on earth and the
saints already in heaven. I talked about John the sailor and about
the old Christian image of life as a sea voyage. Then we began to
make music.

As our house organ and I sang together surrounded by all those
good people, I experienced a healing that was a kind of resurrection. The dedicatory recital became my way of grieving the
ending of John's earthly life and celebrating the hope of his new
one. I was in the presence of *ruach:* Life as it was, as it is, and as
it is to come.

In their individual ways, just about everybody else was feeling
the same thing. They were re-experiencing their own sadnesses
and joys, people they mourned, and loved ones on the journey
who made them glad to be alive. The instrument, the music, the
evening inspired them to feel and think and afterwards to talk
about all that.

On the surface of it, the pipe organ seems to be a relic from an
ancient world. Nowadays Western ecclesiastical culture and the
general culture too are so deeply inflected by humanistic principles of personal transparency and social tolerance. I think organs
probably remind our contemporaries mostly of eras we reject,
those characterized by social stratification, rigid lifestyles, and
pomp and circumstance. Perhaps pipe organs seem to be the musical counterparts of Sun Kings or propriety in religion.

But every time I play it, every time I notice again its quiet and
beautiful presence in our house, our Brunzema house organ reminds me that organs can be sensitive musical instruments, capable of art which is intimate, simple, emotionally and intellec-
tually honest, and widely evocative.

In reminding us all of that, I think our little organ proclaims hope: life ever renewed and ever renewing, life vibrant and eternal in the winds of the Spirit.

Program
The Dedication of the Brunzema House Organ
in Memory of
John Melbye Wagner
(1948-1984)

Saturday, November 8, 1986
Sunday, November 9, 1986

Prayer of Dedication
Almighty God, whom saints and angels delight to worship in heaven: We remember before you this night all those who have fought the good fight and run the straight race, and who now rest in your peace; especially your child John, in whose memory we humbly and gratefully dedicate this organ. May it give pleasure and wisdom to those who play it and those who hear it; may it always sing Your praise, and reveal to us even now glimpses of Your beauty, assisting us on our journey to that Heavenly City, where at last we shall behold Your radiance face to face, unveiled in all its glory. This we pray through Jesus Christ our Lord, who lives and reigns with you and the Holy Spirit, now and forever. Amen.

Hymn: "The Return Home"
    Text: J. M. Neale (1862) after a Greek hymn
    Tune: "Moritz," by Tom Kolar (1980)

Prelude and Fugue in G Minor . . . Dietrich Buxtehude

Colors of the Organ
    1. *Song* . . . Claudin de Sermisy
       Gedackt 8′
    2. *Dance* . . . Girolamo Frescobaldi
       Gedackt 8′ (bass), Quintade 8′ (treble)
    3. *Pavane* . . . William Byrd
       Rohrflöte 4′

4. *Fantasia* . . . Orlando Gibbons
    Gedackt 8′ and Quinte 1⅓′

Two Songs of Longing
    "Home Once More" (French Canadian) . . . arr. Healey Willan
    "Loch Lomond" (Scottish) . . . arr. Healey Willan

Sonata No. 4 in A Minor . . . Josef Rheinberger
    Tempo moderato
    Andantino (intermezzo)
    Tempo moderato (chromatic fugue)

Chorale from *Petite Suite for Two Keyboards* . . . Michael
McCabe

Hymn: "They Whose Course on Earth Is O'er"
    Text: J. M. Neale (1843, 1866) and others (1906)
    Tune: "East Grinstead," by Mark Hankey (1966)

Musicians
Edward Wagner, organ
Barbara Riihimaki, piano
Susan Casper, soprano

❖ 18

An Interview with Gerhard Brunzema

Craig Cramer

Craig Cramer: *Tell us about your training and background.*
Gerhard Brunzema: I was brought up in the northern part of West Germany close to the coastal area, which has an abundance of historic organs. For many years my relatives played the Schnitger organ in Weener, so I grew up with organ music in my family background.

After World War II, I apprenticed for three and a half years with Paul Ott in Göttingen. Before I went into business with Jürgen Ahrend in Leer, I attended technical college in Braunschweig where I worked in an acoustical laboratory for half a year to gain additional knowledge in room and organ acoustics.

Do you enjoy that aspect of your work?
Yes, it is very interesting. There are limitations to the scientific approach because the human ear has to be the final judge. I usually apply the science of acoustics first to find out what is most appropriate for human ears, and then I try to apply the results by

doing something with the room or with organ pipes. This is a somewhat more complicated approach, but it gives certain assurances that one does not have otherwise. That knowledge is helpful, especially when we work in extreme situations such as organs in very small or very large rooms. The knowledge that an organbuilder accumulates by hands-on experience is sometimes not applicable in extreme circumstances.

Where did you meet Jürgen Ahrend, and when did you form your firm?
Jürgen also worked for Paul Ott, and we started our firm in 1953.

When did you come to Casavant?
In 1972.

When did you form your own firm, and how many people do you employ?
We started in 1980, and we presently are a four-man shop.

Which historic organs influenced your thinking the most?
My favorite organs are the ones built before Schnitger, such as the ones in the province of Groningen and in the area north of my hometown, Emden. We restored some of these organs. I visited historic organs often, so with frequent exposure I was able to learn and memorize their sounds.

Do any specific ones stand out for you?
Yes, we restored the organs in Rysum, in Westerhusen, and in Uttum, and I have a very close knowledge of some organs in the province of Groningen as well.

How about the Schnitger organs?
I worked on the Schnitger organ in Norden when Paul Ott did some restoration work on that instrument. That restoration was not always up to today's highest standards, but at least I got to know that organ. I know the organ in Weener, where my relatives were organists when I was going to school, and I know the sound of other Schnitger organs from visiting them once in a while.

You were perhaps the first builders in this century to work from a decidedly historic viewpoint by trying to recreate the best of historicism—the sound.

We tried to utilize to a maximum what previous generations had explored and followed up. We do not have direct transmission of knowledge through a teacher-pupil or master-apprentice relationship, since tracker organbuilding was dormant during the period of factory-made organs. Through the knowledge that we gained restoring important historic organs, we were able to apply historic principles in a controlled fashion.

We studied historic organs and then tried to reproduce those sounds in new organs. We were not trying to copy historic instruments; instead, we wanted to make use of every conceivable detail from historic organs that seemed to influence the tone of the organ. We made our own pipes and reeds, and we tried once in a while to copy some details. In order to see if we succeeded, we took our new pipes to historic organs and set them beside old pipes to see how close our work came to the original. We also did this with some technical details to find out what contributes a lot, what has a marginal effect and what has only mystical advantages.

Did people consider you the enfants terribles of the time?

Yes, and we were criticized. We knew better than to emphasize too many details of our work that were rooted in historicism. We felt that we were making important contributions to quality organbuilding, and we wanted our organs to speak for themselves. An organ is an aggregate of many small details, and we did not want to divert attention from the sound of the instruments.

However, we were relatively rigid in using ideas that were developed in historic organs: historic temperaments, pipes cut to length, soldered stoppers on stopped pipes, and reeds with no adjustment at the resonators. This, of course, was an entirely new approach at that time.

Certain builders in the United States and Canada have been labeled as historic organbuilders. Did you ever feel that you were trapped in that syndrome?

No, we carefully avoided that. However, we did not build copies as some builders do today. It is dangerous to build copies, because in order to make an honest copy you have to include some details which you might consider questionable. We tried to integrate what we learned from historic organs into modern organbuilding without being attached to one specific style.

Building copies of historic organs is almost beyond human capability. Is it really possible to copy a Renaissance organ this year and a Cavaillé-Coll the next? You end up dealing with technologies and tonal approaches that are widely divergent and separated by perhaps hundreds of years of development. Historic organs were made by people who did just that type for years and years, over and over, with only slight differences from one organ to the next. The differences between two Schnitgers built ten years apart is very slight; they share the same basic approach.

On the other hand, we felt the need to react strongly against the *Orgelbewegung* ideals of low pressures, low cut-ups and no nicking in the voicing. These were reactions against the Romantic organ. We soon realized that historic organs did not produce chiffy sounds. Actually, most historic organ pipes produce the fundamental tone more prominently than the harmonics. *Orgelbewegung* voicing produces sounds from principal, octave, and mixture pipes which have more octave harmonics than fundamental. If you listen to an organ in which the 4′ Principal sounds like a 2′ Octave, and the 2′ sounds like a 1′, that results in a sound that is quite different from historic organs.

How do you feel about the eclectic approach in organbuilding?

There are two forms of eclectic organbuilding. The first includes several styles in the context of one organ, such as the American Classic builders try to do. The other is to place several faithful copies of historic organs in the same room. Then the player makes the selection by going to a different organ bench.

The latter is the more expensive way.

Yes. However, artistic expression involves making a decision and staying with it as effectively and artistically as possible. Work toward an ideal, choose something which you feel is appropriate and pursue that instead of looking in three or four different directions.

Do you view organbuilding as a continuum?

Yes. An organbuilder has to choose a style and stay with it, so that he not only continues to develop his own skills, but also continues to help improve the skills of the people working with him. This gives the best possibility for building the highest quality instruments without spreading too thin. It is best to concentrate on one approach. Become a master of one thing, get over the initial difficulties very quickly, and then polish your knowledge, the details of which finally add up to a very good result.

Can you speak generally about case design? Do you have a dictum about historic versus modern case design? Is the style of the case dependent on the room, or would you try to convince an organ committee to buy a certain style case because that is what you enjoy building?

In former times there were no historic cases—all cases were made according to the newest style. In that respect, our company is very historic. If you read design proposals or contracts from the old builders, in practically all instances they said the organ will be built according to the newest way of making organ cases. Many people think the organ design should reflect the style of the building. This was usually not done in historic times. For example, there were Romanesque churches with Baroque façades. When the organ was built in Baroque times, the case design showed all of the fashionable Baroque details, and there was a Baroque façade whether the church was 600 years old, 300 years old, or brand new.

So, an organ that is built today should look like it came from [the present].

Yes. If you compare Schnitger's façades, they basically look alike. He developed his own style. There was some deviation from one organ to the next, if you will, but the façades are very similar. They differed in the lengths of the pipes, and some organs had more elaborate details, but the style was basically the same.

When I work with organ committees, the questions that loom largest are economic ones: how much will the organ cost, how long will it last, will it be reliable, will it require much maintenance? However, these questions are very different from the ones that organists ask: how will it sound, how will the action feel, what kind of stops will there be? How do you, as the builder, reconcile the two?

The questions of cost, durability, and maintenance are easy to answer. The cost depends on the size of the instrument, and larger instruments provide more variety in the selection of sounds. In financially tight situations we normally suggest building one-manual organs with one pedal stop or pull-down pedals. Such instruments provide high quality, high durability, and require minimal maintenance. In addition the organ can accompany choral and congregational singing easily. If performing a broader range of literature is desired, then a two-manual organ is necessary, so the cost will be more.

I like to see the room where the organ will be located in order to determine what is physically possible and what seems to be appropriate for the acoustical situation. Do we need a large sound, or is a chamber music approach more appropriate? The answers to these questions dictate the concept and the specification.

Do you think we will reach a time on this continent when the majority of organists accept unequal temperaments, flat pedalboards, cone tuning, and similar things that seem to be such large issues today?

That largely depends on the education of future organists. If the tendency of educational institutions is to train traveling virtuosos, then standardized instruments with mechanical assists will continue to be built. There will always be organists who want four-manual electropneumatic organs with all the gadgets. However, that might be contrary to what most churches need, which is an instrument that sounds pleasant, is long-lasting, and requires little maintenance. In that respect, many small churches are well suited for organs that do not need continuous maintenance. In North America, service people often have to travel great distances to repair and tune organs. For that reason, I think that small mechanical-action organs hold hope for the future in many situations.

Have you ever built a tracker organ with electric stop action?

We have not done that, and I would be a little hesitant to go into that. What you do is introduce electricity with big magnets to move the sliders, which is one different technology from the mechanical system. On top of that you introduce the electronics technology for storing the registration memory system, so you have two additional technologies.

Neither of which will last as long as the organ's playing system.
That is right, because the machine becomes more complex. If people absolutely want a combination action, the disadvantages can be avoided to a great extent by having a mechanical stop action with the electronic components and memory as a piggyback system. This way they do not interfere directly with the organ. Then you can always use the mechanical stop action in case the electric system fails. However, this is expensive. It costs twice as much for the stop action because you make everything double. In a small organ it costs about the price of one or two stops. In a large organ of 45 or 50 stops, some people think it is worth it.

What are the larger questions that organists and organbuilders need to address?
The more specifically you build tracker organs, the better the chances for long-term success. If organists accept that not as a limitation but as a fact of artistic life, then this approach will succeed. Play the organ on its own terms. Develop a music program that conforms to the organ. Select something that you and the congregation are comfortable with and try to develop the choral literature to its fullest potential. Some people in North America say, "Oh, we can't do that—we have a large, broad literature at our disposal, and we have to include everything." All-inclusive art is not art at all. It is a contradiction in terms. It is not possible. Art is selection. It is preference for something.

After you have built as many organs as you have, how do you keep fresh?
You always try to improve your skills, improve details and gain more profound knowledge of this art. Sometimes you did something intuitively and it turned out right. Later, you do something with reason and justification, which is the foundation of good organbuilding.

What constitutes a good organ?
An organ should produce the right volume, it should feel comfortable and the organist should get confident excitement while playing it.

How did you and Jürgen Ahrend go about building organs as partners?

I was heavily involved with the design of the organs, and the tonal finishing was done with one of us at the console and the other doing the voicing. We tried to reach a consensus on what we wanted to achieve tonally.

I am fascinated with the changes of direction that large firms often take when they get new tonal directors. How is it possible for them to maintain quality in their work?

Electropneumatic organs allow more diversity in tonal approaches and more freedom in tonal design because they do not demand as strict a discipline in making specifications and in arranging pipes as in mechanical organs. Making electropneumatic organs in a large company seems to be more profitable than making mechanical organs. There is less design time and less fine tuning in the specification, layout, and position of the organ. While I was at Casavant, total production at one time was 50 percent mechanical organs, which was as high as it had been in a long time. Since then, it appears that they mainly sell electropneumatic organs.

Is it possible for a firm to build quality trackers and electropneumatic organs at the same time?

I suspect that building trackers with the left hand only will not work in the long run. Too many people leave the firm because they are dissatisfied with one or the other type of instrument. Therefore, the expertise necessary to build both types of organs well is not continuously available.

While you were at Casavant, did you miss building the instruments yourself in a small tracker shop?

Yes. However, my time at Casavant gave me the opportunity to influence the American scene. The *Orgelbewegung* voicing approach which Lawrence Phelps advocated was drastically changed, and in that respect I think I had a strong influence on the American market.

How do you use a North German organ?

Many of the registrations on Baroque organs were probably

developed through improvisation. North German organists played on manual flues, with reeds in the pedal for contrast. The robust pedal reeds also encouraged playing pedal solos. Every organist who has a quality organ will explore and find these possibilities.

Do you think pedal mixtures were used in fugues when a mixture was drawn on the manual?

If you look at specifications of historic organs, pedal mixtures are relatively rare. On the organ in which the Great and Pedal share the same chest it does not make sense to have a pedal mixture, because the pedal mixture stands right beside the manual mixture. The pedal mixture is redundant; it is a luxury. A small pedal division with only five stops, such as a 16', 8', 4', and reeds 16' and 8', is useful for most literature. If mixture sound is called for in the pedal, the Great to Pedal coupler gives sufficient possibilities in most cases. In a larger organ, especially ones with separate pedal cases, it is possible to include a mixture that can be designed so that it is in proper pitch relation to the façade pipes of that division.

How were 16' manual stops used?

Sixteen-foot manual stops make the Great sound full and fundamental. If a piece sounds extremely dark and unclear, that is a good indication not to use the 16' stop. Sixteen-foot stops should be played with the hands somewhat separated. Whenever you use the 16' Bourdon, you should add the 2⅔' and 2' so that the basic pitch of the mixture is transformed to the 16' fundamental. The 16' is not supposed to tint or color the sound of an otherwise 8' manual setup. It is a completely different approach in which the music demands a 16' basis instead of playing on 8' with a remote 16' Bourdon sound with it. If a builder misunderstands the function of the 16', then he tends to make this stop so soft that it allows the organist to play the same way whether the 16' is drawn or not.

How about manual reeds?

The addition of a trumpet to the principal chorus demands a different quality of playing in highly polyphonic music. There is a lot of literature which can be well understood if a reed is added to the registration. It adds a nice clarity; you can follow the inner voices because the sound no longer blends completely.

What do you think constituted full organ?
Great and Rückpositiv coupled together, with or without reeds, depending on the type of piece.

Do you think the Rückpositiv reeds were used in a plenum?
No, unless there was an 8′ Trumpet on that division.

Was the Waalse Kerk organ in Amsterdam an interesting restoration project?
Yes, and there was a great deal of substance available with which to work. There was not much missing.

Unlike the Ebert organ in Innsbruck?
The Ebert organ was well preserved tonally. There were quite a few missing small pipes, but replacing and voicing those pipes was not difficult. I am confident that whatever has been replaced there is extremely close to the original.

What about Rysum?
Rysum has four basically untouched old stops. There is a very narrow 8′ Gedackt with soldered caps. Obviously, there was not much chance for anyone to modify that stop. It is a lovely, colorful sound. I do not think anyone harmed the 8′ Principal either. The Octave 4′ and the Octave 2′ were also old. We made three new stops: a small Sesquialtera, an 8′ Trumpet, and the Mixture. There were some extant mixture pipes, but they dated from the nineteenth century and were constructed completely differently than old mixtures that we had examined, so we patterned the new mixture pipes on the Octave 2′.

How about Uttum?
Uttum had basically existing old pipes, and there really was not much change to it either.

Did you encourage your son to become an organbuilder?
No. Actually, my father told him that if he wanted to learn the trade he should do that before going to the university. He thought

it would be better to apprentice while he was young, and if he wanted to study he could do that anytime. So, that is what he did. Of course, I am very pleased to have him in our shop.

You seem fortunate in your career always to have been in the right place at the right time.

Yes, I was. The time at Casavant represented a completely different approach, and it gave me many opportunities to work with very large organs. We did not have those opportunities very often in Germany. Most of the organs we worked on and restored were usually not larger than 25 stops. Basic organ design cannot be learned through restoration work because the design was made by someone else. Obviously, conscientious restoration depends on keeping the same design parameters laid out by the original builder. That is something difficult to accept if you happen not to agree with all of the details.

(Chapter reprinted from Cramer 1989, 46-49)

❖ 19

Transcript of "Castles of the Soul: The Organs of Gerhard Brunzema"

Jan Overduin (Organist): Bob Kerr once on the CBC (Canadian Broadcasting Corporation) referred to the way an organ looks as a "fairy castle." And there is something so fascinating about the looks of an organ as well: All these pipes just standing there silently and waiting to be brought to life.

Joyce Knarr (Music Director, Blessed Sacrament Parish, Kitchener, Ontario): Every time I play it [Opus 12], I realize how well built it is. And in order to justify the dollars that the parish spent on it, the labor of love, and also the work that has gone into it, I feel that I as an organist must do my practicing to be worthy of the instrument.

Jan Overduin: And then when we heard that Brunzema was moving to Fergus, that was kind of special because this famous German organbuilder was going to live so close to Kitchener. It's been wonderful.

Gerhard Brunzema: We started approximately ten years ago and set up shop. I built actually this building. We are making tracker organs here; tracker organs means that the connection between the keys and the distribution part of the organ where the wind is distributed, that connection is made by mechanical means. In this case here [in the Kisten Orgel] there are stickers going down which connect the keys with the windchest, the windchest being the wind distribution part. It is, first of all, relatively simple, and so it can be maintained and repaired, and it can have a long lifespan.

Friedrich Brunzema: It's a system that has proved itself throughout the centuries. I was in Switzerland and saw an organ dating back to I think it was the 1480s that had been restored a few times, but essentially was still playing with the original tracker action; and that's really quite incredible. It speaks for the validity of the system.

Father Edward Sheridan (Pastor, Blessed Sacrament Parish): In 1980 we began the process of working with architects on the design of our church, our office section, and residence, and we were very much concerned about space, having ample meeting areas, and little consideration was given to the interior. We were more concerned about the capacity of our church. Once all the drawings were complete we began to look at the interior, and the thought of the organ, what type of instrument we would have. An organ is a tradition in Catholic churches, and so our choir director at that time was Mary Ann Voisin, and Mary Ann took it upon herself to begin doing some research. She came back one time after a trip to Montréal and said she saw this organ in Montréal that she was most impressed with and it was done by Mr. Brunzema. And at that time we were delighted to find out that his plant was in Fergus. So we went out to Fergus and began to discuss with him the possibility of a pipe organ and he was very interested as well.

Gerhard Brunzema: They had almost decided on buying an electronic organ but they came once here to our shop and saw such a small organ [the Kisten Orgel] that they unanimously decided to go for a pipe organ. It was just before they were pouring the concrete and it was possible to have the wind lines, which connect the organ with the electric blower in the corner, that could be built into the floor so that there were no additional steps there.

Father Edward Sheridan: The tragedy of it all is: Mary Ann Voisin, who was the one who initiated and really was the contact person and poured so much energy into the organ, her funeral was the first funeral from the new church. She died very suddenly in August of 1981. And so Mary Ann never saw or heard the organ, but she knew that we had made the decision and that the organ was being built for the new church.

Gerhard Brunzema: That organ has been designed actually as a one-manual organ, and did service for a couple of years in that fashion, and there was a desire to have a second manual. And since there was room we are presently working on including this second division with three stops.

Leslie Smith (Organbuilder with Brunzema Organs, Inc.): And somehow or other, I developed a fascination that goes back just about as far as I can remember with the sound of an organ. I have inherited from my father, as well, a certain aptitude for mechanical things. My father was a mechanic and as a kid I was able to watch him at his work, and that always fascinated me: things that bump and twiddle and knock something else and everything just kind of works together. So it's a way of satisfying my curiosity about sound and also about physics, I guess, or about something that moves. It's also an opportunity to make something with your hands. An organ is something that—at least here [in this shop]—we fabricate with our own hands. The technology is pretty primitive but it all depends on the execution.

Ruth Brunzema: Actually, being the wife of an organbuilder, that means you are involved: directly involved to do some woodworking. I do this [for] about ten years, and I like it very much to make those pipes. And since we have made twenty-four of those small instruments, and one hundred wooden pipes are in [them], then you know that I made more than two thousand of those small little wooden pipes. It's quite an amount. I'm very proud after my long hours when they play for the first time and they sound lovely.

Leslie Smith: It is time-consuming, demanding work, and you have to have patience with it, and that's not always easy, especially when you start as a younger person and you're kind of gung-ho and you see an organ from the outside and you think, "This is great; I want to have something to do with this." But as soon as you get started in as an apprentice you begin to discover all these little details that go into making even the most basic item, and it can be somewhat daunting in the beginning. But it takes a special kind of patience to be able to do that sort of work hour after hour. You always have in mind the final result. You always have in mind that this is only a small part but it contributes to the larger picture.

Gerhard Brunzema: When I started my own business here, I had the possibility to more closely direct the development and closely oversee the quality of the instrument. And we can also try to convince people to select certain details and agree to certain details which have proven in this shop and through my lifetime as being very useful and artistically very valuable.

Peter Nikiforuk (Organist): I am very, very impressed with especially this model [the Kisten Orgel]. I think it is the cleverest design for a portative organ that I've ever seen because it's so compact, and I think that's a tribute to his design skills to get something that compact. It's really a wonderful instrument to play, very enjoyable. It took me a little while to get used to; I've never played an action quite like that. But once you get used to it, it's extremely sensitive. It's neither too heavy nor too light. A lot of mechanical instruments, their action can be so light that if you brush the key they're going to sound; it's like playing on eggshells. And there are a lot of other mechanical-action instruments that are extremely heavy, and prone to induced tendonitis in the performer. This is really quite a pleasure to play. It's exactly the way it should be.

Leslie Smith: The small instrument that we produce on a regular basis, the scales are developed there for a very special situation. The instrument is very small and the pipes have to be made small in dimension—not in length but in width as opposed to length—in order to fit them all in. So that, especially the sounds of the two flute stops in that organ, that produces a very special sound that I don't really think he's aiming for in his larger instruments. It comes as quite a surprise; the first one I worked on, I was really surprised to see how high the mouths were and how hard the pipes were blown. The wind pressure—63 millimeter wind pressure—I knew that wind pressure; we used that in my previous experience in organs in churches seating 800 people, and I thought: 63 millimeters, that's awfully high. But that's what it takes to make those little pipes produce an acceptable sound.

Jan Overduin: I think it always boils down to the sound. If an organ sings, if it has a beautiful singing tone, then it'll be wonderful to hear and, in this case, also to play because he's just a very fine craftsman. I think that has to do with the voicing of an organ, and that part is perhaps the most specialized. You have the windchest, and you put pipes on it, and you have a keyboard, and you push the keys, and the pipes make a sound, but how to fine-tune the sound—not just a matter of tuning although that's part of it—but how they sound, how many overtones they have, and which ones you strengthen, and which ones you weaken, and how one pipe will blend with another, those are things that take years and years to learn and there are actually very few people who are really good at it. And I would say Mr. Brunzema is one of those very few.

Gerhard Brunzema: I grew up in northern Germany, and that area has quite a few historic organs. I was born in Emden, which is a town in the northwestern part not far from the Dutch border, and so I was able to hear many organs from my early days on, in the church and making trips and seeing instruments in Germany and the near vicinity. Now I made a formal apprenticeship time of three and a half years in West Germany at the firm of Paul Ott in Göttingen. That company made tracker organs only, and so I got quite a few technical and practical knowledges of how to make and how to do and some aspects also what not to do.

Leslie Smith: Mr. Brunzema's musical ears were certainly weaned on the sound of North German organs; I mean, they were all around him in the area where he spent his youth and had his musical training and then also his organbuilding training. So they can't help but sound somewhat North German. But I know he is not interested in building replicas of North German organs; he is really concerned about building instruments that work today. So in that respect I would say that his organs sound like Brunzema organs.

Jan Overduin: He has his own ideas. And I would say in general the sound of the recent Brunzemas that I have played—of about this size—is very robust, full, and thrilling. So not shrill and thin, but full and rich in sound.

Joyce Knarr: The Brunzema organs tend to have a more direct sound. They're not harsh as some other tracker organs are, but it is a very full, clean sound. It's excellent in this type of building for leading congregational singing, and that was the way the organ [Opus 12] was designed. It was not designed for organ concerts, it was designed for congregational singing.

Leslie Smith: You have to get the mechanism all working, and the pipes have been installed; usually at some point they have stood inside the organ; and perhaps you have succeeded in making them start to produce a sound. But we usually don't begin the real tonal work until the organ is standing in the room, and then we begin to make final decisions on what direction the work will take based on how our sample notes sound in the room.

Jan Overduin: There is a saying amongst organists that the most important stop on any organ is the room. And each organ is always built for a particular room. It's assembled in the shop of the organbuilder, who already has been to the place where it is to be installed, and with that in mind he builds it, but the final voicing in done in the church. So the answer to your question is, that [the room] is hugely important. You cannot simply take this organ and put it in another church or hall and expect it to sound the same way. It won't.

Joyce Knarr: I think each voicer has their own style of voicing; but it has to also conform to the voicing that's needed for the building. I think he is very good at voicing organs for the building. I've played several of his other instruments, too, and I always felt his voicing suited the building.

Leslie Smith: It's a matter of time, but you can never be overexposed to different instruments, and you really have to be curious enough about other people's work and to be able to go and look at other installations, old and new. It helps to get involved in organ service work; I've always felt this is really an important facet of organbuilding that a lot of organbuilders somewhat ignore. That's really where a young organbuilder gets to see what works and what doesn't work as far as the mechanism and also a chance to evaluate the relative tonal success of that particular builder's approach, and it's only by making those observations of existing instruments that you begin to understand how you can realize your own expectations perhaps, or help Mr. Brunzema realize his expectations.

Gerhard Brunzema: I think it is quite essential for anyone doing some artistic work that you have some kind of early impressions which you can refer to whenever you go later and see something else in other areas. If that is not the case—if there is no personal background from the early times—then you are in danger of being too eclectic.

Peter Nikiforuk: I find it a very compelling sound, and I was exposed to it when I was quite young. And my first experiences with the organ, I went to the church where my piano teacher was the organist, and I used to go up every Sunday and press that cancel button for Mr. Perry and turn off the organ when he was done. From there I started taking organ lessons and it's just something I've always loved.

Friedrich Brunzema: It's something different, and once you get to hear the whole organ, and see how everything works, and you see that you've done a really good job, you see that very quickly in installations, you have that pride, "Oh, this is a job well done," especially if an organist comes and plays the instrument really well. And you say, "This was worth it. All this time, work, and so on; but it was worth it."

Gerhard Brunzema: Yes, I am forty-two years in the field, and so forty-two years gives lots of experience, positive and negative, you know what works and you see also what sometimes is not that advantageous, and you take that into your memory and follow the experiences.

Joyce Knarr: This was the first time that I had an opportunity to work in a church where I felt the instrument, the building, and I were one. And it has been very interesting for me, but I think other musicians now within our parish now appreciate this instrument more that I've had a chance to grow with it, and they are appreciating the variety we can get with the second manual. So I think all in all, it has been a growth experience for the parish, too.

Jan Overduin: Ever since I was a child I loved the sound of an organ. And why do I love it? I've thought about it a lot; I don't really care so much why I do—I know I do. But I think various reasons. One of them is that the spectrum of the sound is so vast: It goes higher than any orchestral instrument and lower than any orchestral instrument. The colors of an organ are so rich; there are reeds and mixtures and mutations and flutes and strings. It's just a wonderful world of sound to live in and work with.

Leslie Smith: It is very hard to let go of them. That's one reason I think why, when the job is done and I know it's good, that I want to leave. They are so much a part of a certain period of your life: You can look at them and say that was eight months or that was six months of my life, and it really becomes like a child. And you know you have to let go of that, you have to let it go, because you did this work for someone else. So the best thing to do is just simply let go and hope that maybe you might be back someday and see how it has developed.

How Gerhard Brunzema Addressed Some of the Problems in Modern Organbuilding

Thomas Donahue

The study of the work of Gerhard Brunzema eventually leads one to consider not only his place in the history of the organ, but also the whole question of building contemporary organs based on historic principles. Many aspects of this organbuilding style emerged as a result of the increased study of the past; however, organbuilding knowledge does not pass through history un-scathed, so the return to these principles is not without its problems. This chapter will examine some of these problems and how Gerhard Brunzema addressed them.

ORGANBUILDING AS ART

To begin with, the very process of designing and constructing organs has its difficulties.

> There are so many ways in which [building organs] can be carried out in concrete instances that it is impossible to make a recipe which can claim exclusive validity.—Rudolf von Beckerath (Beckerath, 14)

> Further examination of the literature will show that we may seek in vain for any consistent and all-embracing theory of musical instrument design. . . . We must face the fact that there can be no universal theory, since a fine musical instrument is a work of art that may be described in rough terms but not explained.—Hugh Gough (Gough, 74)

One key to this problem that is evident particularly in the work of Gerhard Brunzema is something that in many respects is as unexplainable as the art of organbuilding itself: the builder's judgment. Builders who have learned their craft well and have a wide range of experience will have a sense of direction when a dilemma arises. The question may be as simple as, What material would work best for this component? or as far-reaching as, What constitutes good Principal sound? This is one aspect of historic builders of which we can have no direct evidence; we can see a certain building practice in a surviving instrument, but we cannot uncover how the builder thought and why one option was chosen over another. Because of the scarcity of our knowledge about the judgment of historic builders, it becomes easy to assume that all builders in (for example) seventeenth-century northern Germany always agreed on all details related to the organs they built. Similarly, because modern builders are available to tell us what they think, it becomes easy to assume that the judgment of the builder is a modern phenomenon. However, once one gets a sense of the individualism that exists within modern organbuilding, the individualism of historic builders seems all the more likely. While judgment does play a role in contemporary organbuilding (see below), it actually may be one of its more timeless aspects.

Gerhard Brunzema's organbuilding studies led him not to copy, not to transcribe historic organs in modern ways, but to pursue the more fundamental approach of trying to discover why past building practices produced results that were so musical. He incorporated this knowledge in organs that in some ways resembled the instruments he studied, but which were actually modern expressions of his own judgment. He even took this one step further, believing that an organbuilder is an artist who should be given the freedom to exercise judgment in the details of a specific instrument. This adds significance to the fact that we tend to individualize an organ by its builder's name.

> Mr. Brunzema's musical ears were certainly weaned on the sound of North German organs; I mean, they were all around him in the area where he spent his youth and had his musical training and then also his organbuilding training. So they [his instruments] can't help but sound somewhat North German. But I know he is not interested in building replicas of North German organs; he is really concerned about building instruments that work today. So in that respect I would say that his organs sound like Brunzema organs.—Leslie Smith ("Castles of the Soul," pp. 81–82 in this volume)

A MULTITUDE OF OPTIONS

Modern organbuilders have at their disposal too many options from which to choose.

> I find it very difficult to design a given organ because there are so many possibilities but so few of them can be included in one instrument. The more knowledgeable you become, the harder it is to put all your ideas together in one instrument and make it suitable for the diversity of music you might want to play.—Gene Bedient (Cramer 1990, 76)

This overabundance of design features is the result of the complex and diverse history of the organ. The necessity of accommodating a multitude of features in any one organ is fueled by the strong desire by today's organists to be able to play the majority of the organ literature on one instrument. The specific difficulty with this is that it engenders the notion that if an organ simply had enough variety of stops one could play anything. While the stops themselves have a historical basis, eclectic organs do not. Some of the design of an eclectic organ must be directed toward integrating a myriad of varied and sometimes conflicting elements. The problem arises when an instrument has more integration than elements being integrated, more glue than pieces being glued.

On the other hand, Gerhard Brunzema's instruments illustrate what may be referred to as focused design.

> Artistic expression involves making a decision and staying with it as effectively and artistically as possible. Work toward an ideal, choose something which you feel is appropriate and pursue that instead of looking in three or four different directions. . . . It is best to concentrate on one approach. Become a master of one thing, get over the initial difficulties very quickly, and then polish your knowledge, the details of which finally add up to a very good result.—Gerhard Brunzema (Cramer 1989, 47)

A specific example of focused design was the way he concentrated on good organ sound as a universal. The following comments by him show the importance placed on this during the early years in Germany.

> We tried to utilize to a maximum what previous generations had explored and followed up. . . . Through the knowledge that we gained restoring important historic organs, we were able to apply historic principles in a controlled fashion. We studied historic organs and then tried to reproduce those sounds in a new organ. We were not trying to copy historic instruments; instead, we wanted to make use of every conceivable detail from historic organs that seemed to influence the tone of the organ. . . . We knew better than to emphasize too many details of our work that were rooted in historicism. . . . An organ is an aggregate of many small details, and we did not want to divert attention from the sound of the instruments.—Gerhard Brunzema (Cramer 1989, 46)

Other builders have commented on the universal nature of good organ sound.

> There's no reason why, say, the North German organ can't play music from more recent periods. . . . Good voicing and scaling transcends stylistic periods.—Lynn Dobson (Waters, 43)

> All good organs have certain sound-production concepts in common. Organs of different styles and periods have many technical differences—in the mechanics, in qualities of sound and in the voicing—

but in all good styles I have seen, the pipes have open flueways and cutups of generous proportion which permit the pipes to create an energetic sound. The exciting instruments to listen to are those which create open, energetic sounds and have musical subtleties within individual sets of pipes.—Gene Bedient (Cramer 1990, 75)

COPYING AND MODERN TECHNOLOGY

Two approaches that have been used by some modern builders (sometimes as a means of solving the problems already discussed) are copying what was done in the past, and using whatever is the latest technology. Copying historic organs—by which is meant reproducing in a new instrument the details from a particular old instrument as precisely as possible—has its uses, such as allowing builders to understand a certain organbuilding style or to learn the details of a particular builder, and allowing organists to experience to some degree how historic organs sounded and behaved. But in copying, some of what is copied may be musically unessential, and the very act of copying may elevate an atypical or extraneous detail to be more significant than it really is. Also, builders do not get to inject their own ideas, which often leads to the stigma that copying is not a creative activity. Modern technology allows builders to make use of alternative materials and designs, which can have some advantages. But there are also problems, such as promoting the fallacy that new is always better, and the fact that the "state of the art" means today's technology will soon be deposed by something else.

One cannot deny that the techniques of copying and reliance on technology are helpful if used judiciously, but as organbuilding methods in themselves, they are extremes that are probably best avoided. Copying deals with the past, state-of-the-art technology deals with the present; but we cannot select the past or the present and forego the other. Both a historical basis and a contemporary context are necessary.

> It is plain that this complex process [of examining historical instruments] can never become objective. . . . It is hopeless and possibly undesirable to expect to eliminate completely all modern bias in one's judgment and technique.—Frank Hubbard (Hubbard, 11)

> It is perfectly proper to learn from the old masters: We must do so, for no one in one lifetime can do it all. . . . Therefore a modern maker

must go to school with the great masters of the past, though not, I
think, to the point of abdicating from original thought.—Hugh
Gough (Gough, 75)

The necessity of a historical basis rests with the very essence of the organ.

I think you have to recognize that the organ is an entity which must
contain certain elements arranged in a certain way. . . . You have to
come eventually to the realization that if you want to do anything
that's radically new, you'll probably be working with a different instrument.—Lynn Dobson (Waters, 43)

Fidelity to the old [instruments] means in many ways merely fidelity
to the true nature of the organ. This must be so, since the organ is a
specific historical invention like everything else, and too much modi-
fication of the designs achieved centuries ago results in a different
kind of instrument.—Peter Williams (Williams, 111)

Some builders have even noted that a strong historical basis has a quality that extends far beyond the original motivation of reviving a traditional organbuilding practice.

In the years of my organ building practice I have always had the same
experience. . . . The more clearly and purely an organ represents its
own style, the more it is capable of interpreting the music of different
epochs.—Rudolf von Beckerath (Beckerath, 14)

The more specifically you build tracker organs the better the chances
for long-term success. If organists accept that not as a limitation but as
a fact of artistic life, then this approach will succeed. . . . All-inclusive
art is not art at all. It is a contradiction in terms. It is not possible. Art
is selection. It is preference for something.—Gerhard Brunzema
(Cramer 1989, 48)

The necessity of a contemporary context is shown by several
factors. First, regardless of how much we can learn and understand about a past era, we live in the present, so we have a point
of view that is different from a past builder or organist or composer because our vantage point is one of hindsight. Second,
there are a number of factors affecting the design and construction of modern organs that did not exist in the past, such as the

abundance of diverse literature, spaces with poor acoustics, the use of central heating, and installations that require the organ to have multiple functions in spaces with multiple functions. Third, organbuilding cannot be separated from organbuilders, past or present. Modern instruments and modern builders are necessarily related.

Gerhard Brunzema abstracted the essential musical elements from a well-defined class of historical instruments and reapplied these elements artistically and consistently in new instruments that were not associated with a specific historical style. This should be considered no more unusual than the way in which the same organbuilding principles had strikingly different incarnations in the numerous national styles of the past. His designs pay homage to the organs of northern Germany, not only because those instruments are part of his culture and have an intrinsic worth, but also because those designs are straightforward, reliable, and musical. The important point is that regardless of outwardly "historical" features such as mechanical key action, flat/parallel pedal keyboards, and German stop names, his organs are far from being copies. Eighteenth-century organists would find Brunzema's work familiar but his instruments are products of the late twentieth century, a fact that he firmly acknowledged in his organ cases. It is my opinion that his designs will be more influential on future building practice (compared with nonclassical designs) because they show the timelessness of the principles involved, and thus they reveal more of the true nature of the organ.

The approaches discussed do not completely summarize the work of Gerhard Brunzema, nor are they found exclusively in his instruments. Yet, his organs show that an emphasis on these approaches to deal with modern organbuilding problems yields exceptional results. Other builders may use the same and other methods in order to produce fine instruments, but it will be difficult to find anyone who can surpass what Gerhard Brunzema did.

✤ 21

Chorale Prelude on *Schmücke dich, O liebe Seele*

Barrie Cabena

[Ed. note: This piece was written in memory of Gerhard Brunzema and first performed by Bernard Lagacé at a memorial recital on Brunzema Organs Opus 12 in Blessed Sacrament Parish, Kitchener, Ontario, on 20 May 1992.]

Chorale Prelude on *Schmücke dich, O liebe Seele*

Barrie Cabena
Opus 236

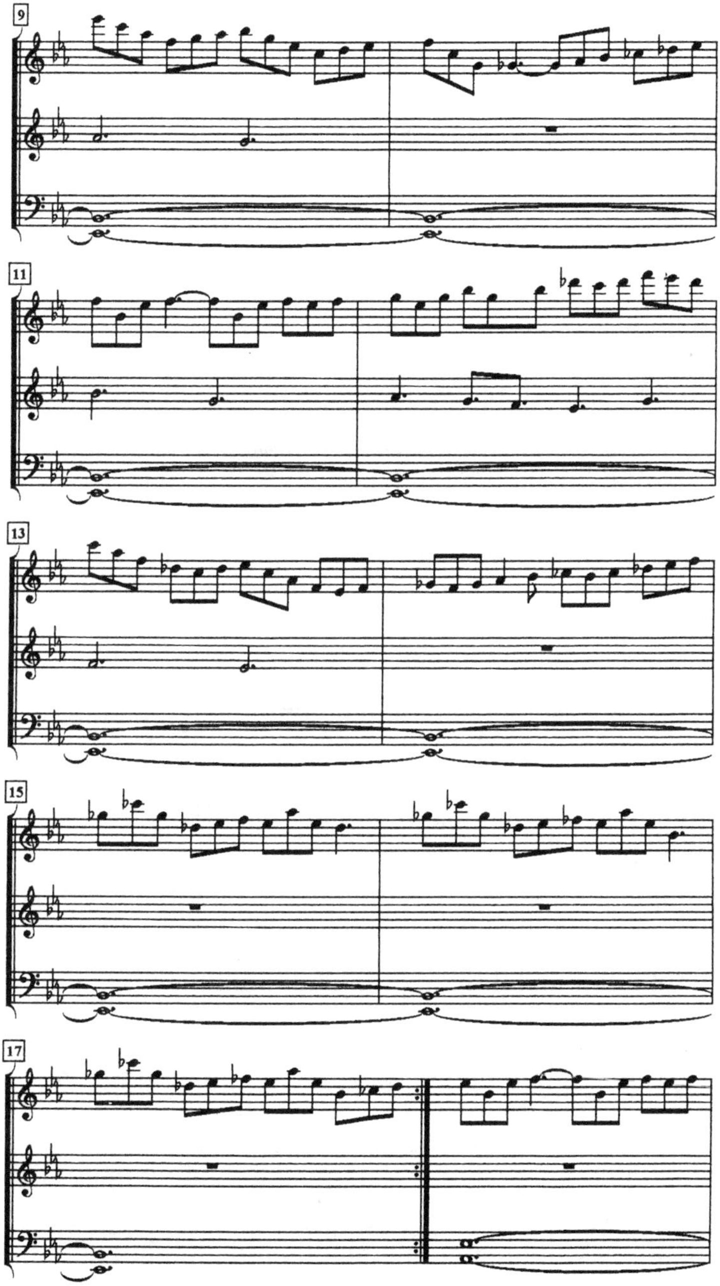
9
11
13
15
17

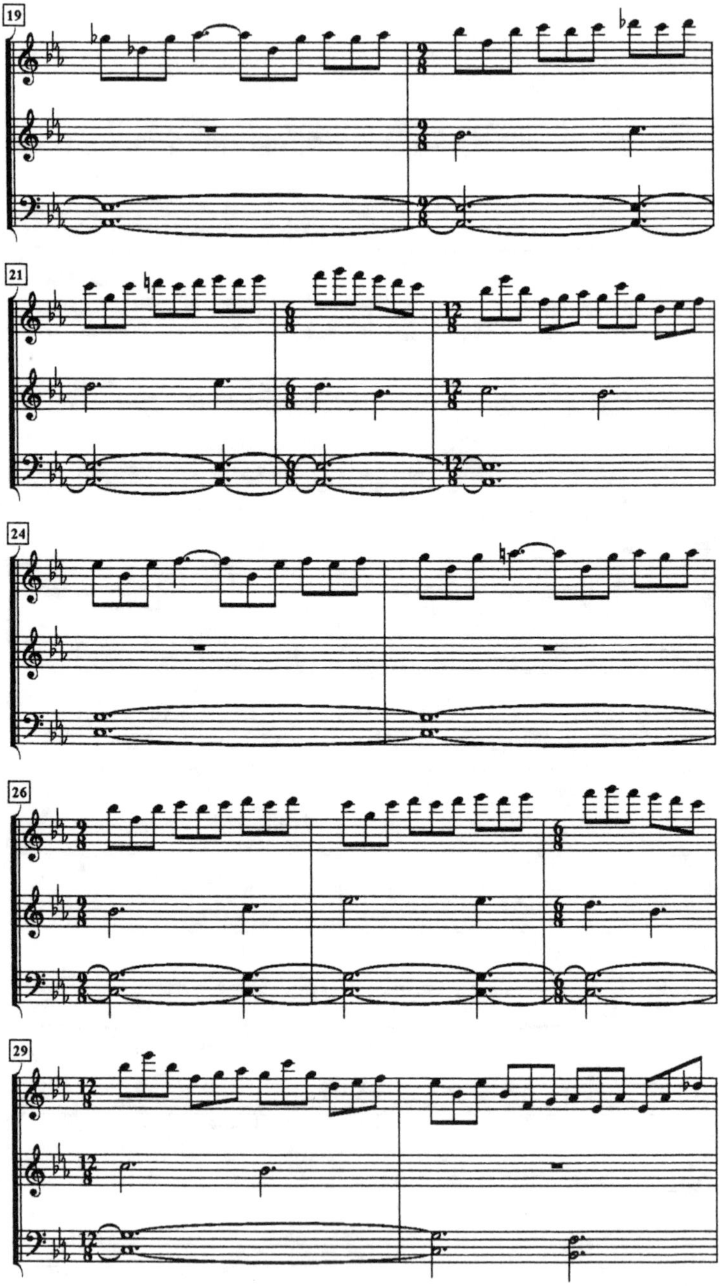
19
21
24
26
29

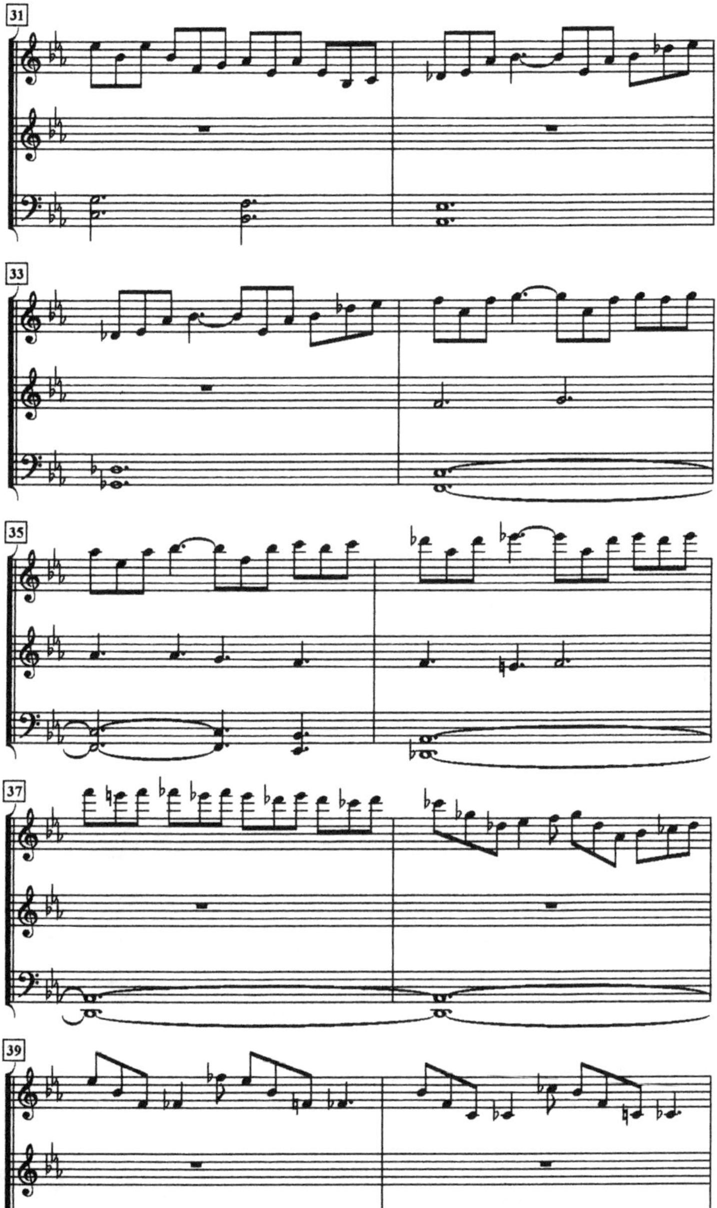
31
33
35
37
39

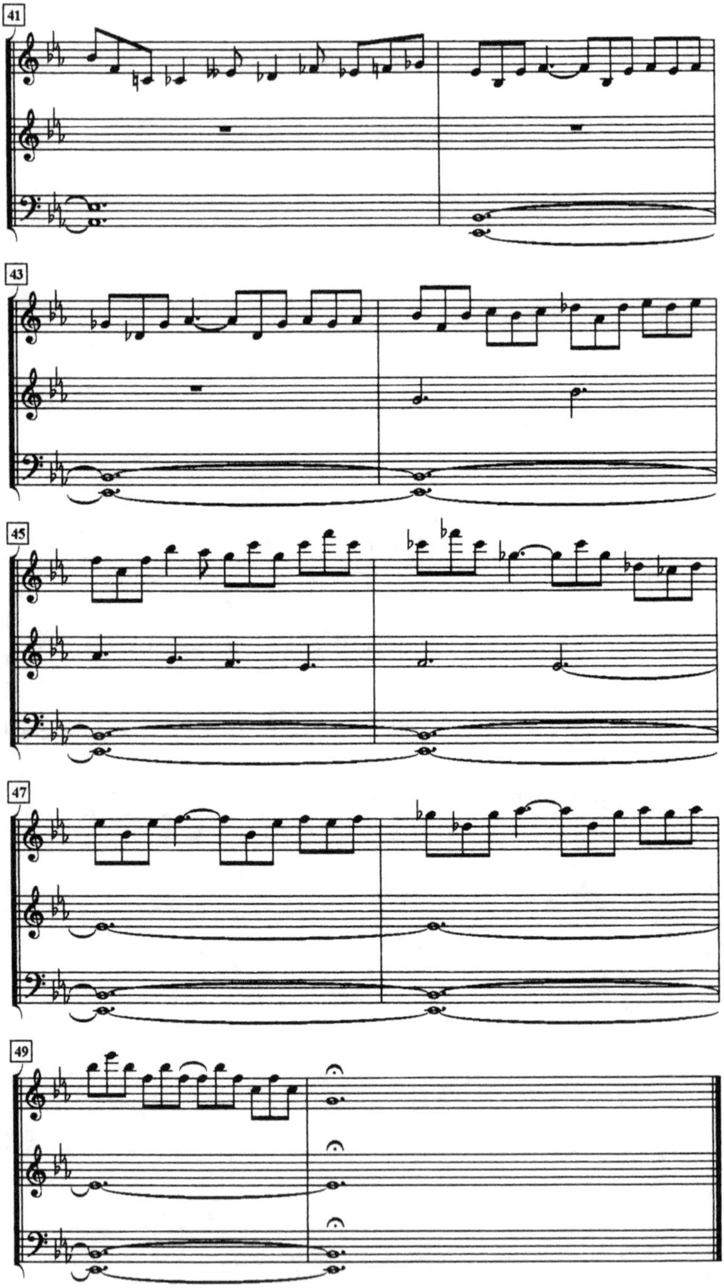
41
43
45
47
49

Part II
THE ORGANS

❖ 22

1954-1971: Orgelbau Ahrend & Brunzema, Leer-Loga, Germany

OPUS LIST

Roman numerals indicate the number of manual keyboards and Arabic numerals indicate the total number of stops. The uppercase letter *P* indicates the presence of a pedal division with independent stops; the lowercase letter *p* indicates the presence of a pedal keyboard but no pedal division (a "pulldown" pedal). Repairs, restorations, and revoicings are noted; all other organs are new. If the organ was a restoration, the years given are those of the original installation and subsequent major rebuilding(s). City and town names not followed by a country are in Germany. An asterisk indicates those organs that appear on a list that Brunzema would send from his Fergus workshop to prospective clients. Superscript numerals refer to the notes at the end of the list. (Sources: Lade, 18, 20, 22; Pape 1972, 28-30; Wallmann and Moe, 24-28)

Opus	Year	Location, Size, and Type
1	1954	Larrelt *Reformierte Kirche*[1] I/P/11 restoration; 1619, 1710, 1848–1855
2	1955	Kirchborgum *Reformierte Kirche* II/P/10 repairs
3	1955	Hohenlimburg *Reformierte Friedhofskapelle* I/3 Positiv
4	1955	Westerhusen *Reformierte Kirche** I/p/7 restoration; 1642–1643
5	1956	Minden *Altsprachliches Gymnasium* II/P/9
6	1956	Iserlohn *Gemeindehaus* In der Grüne I/4 Positiv
7	1956	Münster *Landesverband der Mission* I/3 Positiv
8	1956	Aurich *St. Lamberti* I/4 Positiv (interim organ)
9	1957	Uttum *Reformierte Kirche** I/9 restoration; 1655–1656
10	1957	Veldhausen *Altreformierte Kirche* I/p/6
11	1958	Bremen-Farge *Reformierte Kirche** II/P/11
12	1958	Ennepetal-Milspe *Evangelische Kirche* I/4 Positiv
13	1958	Leer-Heisfelde *Reformierte Kirche* I/4 Positiv
14	1958	Grimersum *Reformierte Kirche* I/4 Positiv (interim organ)
15	1958	Grimersum *Reformierte Kirche* I/p/8
16	1958	Hinte *Reformierte Kirche* I/p/8 new; case from 1776–1781
17	1959	Vienna, Austria *Concentus Musicus* I/1 Kniepositiv ("Knee" positive)
18	1959	Scheveningen, Netherlands *Zorgvlietkerk** III/P/26
19	1959	Bant, Netherlands *Hervormde Kerk* I/4 Positiv

Opus	Year	Location, Size, and Type (*continued*)
20	1959	Rutten, Netherlands *Hervormde Kerk* I/4 Positiv
21	1959	Bath, Somerset, England *Private residence* I/1 Kniepositiv
22	1960	Groningen, Netherlands *Gereformeerd Kerk*[2] I/6
23	1960	Freren *Reformierte Kirche* I/p/8 new; case from 1699
24	1960	Bath, Zeeland, Netherlands *Hervormde Kerk* I/4 Positiv
25	1961	Rysum *Reformierte Kirche** I/7 restoration; 1457, 1736–1737
26	1961	Vienna, Austria *Nikolaus Harnoncourt* I/3 restoration
27	1961	Aurich *St. Lamberti** II/P/25
28	1962	Leer *Kirchsaal Hohe Ellern* I/5
29	1962	Espel, Netherlands *Hervormde Kerk* I/p/7
30	1962	Bremen *St. Martini** III/P/33 new; case from 1615–1619
31	1962	Emden *Schweizer Kirche*[3] II/p/11
32	1962	The Hague, Netherlands *Geemente Museum** I/1 Regal, restoration; seventeenth century
33	1963	Munich *Studio für frühe Musik* I/1 Kniepositiv
34	1963	Wassenaar, Netherlands *Kievitkerk**[4] II/P/21
35	1964	Hatzum *Reformierte Kirche* I/p/7
36	1964	Leer-Loga *Friedenskirche* II/P/13
37	1965	Celle *Reformierte Kirche* II/P/14 restoration
38	1965	Wybelsum *Reformierte Kirche* I/p/6

Opus	Year	Location, Size, and Type (*continued*)
39	1965	Gildehaus *Reformierte Kirche* II/P/15
40	1965	Groningen, Netherlands *Magnaliakerk* II/p/13
41	1965	Amsterdam, Netherlands *Oude Kerk* (small organ)* II/P/17 new; case from 1658
42	1965	The Hague, Netherlands *Johanneskapel* II/P/14
43	1965	Amsterdam, Netherlands *Waalse Kerk**5 II/P/26 restoration; 1680, 1733–1734
44	1966	Leer *Große Kirche* III/P/37 revoicing
45	1966	Bremen *Evangelische Kirche Oberneuland** II/P/22
46	1966	Bösperde *Evangelische Kirche* II/P/9
47	1967	Georgsdorf *Reformierte Kirche* I/9 restoration
48	1967	Los Angeles, Calif., U.S. *Residence organ** II/P/11
49	1967	Castrop-Rauxel *Kirche Schwerin-Frolinde** III/P/27
50	1967	Bremerhaven *Reformierte Kirche* I/6
51	1968	Aalten, Netherlands *Gereformeerd Zuiderkerk** II/P/16
52	1968	Berkeley, Calif., U.S. *University of California** I/4 Truhenorgel (cabinet organ)
53	1968	Berkeley, Calif., U.S. *University of California* I/1 Regal
54	1968	Vienna, Austria *Concentus Musicus* I/1 Regal
55	1968	Amsterdam, Netherlands *Private residence* I/1 Kniepositiv
56	1968	Berkeley, Calif., U.S. *University of California* I/1 Kniepositiv
57	1968	Gütersloh *Evangeliumskirche** II/P/20

Opus	Year	Location, Size, and Type (*continued*)
58	1968	Haarlem, Netherlands *Doopsgezinde Kerk**6 III/P/24
59	1969	Leer-Bingum *St. Matthäi* II/P/13
60	1969	Bremen *St. Martini* I/4 Truhenorgel
61	1969	Bremen *St. Martini* I/1 Regal
62	1969	Hamburg *Reformierte Kirche Altona** II/P/13
63	1969	Leer-Loga *Reformierte Kirche* I/P/9
64	1969	Schluderns, Italy *Schloss Churburg** I/7 chamber organ, restoration; sixteenth century
65	1969	Marienhafe *St. Marien* II/p/20 restoration; 1710
66	1969	Jennelt *Reformierte Kirche* I/p/8 restoration; 1738
67	1970	Vienna, Austria *Private owner** I/5 chamber organ, restoration; c1700
68	1970	Frankfurt/Main *Cantate Domino** III/P/32
69	1970	Uelsen *Reformierte Kirche** II/P/20 new; old case
70	1970	Innsbruck, Austria *Hofkirche**7 II/p/15 restoration, first stage; 1555–1561
71	1971	Kamp-Lintfort *Evangelische Kirche Hoerstgen** I/11 restoration; 1732
72	1971	Westerstede *St. Peter* II/P/23
73	1971	Groothusen *Reformierte Kirche* II/P/19 repairs
74	1971	Leer *Reformierte Kirche* III/P/37 revoicing
87	1975	Berkeley, Calif., U.S. *University of California**8 II/P/12

NOTES ON THE OPUS LIST

1. Larrelt, Opus 1: revoiced by Ahrend in 1988
2. Groningen, Opus 22: moved to Walburgskerk, Zutphen, The Netherlands
3. Emden, Opus 31: pedal stops added by Ahrend in 1985
4. Wassenaar, Opus 34: a Rückpositiv added by Van Vulpen in 1991
5. Amsterdam, Opus 43: retuned to a Neidhardt temperament in 1976
6. Haarlem, Opus 58: retuned to a Werckmeister temperament in 1975; unspecified additions in 1985
7. Innsbruck, Opus 70: second stage of restoration completed by Ahrend in 1976
8. Berkeley, Opus 87: finished in 1971 but not installed until 1975

SELECTED RESTORATIONS

Reformierte Kirche Westerhusen, Germany

Jost Sieburg, Göttingen, 1642-1643
Ahrend & Brunzema, 1955

MANUAL		PEDAL
8	Gedackt	pulldowns
8	Quintadena	
4	Principal	
2	Oktave	
1⅓	Quinte	
	Mixtur IV (highest rank 1955)	
8	Trompete	

Mixtur:	C	1	⅔	½	⅓
	c′	2	1⅓	1	⅔
	c″	4	2	1⅓	1

Cimbelstern
Manual compass: C-c‴ (49 notes)
Wind pressure: 76 mm (3 inches)
Temperament: Meantone
Source: Wallmann and Moe, 35

Reformierte Kirche St. Paulus Uttum, Germany

?, 1655-1656
Ahrend & Brunzema, 1957

MANUAL

16	Quintadena
8	Praestant
8	Gedackt
8	Quintadena
4	Oktave
2	Oktave
	Sesquialtera II (1957)
	Mixtur III–IV (4th rank 1957)
8	Trompete

Sesquialtera:	C	$1\frac{1}{3}$	$\frac{4}{5}$		
	b′	$2\frac{2}{3}$	$1\frac{3}{5}$		

Mixtur:	C	$1\frac{1}{3}$	1	$\frac{2}{3}$	
	G	2	$1\frac{1}{3}$	1	
	c	$2\frac{2}{3}$	2	$1\frac{1}{3}$	
	g′	4	$2\frac{2}{3}$	2	$1\frac{1}{3}$
	c″	4	4	$2\frac{2}{3}$	2

Tremulant (old)
Manual compass: CDEFGA–c‴ (45 notes)
Wind pressure: 78 mm (3 inches)
Temperament: Meantone
Sources: Lade, 30; Wallmann and Moe, 35; Gustav Leonhardt RCA
SEON RL 30765 (recording)

Reformierte Kirche   **Rysum, Germany**

?Master Harmannus, Groningen, 1457
Mathias Amoort, Groningen, 1736–1737
Ahrend & Brunzema, 1959–1961

MANUAL

8	Praestant
8	Gedackt
4	Oktave
2	Oktave
	Sesquialtera II (1959–1961)
	Mixtur III–V (1959–1961)
8	Trompete (1959–1961)

Manual compass: CDEFGA-g″a″ (41 notes)
Wind pressure: 70 mm (2¾ inches)
Temperament: Meantone
Sources: Lade, 32; Wallmann and Moe, 35; Gustav Leonhardt RCA
SEON RL 30765 (recording)

Waalse Kerk   **Amsterdam, Netherlands**
  Nicolas Langlez, Ghent, 1680
  Christiaan Müller, Amsterdam, 1733–1734
  Ahrend & Brunzema, 1965

HAUPTWERK
16	Prestant I-II	1734; doubled ranks from g′
8	Prestant I-II	1734; doubled ranks from f
8	Roerfluit	1734
8	Quintadeen	1734
4	Octaaf	1734
3	Quint I-II	1734; doubled ranks from c′
2	Gemshoorn	1734
2	Mixtuur IV-VI	1734
16	Trompet	1734, 1965
8	Trompet	1734
8	Vox humana	1734

RÜCKPOSITIV
8	Prestant I-II	1734; from G
8	Holpijp	1680; C-F stopped; remainder Rohrflöte
4	Octaaf	1680
3	Quint I-II	1965; doubled ranks from c′
2	Octaaf	1734
1⅗	Terts	1965; from c
1½	Mixtuur II-IV	1965
	Scherp VI	1965

PEDAL
16	Bourdon	1680
8	Prestant	1680, 1965
6	Roerquint	1680
4	Octaaf	1734
2	Nachthoorn	1734
16	Fagot	1734
8	Trompet	1734

HW Mixtur:	C	2	1⅓	1	⅔		
	c	2⅔	2	1⅓	1		
	c'	4	4	2⅔	2⅔	2	2

Two tremulants (quick, slow)
Couplers: RP→HW HW→P
Manual compass: C–c''' (49 notes)
Pedal compass: C–d' (27 notes)
Wind pressure: 84 mm (3⅓ inches)
Sources: Lade, 35; Williams 1966, 47–48; Visser, 58, 60; Gustav
Leonhardt, RCA SEON GL 71051 (recording)

"The [Waalse Kerk] organ was a rebuild of what appears to have
been a conventional French-Belgian two-manual, pedal-less organ of the late seventeenth century. In both [the Waalse Kerk
and the St. Bavo, Haarlem] organs Müller gave the Hauptwerk a
Prinzipal chorus based on a 16', 8' and 4', the Mixtures in both
cases demanding the 16' Praestant since they over-thicken the 8'
tone. The main Hauptwerk reeds are similarly 16' Trompeten—
the 8' Trompete, like the Praestant 8', rather less forceful and
rounder than the 16' ranks. The 16' Praestants are beautifully
rich in the treble, due partly to the doubling; both Hauptwerk
choruses are best suited by large, slow, powerful chords such as
would be used in hymn accompaniment. Subtle chorale-prelude
registrations are not easy to obtain, though the dark, sombre,
unique sound of the Haarlem 16.16.8.5⅓.4 combination must
have attracted organists. . . . The Amsterdam organ is much less
subtle [than the Haarlem organ], and though some stops are un-
deniably charming (Rohrflöte 8', Vox humana, Holpijp), very little could be called delicate. Other stops are brilliant and stag-
geringly forceful (Hauptwerk Mixtur, pedal Trompete) and the two
manual choruses hit the listener's ear with the force of a hell-fire
evangelist, their tone unsurpassable for controlling an eighteenth-
century Protestant congregation. The pedal is no match for the
Hauptwerk even with its dominant Trompete 8' à la bra-
bançonne, a firm 2' and a manual coupler. Even the Quintadena
is strong—not with its fifth-overtones, but in general character,
adding good definition to an Hauptwerk accompaniment of 8' +
8' when a solo line is played by Rückpositiv 8' + 4' + Tierce. The
new Scharf is usable only when the two manuals are coupled together, but the Rückpositiv chorus is otherwise relatively mild,

its Prinzipalen having something of Silbermann's Gamba tone."
(Williams 1966, 47–48)

Schloss Churburg   Schluderns, Italy
> The Baldachin chamber organ
> Michael Strobel, 1559
> Ahrend & Brunzema, 1969

"At Schloss Churburg near Schluderns, Vintschgau, South Tirol,
Italy, is to be found a most interesting and valuable Renaissance
organ built in 1559 by Michael Strobel (from Amberg near Brau-
nau-am-Inn, Austria) for the Knight Jakob Trapp. Since the sixteenth century the castle, built three hundred years previously for
the Chur bishops, has been in the possession of the Counts
Trapp; the little organ is essentially unaltered. Moved in 1915 because of the danger of war-damage, the instrument has suffered
externally but was completely restored in 1969 by the well-
known restorers and builders Ahrend & Brunzema.

  "The chamber organ, completely enclosed in a canopy most
artfully made, pierced here and there with lattice work which is
lined with an ancient velvet-like material, contains seven speaking stops and two speaking accessories, all divided in bass and treble. The stops are made to sound by pulling out knobs protruding from the lower part of the case fixed to the end of the sliders
to the player's left (bass) and right (treble). From front to back the
ranks are placed thus, according to their name-initial written
above the coloured knobs:

R	white	Regal	8	Trichterregal (Ahrend & Brunzema, reconstruction)
O	dark	Oktave (Prinzipal)	2	Largest open tin pipes
Z	white	Zimbel 1	¼	C36 f29 f′22 or,

$$\begin{array}{ccc} C & f & f' \\ \tfrac{1}{4} & \tfrac{1}{2} & 1 \end{array}$$

Z	dark	Zimbel 2	⅙	C40 f33 f′26 f″19 or,

$$\begin{array}{cccc} C & f & f' & f'' \\ \tfrac{1}{6} & \tfrac{1}{3} & \tfrac{2}{3} & 1\tfrac{1}{3} \end{array}$$

Q	white	Quindecima	1	Prinzipal oktave
F	dark	[Filomela or] "Nachtigall"		A little pipe for treble and bass, placed in a beaker of water
C	white	Copl	2	Rohrflöte with short, narrow chimney closed by soldering, no ears
G	dark	"Gezwitscher" (twitter)		Three very small pipes for treble and bass, giving a twittering sound
C	white	Copl	4	Stopped pipes, the foundational stop

The stops F and G are accessory speaking stops for nightingale-warbling and bird-twittering, fed with wind from all the channels of the natural keys. A Tremulant "in the wind" (*Tremblant doux*), called *Zitter* in the renaissance period and giving a quick undulation, is brought on by pulling out an ivory knob on the lower right-hand panel.

"The keyboard has a compass of [CDEFGA–g″ a″, 41 notes], has ivory-plated naturals and ebony-plated sharps, and can be slid to the right a whole tone. The organ is tuned with thirds pure, which means that only certain keys are playable. The transposing device obviously has the aim of making more keys available, quite apart from the question of their absolute pitch.

"The mechanism is also remarkable. The pipe-ranks are longer than the keyboard, and by means of stickers, each key tilts two connected squares which lie inside the chest and which radiate fan-wise from keyboard to pipe-ranks. The second square pulls down the pallet not as usual longitudinally but sideways; its little tracker pulling the pallet is fixed to one side (left) while the pallet is hinged to the channel-wall along the other (right). This is necessary to give the right amount of wind to all the separate wind conducts which have been made in each channel by dividing bars. A normal longitudinal pallet would not give the conducts near its hinged short side their required wind.

"Two wedge-shaped bellows, each of which have seven folds and are provided with removable lead weights, work in alternation;

they are raised by little wooden handles and in falling deliver wind at a pressure of 80 mm [3⅛ inches]. The wide scale of the bass pipes is remarkable, as are the high cut-ups. Scaling is almost halving-at-the-octave, but there is a small, distinctive addition-constant in the scale. The mouth-widths are independent, and also notable is the considerable raising of the "tonal ceiling," something rarely met with in the Alpine countries: here, both the Quindecima and Zimbel go above the ceiling of ⅛' [or, 1½" speaking length].

"The sound of the organ is typical Renaissance-like, full, compact, vital, lovely. The Churburg organ is indeed one of the most valuable representatives of the Renaissance period still extant." (Krauss 77–79)

St. Marien   Marienhafe, Germany

Gerhard von Holy, Aurich, 1710
Ahrend & Brunzema, 1966, 1969

MANUAL		RÜCKPOSITIV		PEDAL
16	Qvintaden (new)	8	Rohr-Flevte	pulldowns
8	Principaal	4	Principaal	
8	Gedact	4	Blok-Flevte	
4	Octave	2	Octave	
4	Spits-Flevte	1½	Qvinte	
3	Qvinte	1	Sifflevte	
2	Octave		Scharf II	
2	Spits-Flevte	8	Krvmhorn	
	Sesquialter II			
	Mixtuur IV–VI			
	Cymbel III			
8	Trompete (new)			

Tremulant
Two Cymbelsterne
Scheibekoppel ("push" coupler)
Manual compass: CDEFGA–c''' (45 notes)
Pedal compass: CDEFGA–d' (23 notes)
Wind pressure: 63 mm (2½ inches)
Pitch: almost one semitone above a' = 440 Hz
Temperament: Meantone (modified)

Drawknob layout:

	Left			Right	
	RP	HW		HW	RP
	Tremulant	8 Principaal	16	Qvintaden	Ventil Manual
	Cymbelstern	8 Gedact	4	Octave	Ventil RP
4	Principaal	4 Spits-Flevte	3	Qvinte	8 Rohr-Flevte
4	Blok-Flevte	2 Octave	2	Spits-Flevte	2 Octave
1½	Qvinte	Sesquialter		Mixtuur	1 Sifflevte
	Scharf	Cymbel	8	Trompete	8 Krvmhorn

Sources: Jongepier 1989, 206; Lade, 37; Williams 1974, 111; Gustav Leonhardt RCA SEON GL 71051, RCA SEON GL 30765 (recordings)

Hofkirche Innsbruck, Austria

Jörg Ebert, Ravensburg, 1555–1561
Ahrend & Brunzema, 1970
Jürgen Ahrend, Leer-Loga, 1976

Original Terminology	*Modern Equivalent*		*Pipes (original/new)*
"IM GROβEN CORPUS"	HAUPTWERK		
Principal	8	Prinzipal (façade)	41/0
Deckt Fleten	8	Gedackt	41/0
Octaf	4	Oktave	39/2
Quint	3	Quinte	40/1
Quintez	2	Oktave	41/0
Hindersaz		Hintersatz V-X	213/90
Ziml		Zimbel II	16/66
Hörnndl		Hörnlein II	34/48
Trumetten	8	Trompete	0/41
Regal	8	Regal	0/41
"IM RUGGPOSITIF"	RÜCKPOSITIV		
Offen Fletl	4	Prinzipal (façade)	36/2
Zudeckt Fleten	4	Gedackt	38/0
Mixtur		Mixture III–V	51/98
Ziml		Zimbel II	1/75
Hörnndl		Hörnlein II	2/74

PEDAL
pulldowns

HW Hintersatz:

C	2	1⅓	1	½	½					
c#	2	1	1	⅔	½	½				
f#	2	2	1⅓	1⅓	1	1	⅔			
c#'	2	2	2	1⅓	1⅓	1	1	⅔		
f#'	4	2⅔	2	2	2	1⅓	1⅓	1	1	
c#"	4	4	2⅔	2⅔	2⅔	2	2	2	1⅓	1⅓
f#"	4	4	4	2⅔	2⅔	2⅔	2	2	2	2

HW Zimbel:

C	⅓	¼
c#	½	⅓
f#	⅔	½
c#'	1	⅔
f#'	1⅓	1
c#"	2	1⅓
f#"	2⅔	2

HW Hörnlein:

C	1⅓	⅘
f#'	2⅔	1⅗

RP Mixtur:

F	2	1⅓	1		
a	2	1⅓	1	⅔	
a'	2	2	1⅓	1⅓	1
e"	4	4	2⅔	2	1⅓

RP Zimbel:

F	⅔	½
e'	1	⅔
a'	1⅓	1
e"	2	1⅓

RP Hörnlein:

F	⅔	⅖
a	1⅓	⅘
a'	2⅔	1⅗

Zitter (Tremulant)
HW compass: CDEFGA-g"a" (41 notes)
RP compass: FGA-g"a" (38 notes)

Pedal compass: CDEFGA-b♭ (19 notes)
Wind pressure: 90 mm (3½ inches)
Temperament: Meantone
Seven or eight bellows in the original organ
Pitch: a' = 445 Hz at 11°C (52°F)
Pedal keys activate a second row of pallets in HW windchest
Regal is on its own windchest in the Brustwerk position, divided at e-f
Rückpositiv windchest extends under pedal keyboard into the main case, where the inverted pallets are pulled up by the lower keyboard
Sources: Hradetzky, 691-720; Salmen, 234; Williams and Owen, 86, 89, 91

"The Innsbruck organ is very strong in tone, neither manual proving useful for accompanying a choir. The cases are shallow (Rückpositiv less than 50 cm [20 inches]), the chests spacious, the organs contained in resonant wooden boxes. Since all the Chair organ stops have close equivalents in the Great organ, yet at only 4' pitch (as so often during the sixteenth century and late fifteenth), the two manuals can be regarded partly as extensions of each other in different directions. . . . The stopped pipes at Innsbruck are very strong in tone, with a big mouth and a tone-colour ranging from wide, vague flute sound in the bass to strong, breathy treble colour. The two Hörnli stops are very keen, repeating Terzzimbeln. Throughout the organ there is a distinct change of tone from bass to treble, enabling the Hauptwerk bass keys to produce a different quality of sound from the right-hand solo lines in the treble." (Williams and Owen, 89)

SELECTED NEW ORGANS

All mixture compositions except for Aalten (Opus 51) and Haarlem (Opus 58) are from the Brunzema Archives.

Altreformierte Kirche **Veldhausen, Germany**

Opus 10, 1957

MANUAL					PEDAL
8	Praestant				pulldowns
8	Gedackt				
4	Oktave				
2	Oktave				
1	Mixtur IV				
8	Trompete (horizontal)				

HW Mixtur:	C	1	⅔	½	⅓
	c	1⅓	1	⅔	½
	c′	2	1⅓	1	⅔
	c″	2⅔	2	1⅓	1
	a″	4	2⅔	2	1⅓

Source: Pape 1972, 31

Reformierte Kirche   Bremen-Farge, Germany

Opus 11, 1958

HAUPTWERK		BRUSTWERK		PEDAL	
8	Prinzipal	8	Gedackt	16	Subbass
8	Rohrflöte	4	Flöte	4	Vox humana
4	Oktave	2	Quintadena		
1	Mixtur III–II	1	Prinzipal		
8	Trompete				

Couplers: BW→HW HW→P BW→P
Source: Pape 1972, 31

Zorgvlietkerk   Scheveningen, Netherlands

Opus 18, 1959

HAUPTWERK		RÜCKPOSITIV	
8	Praestant I–II	8	Gedackt
8	Gedackt	4	Praestant
4	Oktave I–II	4	Hohlflöte
2	Oktave	2	Waldflöte
	Mixtur IV	1⅓	Spitzquinte
8	Trompete		Sesquialtera II
	(horizontal)		Scharf II–III
		8	Krummhorn
			Tremulant

BRUSTWERK		PEDAL	
8	(Spitz) Gedackt	16	Bourdon
4	Gedacktflöte	8	Oktave
2	Prinzipal	4	Nachthorn
1	Oktave	2	Gedackt
16	Rankett	16	Posaune
8	Regal	4	Schalmey
	Tremulant		

HW Mixtur:	C	1	⅔	½	⅓
	c	1⅓	1	⅔	½
	c′	2	1⅓	1	⅔
	c″	4	2⅔	2	1⅓

RP Scharf:	C	⅔	½	
	c	1⅓	1	
	g	2	1	⅔
	c′	2	1⅓	1
	c‴	2⅔	2	1⅓

Couplers: RP→HW BW→HW HW→P RP→P
Two Zimbelsterne
Case: painted oak
Dimensions (height × width × depth)
  Main case: 577 × 338 × 97 cm (227 × 133 × 38 inches)
  Rückpositiv case: 175 × 175 × 64 cm (69 × 69 × 25 inches)
Sources: Pape 1972, 32; *The Diapason* 53 (February 1962): 35;
Blanton, 49

Gereformeerd Kerk Groningen, Netherlands

Opus 22, 1960

MANUAL		PEDAL
8	Praestant	pulldowns
8	Gedackt	
4	Oktave	
4	Rohrflöte	
2	Oktave	
	Mixtur IV	

Source: Pape 1972, 31

Reformierte Kirche   **Freren, Germany**

Opus 23, 1960

MANUAL		PEDAL
8	Prinzipal	pulldowns
8	Gedackt	
4	Oktave	
2	Oktave	
2	Gemshorn	
	Sesquialtera II	
1	Mixtur III	
8	Trompete	

Case of 1699
Source: Pape 1972, 31

St. Lamberti   **Aurich, Germany**

Opus 27, 1961

HAUPTWERK		RÜCKPOSITIV		PEDAL	
16	Quintadena	8	Quintadena	16	Subbass
8	Praestant	8	Gedackt	8	Oktave
8	Hohlflöte	4	Praestant	4	Oktave
4	Oktave	4	Rohrflöte		Mixtur
4	Spitzflöte	2	Gemshorn	16	Posaune
2⅔	Quinte	1⅓	Quinte	8	Trompete
2	Oktave		Sesquialtera	4	Schalmei
	Mixtur IV		Scharf II–III		
8	Trompete	16	Dulzian		

HW Mixtur:	C	1⅓	1	⅔	½
	a#	2	1⅓	1	⅔
	g′	2⅔	2	1⅓	1
	c″	4	2⅔	2	1⅓

RP Scharf:	C	⅔	½		
	c	1⅓	1		
	g	2	1	⅔	
	c′	2	1⅓	1	
	c″	2⅔	2	1⅓	

Manual compass: C-f ″′ (54 notes)
Pedal compass: C-f′ (30 notes)

Sources: *The Diapason* 53 (September 1962): 29; Lade, 33; André Isoir, *L'Œuvre de J. S. Bach,* Volume 8, Calliope CAL 1708 (recording)

Hervormde Kerk   **Espel, Netherlands**

Opus 29, 1962

MANUAL		PEDAL
8	Prinzipal	pulldowns
8	Gedackt	
4	Oktave	
4	Rohrflöte	
2	Oktave	
2	Gemshorn	
1	Mixtur III	

1-7 of Prinzipal from Gedackt
Source: Lade, 33

St. Martini   **Bremen, Germany**

Opus 30, 1962

HAUPTWERK		RÜCKPOSITIV	
16	Bordun	8	Gedackt
8	Praestant	4	Praestant
8	Hohlflöte	4	Rohrflöte
4	Oktave	2	Oktave
4	Spitzflöte	2	Waldflöte
2	Oktave	1⅓	Nasat
	Rauschpfeife		Sesquialtera II
	Mixtur V-VI		Scharf III
16	Dulcian	8	Krummhorn
8	Trompete		

BRUSTWERK		PEDAL	
8	Gedackt	16	Praestant
4	Flöte	8	Oktave
2	Prinzipal	4	Oktave
1	Blockflöte	2	Flöte
	Zimbel II		Mixtur IV-V
8	Regal	16	Posaune
		8	Trompete
		4	Trompete

HW Mixtur:

C	1⅓	1	⅔	½	⅓	
c	2	1⅓	1	⅔	½	
a	2	1⅓	1	⅔	⅔	½
c′	2⅔	2	1⅓	1	⅔	⅔
c″	4	2⅔	2	1⅓	1⅓	1
c‴	4	2⅔	2	2	1⅓	1⅓

RP Scharf:

C	⅔	½	⅓
c	1⅓	1	⅔
g	2	1⅓	1
c″	2⅔	2	1⅓

BW Zimbel:

C	⅓	¼
c	⅔	½
g	1	⅔
c′	1⅓	1
g′	2	1⅓
c″	2⅔	2

P Mixtur:

C	1	⅔	½	½
c	1⅓	1	⅔	½	½
c′	2	1⅓	1	⅔	⅔

Tremulant
Source: Pape 1972, 34

Oude Kerk (small organ)   Amsterdam, Netherlands

Opus 41, 1965

HOOFDWERK		BORSTWERK		PEDAAL	
8	Prestant	8	Gedekt	16	Bourdon
8	Holpijp	4	Prestant	8	Octaaf
8	Quintadeen	2	Octaaf	8	Trompet
4	Octaaf	8	Dulciaan		
2⅔	Quint				
2	Octaaf				
2	Gemshoorn				
1⅓	Mixtuur V–VI				
⅔	Scherp IV–V				
8	Trompet				

HW Mixtuur:	C	1⅓	1	⅔	½	½	
	G	1⅓	1	⅔	⅔	½	
	c	2	1⅓	1	1	⅔	
	g	2	1⅓	1⅓	1	⅔	
	c'	2⅔	2	2	1⅓	1	1
	g'	2⅔	2	1⅓	1⅓	1	1
	c"	4	2⅔	2	2	1⅓	1⅓
	g"	4	2⅔	2⅔	2	2	1⅓

BW Scherp:	C	⅔	½	⅓	¼	
	G	1	⅔	½	⅓	
	c	1⅓	1	⅔	½	
	c'	2	1⅓	1	1	⅔
	c"	2⅔	2	1⅓	1⅓	1
	g"	2⅔	2	2	1⅓	1⅓

Tremulant to the whole organ
Coupler: HW→P
Manual compass: C-d‴ (51 notes)
Pedal compass: C-d′ (27 notes)
Case from 1658
Specification by Gustav Leonhardt, with reference to that of 1658
Sources: Pape 1972, 32; Visser, 56

Johanneskapel   The Hague, Netherlands

Opus 42, 1965

HAUPTWERK		BRUSTWERK		PEDAL	
8	Prinzipal	8	Gedackt	16	Bourdon
8	Hohlflöte	4	Rohrflöte	8	Pommer
4	Oktav	2	Gemshorn	4	Schalmey
4	Flöte	1	Oktave		
2	Oktave	8	Regal		
1	Mixtur IV				

Couplers: BW→HW HW→P BW→P
1-5 of Prinzipal from Hohlflöte
Source: Pape 1972, 31

Evangelische Kirche Oberneuland   **Bremen, Germany**
Opus 45, 1966

HAUPTWERK		RÜCKPOSITIV		PEDAL	
16	Quintadena	8	Gedackt	16	Subbass
8	Praestant	4	Praestant	8	Oktave
8	Hohlflöte	4	Rohrflöte	4	Oktave
4	Oktave	2	Gemshorn	16	Posaune
4	Spitzflöte	1⅓	Quinte	8	Trompete
2	Oktave		Sesquialtera	2	Kornett
	Mixtur		Scharf		
8	Trompete	8	Dulzian		
			Tremulant		

Couplers: RP→HW HW→P RP→P
Source: Herbert Tachezi, *Die Kunst der Fuge,* TELDEC 8.43771 (recording)

Kirche Schwerin-Frolinde   **Castrop-Rauxel, Germany**
Opus 49, 1967

HAUPTWERK		RÜCKPOSITIV	
8	Praestant	8	Gedackt
8	Hohlflöte	4	Praestant
4	Oktave	4	Rohrflöte
2⅔	Quinte	2	Flöte
2	Oktave	1⅓	Nasat
	Mixtur III–IV		Sesquialtera II
8	Trompete		Scharf III
		8	Krummhorn
			Tremulant

BRUSTWERK		PEDAL	
8	Holzgedackt	16	Subbass
4	Spitzgedackt	8	Oktave
2	Prinzipal	4	Oktave
1	Oktave	2	Flöte
16	Rankett	16	Fagott
8	Regal	8	Trompete

Couplers: RP→HW BW→HW HW→P RP→P
Source: Pape 1972, 34

Gereformeerd Zuiderkerk   **Aalten, Netherlands**

Opus 51, 1968

HOOFDWERK

8	Praestant	1–5	from Holpijp
8	Holpijp		Roerfluit in treble
4	Octaaf		
2	Octaaf		
	Mixtuur IV		
8	Trompete		

RUGPOSITIEF

8	Holpijp	1–7	oak
4	Praestant		
4	Roerfluit	1–12	Gedekt
2	Spitsfluit	1–13	Spitsgedekt
	Scherp II–III		
8	Kromhoorn		

PEDAAL

16	Bourdon	oak
8	Octaaf	
4	Octaaf	
8	Trompete	

HW Mixtuur:	C	1	⅔	½	⅓
	c	1⅓	1	⅔	½
	g	2	1⅓	1	⅔
	g′	2⅔	2	1⅓	1
	c″	4	2⅔	2	1⅓
	c‴	4	2⅔	2⅔	2

RP Scherp:	C	⅓	¼	
	G	½	⅓	
	c	⅔	½	
	g	1	⅔	½
	g′	1⅓	1	⅔
	c″	2	1⅓	1
	g″	2⅔	2	1⅓
	c‴	4	2⅔	2

Tremulant
Couplers: RP→HW   HW→P   RP→P

Manual compass: C-f ''' (54 notes)
Pedal compass: C-f' (30 notes)
Case: white oak
Source: Os, 329–331

Evangeliumskirche   **Gütersloh, Germany**

Opus 57, 1968

HAUPTWERK		RÜCKPOSITIV		PEDAL	
8	Praestant	8	Gedackt	16	Subbass
8	Hohlflöte	4	Praestant	8	Oktave
4	Oktave	4	Rohrflöte	4	Oktave
4	Gedackt	2	Gemshorn	2	Flöte
2	Oktave		Sesquialtera II	16	Fagott
	Mixtur IV		Scharf II–III	8	Trompete
8	Trompete	8	Krummhorn		
			Tremulant		

Zimbelstern
Couplers: RP→HW HW→P RP→P
Source: Pape 1972, 32

Doopsgezinde Kerk   **Haarlem, Netherlands**

Opus 58, 1968

HOOFDWERK

8	Praestant	1–7 from Roerfluit
8	Roerfluit	soldered closed; chimneys from c'
4	Octaaf	
2	Octaaf	
	Mixtuur IV–V	
8	Trompet	

RUGWERK

8	Holpijp	soldered closed
4	Praestant	1 and 2 stopped
4	Roerfluit	soldered closed; chimneys throughout
2	Gemshoorn	cylindrical
1⅓	Quint	
	Scherp III	
8	Dulciaan	

BORSTWERK

8	Holpijp	oak
4	Fluit	1-12 stopped, rest open
2	Blokfluit	1-12 Spitsgedekt, rest open conical
1	Octaaf	2' from b''
8	Regaal	

PEDAAL

16	Bourdon
8	Octaaf
4	Octaaf
	Mixtuur III
16	Bazuin
8	Trompet

HW Mixtuur:

C	1	⅔	½	⅓	
c	1⅓	1	⅔	½	
g	2	1⅓	1	⅔	
g'	2⅔	2	1⅓	1	
c''	4	2⅔	2	2	1⅓
c'''	4	2⅔	2⅔	2	2

RW Scherp:

C	½	⅓	¼
c	⅔	½	⅓
g	1	⅔	½
c'	1⅓	1	⅔
g'	2	1⅓	1
c''	2⅔	2	1⅓
g''	4	2⅔	2

P Mixtuur:

C	1⅓	1	⅔
G	2	1⅓	1
c	2⅔	2	1⅓

Tremulant
Source: Jongepier 1974, 337-338

Reformierte Kirche   **Leer-Loga, Germany**
Opus 63, 1969

MANUAL   PEDAL
 8 Prinzipal   16 Subbass
 8 Gedackt   8 Oktave
 4 Oktave
 4 Rohrflöte
 2 Oktave
    Mixtur
 8 Trompete

Coupler: Manual→Pedal
Source: Pape 1972, 31

Cantate Domino   **Frankfurt/Main, Germany**
Opus 68, 1970

HAUPTWERK   RÜCKPOSITIV
16 Bordun   8 Gedackt
 8 Prinzipal   4 Prinzipal
 8 Spitzgedackt   4 Rohrflöte
 4 Oktave   2 Waldflöte
 4 Koppelflöte   1⅓ Spitzquinte
2⅔ Quinte   Sesquialtera II
 2 Oktave   Scharf III–IV
    Mixtur IV–V   8 Krummhorn
    Cornet V   Tremulant
 8 Trompete

BRUSTWERK   PEDAL
 8 Gedackt   16 Prinzipal
 4 Holzprinzipal   16 Subbass
 2 Rohrflöte   8 Oktavbass
 1 Blockflöte   4 Oktave
    Zimbel II   Mixtur V
 8 Regal   16 Posaune
    Carillon   8 Trompete
    Tremulant   4 Clarine

HW Mixtur:	C	1⅓	1	⅔	½	
	f#	1⅓	1	⅔	⅔	
	c#′	1⅓	1	1	⅔	
	f#′	1⅓	1⅓	1⅓	1	1
	c#″	2	2	1⅓	1⅓	1⅓
	f#″	2⅔	2⅔	2⅔	2	2
	c#‴	4	4	2⅔	2⅔	2⅔

RP Scharf:	C	½	⅓	¼	
	F#	½	⅓	⅓	
	c#	½	½	⅓	
	f#	⅔	⅔	½	
	c#′	1	1	⅔	
	f#′	1⅓	1⅓	1	1
	c#″	2	2	1⅓	1⅓
	f#″	2⅔	2⅔	2	2
	c#‴	4	4	2⅔	2⅔

BW Zimbel:	C	¼	⅙
	c#	⅓	¼
	f#	½	⅓
	c#′	⅔	½
	f#′	1	⅔
	c#″	1⅓	1
	f#″	2	1⅓
	c#‴	2⅔	2

| P Mixtur: | C | 2 | 1⅓ | 1 | ⅔ | ½ |
| | c# | 2⅔ | 2 | 1⅓ | 1 | 1 |

Source: Pape 1972, 34

Figure 1
Altreformierte Kirche
Veldhausen, Germany
Ahrend & Brunzema Opus 10, 1957

Figure 2
Zorgvlietkerk
Scheveningen, Netherlands
Ahrend & Brunzema Opus 18, 1959

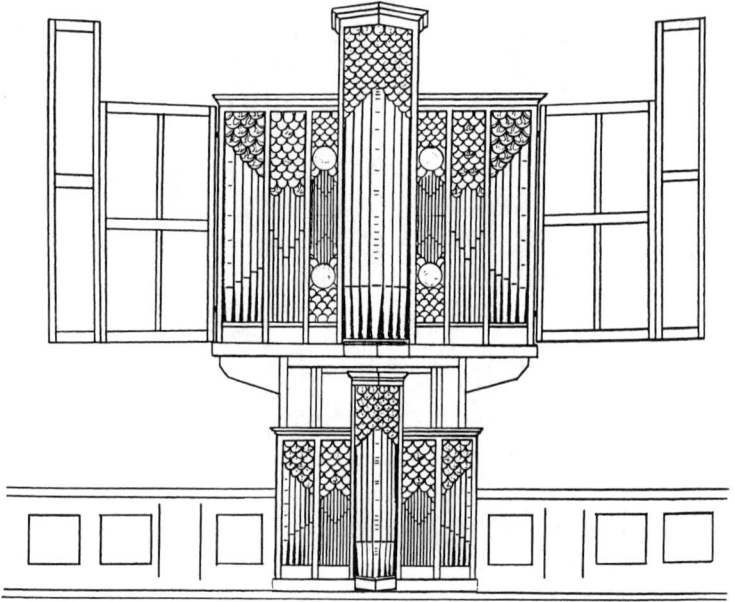

Figure 3
St. Lamberti
Aurich, Germany
Ahrend & Brunzema Opus 27, 1961

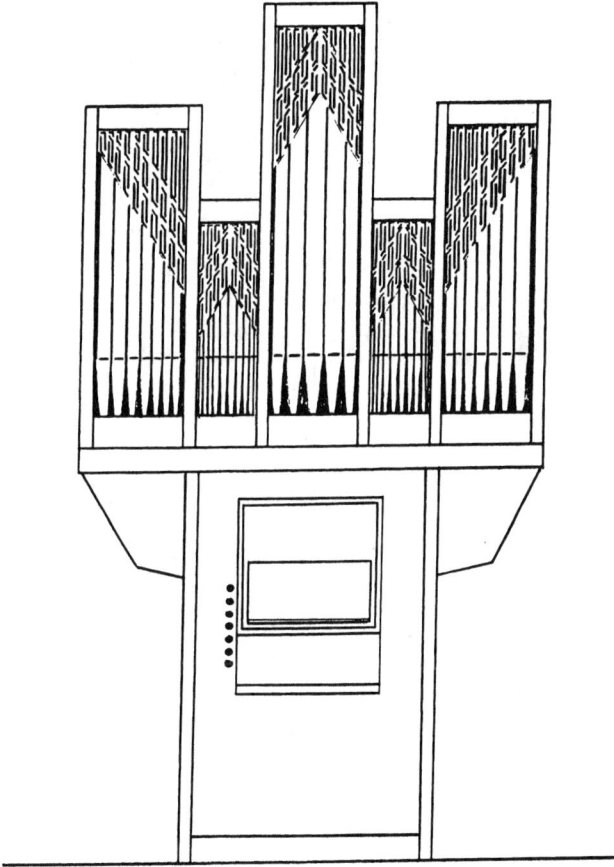

Figure 4
Hervormde Kerk
Espel, Netherlands
Ahrend & Brunzema Opus 29, 1962

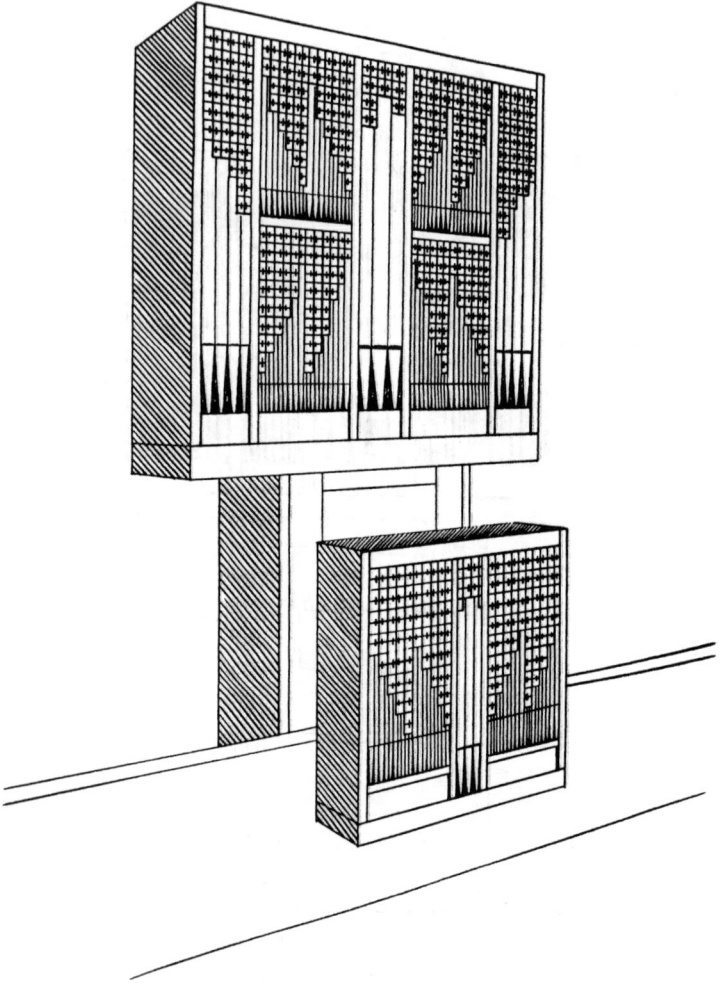

Figure 5
Evangelische Kirche
Bremen-Oberneuland, Germany
Ahrend & Brunzema Opus 45, 1966

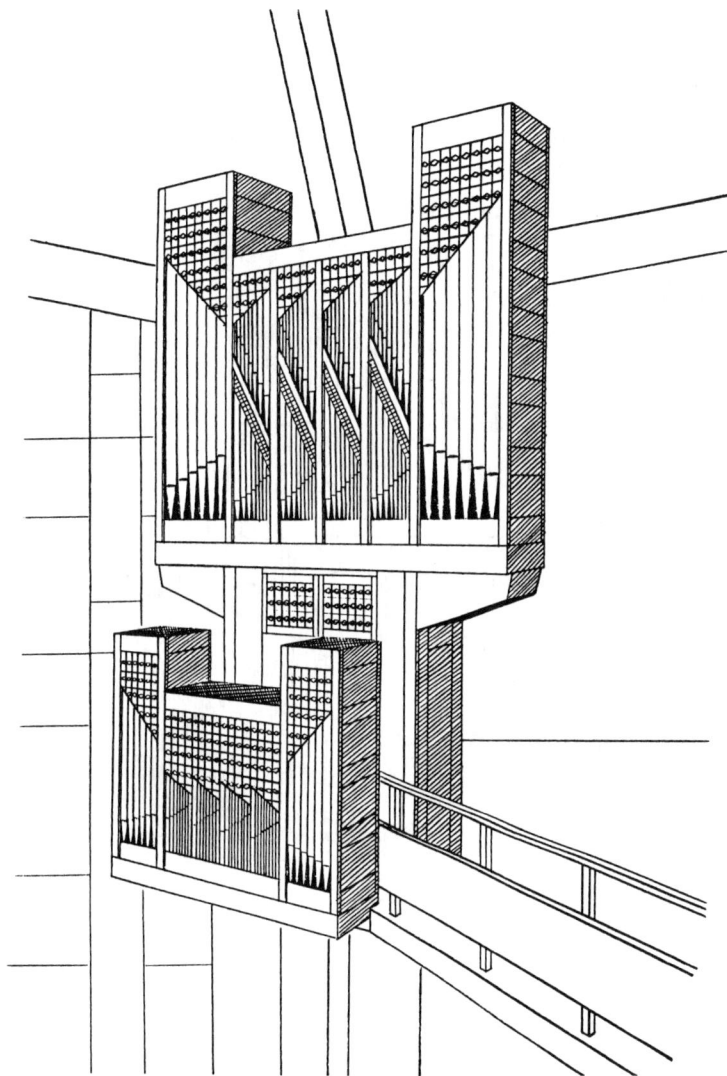

Figure 6
Kirche Schwerin-Frolinde
Castrop-Rauxel, Germany
Ahrend & Brunzema Opus 49, 1967

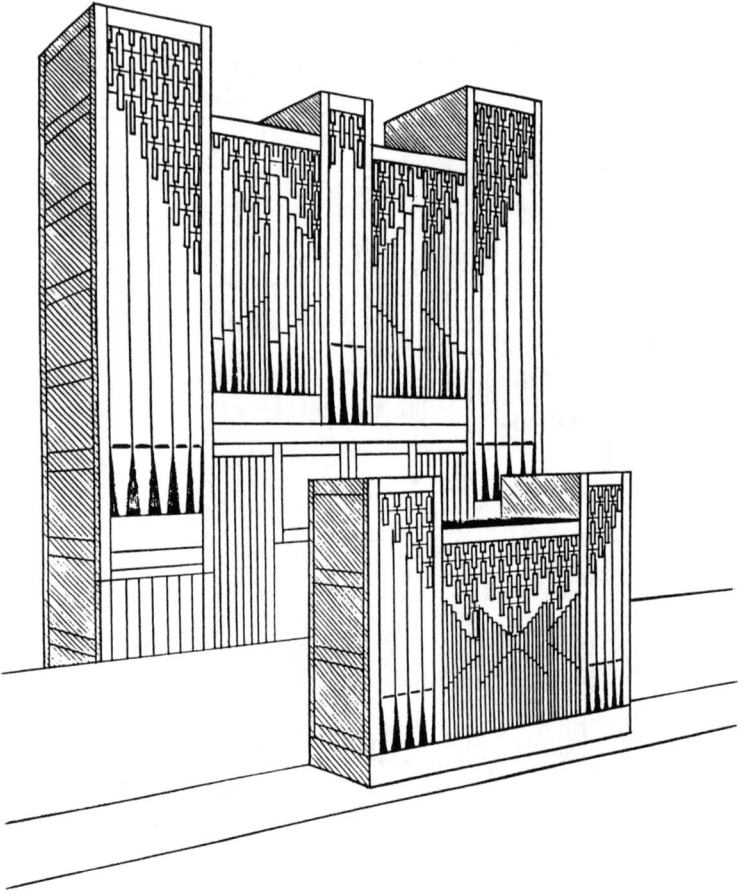

Figure 7
Doopsgezinde Kerk
Haarlem, Netherlands
Ahrend & Brunzema Opus 58, 1968

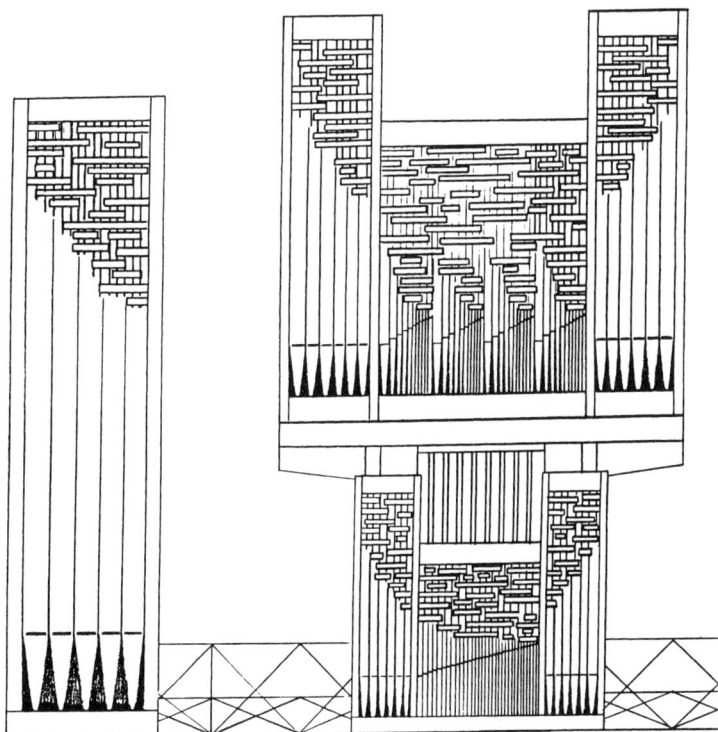

Figure 8
Cantate Domino
Frankfurt/Main, Germany
Ahrend & Brunzema Opus 68, 1970

❖ 23

1972–1979: Casavant Frères, Limitée, Saint-Hyacinthe, Québec, Canada

SELECTED OPUS LIST

Gerhard Brunzema was tonal director of Casavant Frères from 12 April 1972 to 17 August 1979. While many of the instruments have Brunzema's imprint, the organs built by Casavant are products of an entire team of talented people rather than the work of one person. The opus list presented here is based on the information provided by Stanley Scheer, taken from drawings and voicing records. The first drawing that shows Gerhard Brunzema's initials is Opus 3162, dated 28 April 1972. Following that, his initials appear regularly except for Opuses 3164, 3165, and 3171. These three drawings were approved by Eugène Laplante, who worked for Casavant from 1968 to 1984. The last drawing having Brunzema's initials is Opus 3455, dated 8 June 1979. The first voicing sheet with his initials is Opus 3167, although this is an indication for only one stop. The most distinct changeover to Brunzema's handwriting on voicing sheets begins at Opus 3170 and carries through to Opus 3478, dated 17 May 1979. The last contract sent and received prior to Brunzema's departure was Opus 3480. Thus, the following opus list extends from 3162 to 3480, excluding 3164, 3165, and 3171. While the earliest organs from the year 1972 may not have the complete influence of Brunzema, it may be said that the following opus list enumerates the Casavant organs with which Gerhard Brunzema was involved. This includes a total of 315 organs, 107 of which have mechanical action.

Roman numerals indicate the number of manual keyboards and Arabic numerals indicate the total number of stops. The presence or absence of a pedal division is not indicated on Casavant's original list. The letter *M* denotes mechanical-action organs. An asterisk indicates those organs that appear on a list that Brunzema would send from his Fergus workshop to prospective clients. (Primary source: Stanley Scheer, personal communication, 19 July 1996. Secondary sources: D'Aigle [no page numbers]; Pierre Dionne, personal communication, 29 March 1994; Pape 1978, 141–144)

Opus	Year	Location	Size M
3162	1972	Chatham, Massachusetts	
		First Congregational Church	II/16
3163	1972	Falls Church, Virginia	
		First Christian Church	II/26
3166	1972	Keene, Texas	
		Southwestern Union College	II/12
3167	1972	Takoma Park, Maryland	
		Sligo Seventh Day Adventist Church	IV/22
3168	1972	Homer, New York	
		Homer Congregational Church	II/16
3169	1973	Midland, Michigan	
		Saint John's Lutheran Church	II/22
3170	1973	Glens Falls, New York	
		First Presbyterian Church	III/40
3172	1973	Saint Catharines, Ontario	
		Maranatha Christian	
		Reformed Church	II/19
3173	1973	Bloomington, Minnesota	
		Saint Luke's Lutheran Church	II/16

Opus	Year	Location	Size M
3174	1973	Sanford, Florida	
		Holy Cross Episcopal Church	II/18
3175	1973	Islington, Ontario	
		Saint George's Church on the Hill	II/22
3176	1973	Kalamazoo, Michigan	
		Trinity Lutheran Church	II/17
3177	1973	Whitehall, Wisconsin	
		Our Savior's Lutheran Church	II/17
3178	1973	Malden, Massachusetts	
		Central Methodist	
		Church of Malden	III/28
3179	1973	Concord, North Carolina	
		Central United Methodist Church	II/23
3180	1973	Sydney, Nova Scotia	
		Holy Redeemer Church	II/15
3181	1973	Sarnia, Ontario	
		Saint George's Anglican Church	III/26
3182	1975	Wolfville, Nova Scotia	
		Saint John's Anglican Church	II/7
3183	1973	Newton, North Carolina	
		Grace United Church of Christ	II/18
3184	1973	Sherbrooke, Québec	
		Filles de la Charité	
		du Sacré-Coeur de Jésus	II/12
3185	1973	Toronto, Ontario	
		University of Toronto	II/25 M*
3186	1973	Altoona, Pennsylvania	
		Bethany Lutheran Church	II/17
3187	1973	Springfield, Virginia	
		Saint John's	
		United Methodist Church	II/14
3188	1973	Waynesboro, Virginia	
		First Presbyterian Church	II/22
3189	1973	Weston, Ontario	
		Saint John's Anglican Church	II/9
3190	1973	Decorah, Iowa	
		First Lutheran Church	II/25 M
3191	1974	New York, New York	
		Community of the Holy Spirit	II/7 M

Opus	Year	Location	Size M
3192	1974	Santa Barbara, California	
		First Presbyterian Church	IV/57
3193	1973	Austin, Minnesota	
		Our Savior's Lutheran Church	II/29
3194	1973	Seymour, Connecticut	
		Saint Augustine's Church	III/31
3195	1973	Pfaff Town, North Carolina	
		Christian Church	II/12
3196	1974	Fort Worth, Texas	
		University Baptist Church	III/36
3197	1973	Oak Park, Michigan	
		Church of Our Lady of Fatima	II/13
3198	1974	Greenwood, Mississippi	
		First Presbyterian Church	II/31
3199	1973	Kitchener, Ontario	
		New Apostolic Church of Canada	III/40
3200	1973	Moline, Illinois	
		Trinity Lutheran Church	III/32 M*
3201	1974	Worcester, Massachusetts	
		Saint John's Episcopal Church	II/16
3202	1973	Edmonton, Alberta	
		Central Baptist Church	II/24
3203	1974	Glenview, Illinois	
		Holy Trinity Lutheran Church	II/26
3204	1974	Minneapolis, Minnesota	
		Holy Trinity Lutheran Church	II/18
3205	1973	Weston, Connecticut	
		Norfield Congregational Church	II/12 M
3206	1974	Toledo, Ohio	
		Saint Petri Evangelical	
		Lutheran Church	II/20
3207	1974	Santa Barbara, California	
		Emmanuel Lutheran Church	II/13
3208	1974	Silver Spring, Maryland	
		Episcopal Church of Our Savior	II/25
3209	1973	Edmonton, Alberta	
		Church of Saint John	
		the Evangelist	II/13
3210	1974	Québec, Québec	
		Conservatoire de Musique	II/19 M

Opus	Year	Location	Size M
3211	1974	Decatur, Alabama	
		First Baptist Church	II/31
3212	1973	Rome, Georgia	
		First United Methodist Church	II/24
3213	1974	Bellevue, Washington	
		Cross of Christ Lutheran Church	II/10
3214	1974	Bay Head, New Jersey	
		All Saints Episcopal Church	II/13 M
3215	1974	Ann Arbor, Michigan	
		Saint Paul's Lutheran Church	II/22
3216	1974	Everett, Washington	
		Central Lutheran Church	II/14
3217	1974	St. Paul, Minnesota	
		Hamline United	
		Methodist Church	III/45
3218	1974	Toronto, Ontario	
		Saint Peter's Anglican Church	II/18
3219	1974	Edmonton, Alberta	
		Christ Church	II/14
3220	1974	Stillwater, Oklahoma	
		First United Methodist Church	II/19
3221	1974	Pictou, Nova Scotia	
		Pictou United Church	II/14
3222	1974	Cambridge, Ontario	
		Saint Paul's Lutheran Church	II/19
3223	1974	Kingston, Ontario	
		Queen's University	II/16 M
3224	1974	Petersburg, Virginia	
		Saint Mark's United	
		Methodist Church	II/20
3225	1974	Glens Falls, New York	
		Christ Church United Methodist	III/36
3226	1974	Clearwater, Florida	
		Peace Memorial	
		Presbyterian Church	IV/46
3227	1974	Saint Catharines, Ontario	
		Saint Thomas	
		Anglican Church	III/33
3228	1974	West Trenton, New Jersey	
		United Presbyterian Church	II/7

Opus	Year	Location	Size M
3229	1974	Easton, Pennsylvania	
		Saint John's Lutheran Church	III/30
3230	1974	Regina, Saskatchewan	
		University of Saskatchewan	II/7
3231	1974	Corpus Christi, Texas	
		All Saints Episcopal Church	II/10
3232	1974	Regina, Saskatchewan	
		Saint Paul's Cathedral	II/16
3233	1974	Kenosha, Wisconsin	
		Carthage College	II/8 M
3234	1974	Leacock, Pennsylvania	
		Zion Lutheran Church	II/7
3235	1974	London, Ontario	
		First Saint Andrew's	
		United Church	II/7 M
3236	1975	Arlington, Texas	
		University of Texas	III/15
3237	1974	Painesville, Ohio	
		Judith B. Metz residence	II/13
3238	1974	New Haven, Connecticut	
		Yale University	II/7 M
3239	1974	Indianapolis, Indiana	
		Second Presbyterian Church	II/10
3240	1974	North Vancouver, British Columbia	
		Saint Catherine's Anglican Church	II/10
3241	1975	Newton, Iowa	
		United Presbyterian Church	II/17 M*
3242	1976	Rock Island, Illinois	
		Augustana College	I/4 M
3243	1974	Worcester, Massachusetts	
		Church of Christ the King	II/16
3244	1974	Albemarle, North Carolina	
		First Baptist Church	III/35
3245	1975	Rockford, Illinois	
		Our Savior's Lutheran Church	II/15 M
3246	1975	Champaign, Illinois	
		Grace Lutheran Church	II/16 M
3247	1974	Mankato, Minnesota	
		Bethany Lutheran College	II/7 M

Opus	Year	Location	Size	M
3248	1974	Torrance, California		
		Saint Catherine's Church	II/16	
3249	1975	Gainesville, Florida		
		First Baptist Church	III/32	
3250	1974	Chicago, Illinois		
		Saint James Lutheran Church	II/10	
3251	1974	Dearborn, Michigan		
		Our Redeemer Lutheran Church	II/10	
3252	1974	Poynette, Wisconsin		
		Bethel Evangelist		
		Lutheran Church	II/10	
3253	1974	Big Spring, Texas		
		Church of Saint Mary the Virgin	II/11	
3254	1975	Lansing, Michigan		
		Plymouth Congregational Church	III/55	
3255	1974	Livingston, New Jersey		
		Saint Peter's Episcopal Church	II/10	
3256	1975	Waterloo, Ontario		
		Wilfrid Laurier University	II/14	M*
3257	1975	Hot Springs, Arkansas		
		Westminster Presbyterian Church	II/30	
3258	1974	Sioux Center, Iowa		
		Dordt College	II/7	M
3259	1974	Montréal, Québec		
		McGill University	II/7	M
3260	1975	Fort Lauderdale, Florida		
		Christ United Methodist Church	III/42	
3261	1975	Lenoir, North Carolina		
		First Baptist Church	II/27	
3262	1975	Cedar Rapids, Iowa		
		Saint Mark's Lutheran Church	II/13	M*
3263	1975	Westland, Michigan		
		Saint Theodore's Church	III/15	
3264	1975	London, Ontario		
		Saint George's Anglican Church	II/23	
3265	1975	Rochester, Michigan		
		Oakland University	II/21	M
3266	1975	Ann Arbor, Michigan		
		Saint Luke's Lutheran Church	II/11	

Opus	Year	Location	Size	M
3267	1975	Whiting, Indiana		
		Saint John the Baptist		
		Catholic Church	III/23	
3268	1975	Sandpoint, Idaho		
		First Lutheran Church	II/10	
3269	1975	Minnetonka, Minnesota		
		Fairview Lutheran Church	II/11	
3270	1975	Dowagiac, Michigan		
		First United Methodist Church	II/16	
3271	1975	North Palm Beach, Florida		
		Faith Lutheran Church	II/16	
3272	1975	Vancouver, British Columbia		
		Christian Apostolic Church	II/7	
3273	1975	McFarland, Wisconsin		
		McFarland Lutheran Church	II/16	
3274	1975	Youngstown, Ohio		
		Christ United		
		Presbyterian Church	II/21	
3275	1975	Williamsburg, Virginia		
		Williamsburg Presbyterian		
		Church	II/17	M
3276	1975	Kenosha, Wisconsin		
		Carthage College	IV/41	M*
3277	1975	Farmington, Connecticut		
		Saint James Episcopal Church	II/17	
3278	1975	Fort Madison, Iowa		
		First United Methodist Church	II/18	
3279	1975	Fresno, California		
		First Armenian		
		Presbyterian Church	II/16	
3280	1975	Sharon, Pennsylvania		
		First Presbyterian Church	III/37	
3281	1975	Bloomsburg, Pennsylvania		
		Saint Paul's Episcopal Church	II/18	
3282	1975	Sayville, New York		
		Saint Ann's Episcopal Church	II/14	
3283	1975	Sparks, Nevada		
		Saint Paul's Episcopal Church	II/10	

Opus	Year	Location	Size	M
3284	1975	Manakin-Sabot, Virginia		
		Dover Baptist Church	II/7	
3285	1975	Newport, Arkansas		
		Saint Paul's Episcopal Church	II/10	
3286	1975	Hamilton, Ontario		
		McMaster University	II/7	M
3287	1975	Daytona Beach, Florida		
		Lutheran Church of		
		Christ the King	II/25	
3288	1975	Scarborough, Ontario		
		Saint Rose of Lima Church	II/17	
3289	1975	Ashburn, Georgia		
		United Methodist Church	II/10	
3290	1975	Barron, Wisconsin		
		First Lutheran Church	II/17	
3291	1975	Sydney, Nova Scotia		
		Westminster Presbyterian		
		Church	I/6	M
3292	1975	Saint John's, Newfoundland		
		Saint James United Church	II/17	
3293	1975	Alpena, Michigan		
		First United Methodist Church	II/10	
3294	1975	Saginaw, Michigan		
		Richard Heuschele residence	II/13	
3295	1975	Rockford, Illinois		
		Ronald Burmeister residence	II/7	M*
3296	1975	Lawrence, Kansas		
		University of Kansas	II/7	M
3297	1976	Springfield, Illinois		
		Our Savior's Lutheran Church	II/8	M*
3298	1976	Denver, Colorado		
		Saint John's Catholic Church	I/4	M
3299	1976	Iowa City, Iowa		
		Sven Hansell residence	I/4	M
3300	1976	Madison, Wisconsin		
		Blessed Sacrament Church	II/10	
3301	1976	Detroit, Michigan		
		Old Christ Church	III/30	

Opus	Year	Location	Size	M
3302	1976	St. Paul, Minnesota		
		Church of the Maternity of		
		the Blessed Virgin	II/18	M*
3303	1976	Lewiston, Minnesota		
		Saint John's Lutheran Church	II/10	
3304	1976	Panama City, Florida		
		First United Methodist Church	II/29	
3305	1976	Saint Catharines, Ontario		
		Brock University	I/4	M
3306	1976	Milwaukee, Wisconsin		
		Fox Point		
		Evangelical Lutheran Church	II/15	M*
3307	1976	Lincoln, Nebraska		
		Westminster Presbyterian Church	IV/54	
3308	1976	Vancouver, British Columbia		
		Central Presbyterian Church	II/10	
3309	1976	Cincinnati, Ohio		
		Indian Hills		
		Episcopal Presbyterian Church	II/21	
3310	1976	Holland, Michigan		
		Faith Christian Reformed Church	II/23	
3311	1976	Mexico City, Mexico		
		Basilica de Santa Maria		
		de Guadelupe	II/17	
3312	1976	Mexico City, Mexico		
		Basilica de Santa Maria		
		de Guadelupe	V/123	
3313	1976	St. Paul, Minnesota		
		Blessed Sacrament Parish	II/10	
3314	1976	Ottumwa, Iowa		
		First Lutheran Church	II/23	
3315	1976	Montréal, Québec		
		Saint John's		
		Estonian Lutheran Church	II/8	M
3316	1976	Casper, Wyoming		
		First United Methodist Church	III/30	M*
3317	1976	Islington, Ontario		
		Church of Our Lady of Peace	II/17	

Opus	Year	Location	Size M
3318	1976	Muscatine, Iowa	
		Trinity Episcopal Church	II/15
3319	1976	Willowdale, Ontario	
		Northminster United Church	II/17
3320	1976	Winchester, Massachusetts	
		First Baptist Church	II/17
3321	1976	Shrewsbury, Massachusetts	
		Trinity Church	II/17
3322	1976	Grand Forks, North Dakota	
		Calvary Lutheran Church	II/17
3323	1976	New Haven, Connecticut	
		Bethesda Lutheran Church	II/18
3324	1976	Chicago, Illinois	
		Norwood Park	
		Lutheran Church	II/17
3325	1976	Kiester, Minnesota	
		Our Savior's Lutheran Church	II/10
3326	1976	St. Paul, Minnesota	
		Gethsemane Lutheran Church	II/21
3327	1976	Iowa City, Iowa	
		Our Redeemer Lutheran Church	II/8 M
3328	1976	Ottawa, Ontario	
		Saint Peter's Lutheran Church	II/15 M*
3329	1976	Toronto, Ontario	
		Saint John's	
		Latvian Lutheran Church	II/19
3330	1976	Colonia Mixcoac, Mexico	
		La Capilla de las Madres	
		Franciscanas	II/10
3331	1976	Rice Lake, Wisconsin	
		Bethany Lutheran Church	II/17
3332	1976	Homewood, Alabama	
		All Saints' Episcopal Church	II/17
3333	1974	Decorah, Iowa	
		Good Shepherd Lutheran Church	I/4 M
3334	1977	Seattle, Washington	
		Green Lake	
		Seventh-Day Adventist Church	III/31

Opus	Year	Location	Size	M
3335	1977	Omaha, Nebraska		
		Saints Peter and Paul Church	II/16	M*
3336	1977	Bennettsville, South Carolina		
		First United Methodist Church	III/35	
3337	1977	Tuscaloosa, Alabama		
		First Presbyterian Church	III/39	
3338	1977	Truro, Nova Scotia		
		First Baptist Church	III/23	
3339	1977	Three Rivers, Massachusetts		
		Church of Saints Peter and Paul	II/16	
3340	1977	St. Louis, Missouri		
		Fergusson Presbyterian Church	II/17	M
3341	1977	Reedley, California		
		First Mennonite Church	II/17	
3342	1977	Pittsburgh, Pennsylvania		
		Church of the Holy Cross	II/17	
3343	1976	Camilla, Georgia		
		First Baptist Church	II/24	
3344	1977	Taylorsville, North Carolina		
		Friendship Lutheran Church	II/13	
3345	1977	Salt Lake City, Utah		
		Westminster College	I/4	M
3346	1977	Toronto, Ontario		
		Festival Singers of Canada	I/4	M
3347	1977	Madison, Wisconsin		
		University of Wisconsin	I/4	M*
3348	1977	Pennington, New Jersey		
		First United		
		Presbyterian Church	II/13	
3349	1977	Peterborough, Ontario		
		Trinity United Church	II/39	
3350	1977	Winston-Salem, North Carolina		
		Mount Tabor		
		United Methodist Church	II/17	
3351	1977	Saint John's, Newfoundland		
		Memorial University	II/7	M
3352	1977	Waverly, Iowa		
		Redeemer Lutheran Church	II/17	

Opus	Year	Location	Size	M
3353	1977	Erie, Pennsylvania		
		Saint Peter's Cathedral	III/64	
3354	1977	Evanston, Illinois		
		Saint Matthew's Episcopal Church	II/25	M*
3355	1977	Nassau, Bahamas		
		Our Lady's of the		
		Holy Souls Church	II/13	
3356	1977	Marquette, Michigan		
		Messiah Lutheran Church	III/25	
3357	1977	Saint Thomas, Ontario		
		Trinity Anglican Church	II/17	
3358	1978	Edmonton, Alberta		
		University of Alberta	III/36	M*
3359	1977	Baden, Pennsylvania		
		Saint John the Baptist Church	II/13	
3360	1978	Sioux Center, Iowa		
		Dordt College	III/37	M*
3361	1977	Burlington, Vermont		
		Cathedral of the		
		Immaculate Conception	II/10	M*
3362	1977	Toledo, Ohio		
		Saint Matthew's Episcopal Church	II/11	
3363	1977	Mabel, Minnesota		
		First Lutheran Church	II/10	M
3364	1978	Princeton, New Jersey		
		Trinity Church (Episcopal)	IV/42	M*
3365	1977	Bristol, Connecticut		
		Congregational Church	II/18	
3366	1978	Grande Prairie, Alberta		
		Faith Lutheran Church	II/7	
3367	1978	Colfax, Wisconsin		
		Lutheran Church	II/10	
3368	1977	Bethlehem, Pennsylvania		
		Church of Saints Simon and Jude	II/17	
3369	1978	Cape Girardeau, Missouri		
		Southeast State University	II/3	
3370	1978	Kenmore, Washington		
		Saint John Vianney Church	I/6	M

Opus	Year	Location	Size	M
3371	1977	Tullahoma, Tennessee		
		Saint Barnabas Episcopal Church	II/17	
3372	1978	Boulder, Colorado		
		First Presbyterian Church	III/31	M*
3373	1978	Carlinville, Illinois		
		Zion Lutheran Church	I/7	M
3374	1978	Jackson, Minnesota		
		Our Savior's Lutheran Church	II/10	
3375	1977	Edmonton, Alberta		
		University of Alberta	I/4	M
3376	1981	New York, New York		
		Church of Saint Luke in the Fields	I/4	M
3377	1978	Princeton, New Jersey		
		Westminster Choir College	I/4	M
3378	1978	Saskatoon, Saskatchewan		
		Saint James Anglican Church	II/17	
3379		not used		
3380	1978	Grand Rapids, Michigan		
		Trinity United Methodist Church	III/36	
3381	1978	Louisville, Kentucky		
		Second Presbyterian Church	III/36	
3382	1978	Toronto, Ontario		
		Saint Elizabeth of		
		Hungary Church	II/17	
3383	1978	Valparaiso, Indiana		
		Saint Paul's Church	III/34	
3384	1978	Falmouth, Maine		
		Church of Saint Mary the Virgin	II/20	M*
3385	1977	Davenport, Iowa		
		Saint Ambrose College	I/5	M
3386	1978	Kalamazoo, Michigan		
		Zion Lutheran Church	III/31	M*
3387	1978	Mississauga, Ontario		
		Saint Catherine of Siena Parish	II/14	
3388	1978	North Conway, New Hampshire		
		Christ Church (Episcopal)	II/12	M
3389	1978	Sarnia, Ontario		
		Our Lady of Mercy Church	II/17	

Opus	Year	Location	Size	M
3390	1978	Raleigh, North Carolina		
		Brock Downward residence	II/4	M
3391	1978	Austin, Texas		
		All Saints Episcopal Church	III/31	
3392	1978	Caseyville, Illinois		
		Saint Stephen's Church	II/17	
3393	1978	Toronto, Ontario		
		Church of the Messiah	III/25	
3394	1978	Shawnee, Oklahoma		
		First Presbyterian Church	III/21	
3395	1978	Princeton, New Jersey		
		Trinity Church (Episcopal)	I/4	M
3396	1978	White Marsh, Pennsylvania		
		Saint Thomas Episcopal Church	I/4	M
3397	1978	Stony Brook, New York		
		State University of New York	I/4	M
3398	1978	Sackville, New Brunswick		
		Mount Allison University	I/4	M
3399	1978	Kobe, Japan		
		Kobe College of Music	II/7	M
3400	1978	Edmonton, Alberta		
		Carol Otto residence	II/7	M
3401	1978	Kobe, Japan		
		Kobe Women's College	II/7	M
3402	1978	St. Paul, Minnesota		
		College of St. Thomas	II/7	M
3403	1978	Cedar Falls, Iowa		
		University of Northern Iowa	II/7	M
3404	1978	Winnipeg, Manitoba		
		Elim Chapel	III/25	
3405	1978	Adelaide, Australia		
		University of Adelaide	III/36	M*
3406	1979	Wayne, Nebraska		
		Grace Lutheran Church	III/30	M*
3407	1979	Sioux City, Iowa		
		Grace United Methodist Church	III/35	
3408	1979	Crystal Lake, Illinois		
		First United Methodist Church	II/17	

Opus	Year	Location	Size	M
3409	1979	Bedford, Virginia		
		Baptist Church	III/27	
3410	1978	St. Petersburg, Florida		
		Saint Matthew's Episcopal Church	II/16	
3411	1978	Charleston, North Carolina		
		Saint Philip's Church	III/33	
3412	1979	New York, New York		
		Church of Saint Luke		
		in the Fields	II/23	M*
3413	1979	Hemlock, Michigan		
		Saint Peter's Lutheran Church	II/17	
3414	1979	Scranton, Pennsylvania		
		Saint Peter's Cathedral	III/37	M*
3415	1979	Streator, Illinois		
		Park Presbyterian Church	II/23	
3416	1979	Brooklyn, New York		
		Hanson Place		
		Seventh-Day Adventist Church	III/28	
3417	1979	Kumamoto, Japan		
		Kumamoto Junior		
		College of Music	II/4	M
3418	1979	Denver, Colorado		
		Wellshire Presbyterian Church	III/38	
3419	1979	Setagaya, Japan		
		Holy Ecclesia of Jesus	II/10	M
3420	1979	Gifu City, Japan		
		Holy Spirit Church	II/10	M
3421	1979	Swarthmore, Pennsylvania		
		Trinity Episcopal Church	II/13	
3422	1980	Charlotte, North Carolina		
		Central Steele Creek Presbyterian	II/17	M
3423	1979	Rockford, Illinois		
		Our Savior's Lutheran	I/4	M
3424	1980	Nashville, Tennessee		
		First Presbyterian Church	I/4	M
3425	1985	Philadelphia, Pennsylvania		
		Michael Korn residence	I/4	M
3426	1980	Mistassini, Québec		
		Les Pères Trappistes	I/4	M

Opus	Year	Location	Size	M
3427	1979	Nagaro, Japan		
		Nagaro Prefecture's		
		Cultural Hall	II/7	M
3428	1979	Osaka, Japan		
		Soai College	II/7	M
3429	1979	Edmonton, Alberta		
		Karl Heinz Rose residence	II/7	M
3430	1979	Princeton, New Jersey		
		Susan Grainger residence	II/7	M
3431	1979	McKinney, Texas		
		First Presbyterian Church	II/17	
3432	1979	Adams, Massachusetts		
		Saint Stanislas Kostka Church	II/20	
3433	1980	Menomonie, Wisconsin		
		Our Savior's Lutheran Church	II/18	M*
3434	1980	Melbourne, Australia		
		Victoria Arts Centre	IV/60	M*
3435	1979	Odessa, Texas		
		First Presbyterian Church	III/27	
3436	1979	Wyoming, Pennsylvania		
		Saint Joseph's Church	II/11	M*
3437	1979	Salt Lake City, Utah		
		Church of Jesus Christ		
		of Latter-Day Saints	II/8	M
3438	1979	Bowling Green, Ohio		
		State University	II/7	M
3439	1979	Osaka, Japan		
		Pool College	II/8	M
3440	1979	Milwaukee, Wisconsin		
		Saint John's Lutheran Church	II/21	
3441	1979	Edmundston, New Brunswick		
		Cathédrale de la		
		Immaculée Conception	I/7	M
3442	1979	Houston, Texas		
		Saint Francis de Sales Church	II/13	
3443	1979	Ontario, California		
		Christian Reformed Church	II/19	
3444	1979	Panama, Florida		
		First United Methodist Church	II/30	

Opus	Year	Location	Size	M
3445	1979	Traverse City, Michigan		
		Carmelite Monastery	II/8	
3446	1979	Downer's Grove, Illinois		
		Saint Andrew's Episcopal Church	II/15	
3447	1979	Chattanooga, Tennessee		
		First Church of Christ, Scientist	II/10	
3448	1980	Oxford, Mississippi		
		First Presbyterian Church	II/22	
3449	1979	Jackson, Missouri		
		Emmanuel		
		United Church of Christ	II/17	
3450	1979	Nishinomiya, Japan		
		Kwansei Gakuin University	II/9	M
3451	1979	Rapid City, South Dakota		
		First United Methodist Church	II/18	
3452	1979	Tampa, Florida		
		Saint Clement's Church	II/12	
3453	1980	Western Springs, Illinois		
		First Congregational Church	III/32	
3454	1979	Saint Clair, Michigan		
		Emmanuel Lutheran Church	II/11	
3455	1980	Davenport, Iowa		
		First Presbyterian Church	III/40	
3456	1980	Kyoto, Japan		
		Doshisha Women's College	III/36	M*
3457	1980	Nagoya, Japan		
		Kinjo Gakuin Church	II/19	M*
3458	1979	Grand Rapids, Michigan		
		Faith United Methodist Church	II/13	
3459	1979	Provo, Utah		
		Brigham Young University	I/6	M
3460	1981	Columbia, South Carolina		
		Columbia College	III/22	M
3461	1980	Dallas, Texas		
		Episcopal Church of		
		the Good Shepherd	II/17	
3462	1980	Stoughton, Wisconsin		
		Covenant Lutheran Church	II/9	M

Opus	Year	Location	Size	M
3463	1980	Newton, Massachusetts		
		First Church of Christ, Scientist	II/28	
3464	1980	Deerfield, Illinois		
		Trinity Evangelical		
		Divinity School	II/22	
3465	1980	Glencoe, Illinois		
		Glencoe Union Church	II/21	
3466	1980	Ames, Iowa		
		First United Methodist Church	II/24	
3467	1980	Elon College, North Carolina		
		Elon College Community Church	II/17	
3468	1979	Toyohashi, Japan		
		Toyohashi Takasagoden	I/5	M
3469	1979	Nagoya, Japan		
		Nagoya Takasagoden	I/5	M
3470	1979	Takamatsu, Japan		
		Takamatsu Church	I/5	M
3471	1979	Urawa, Japan		
		Kita-Urawa Catholic Church	II/4	M
3472	1979	Tokyo, Japan		
		Nippon Gakki Company	II/4	M
3473	1980	Simcoe, Ontario		
		Trinity Anglican Church	II/15	
3474	1980	Pennsburg, Pennsylvania		
		Pennsburg United Church of Christ	II/10	
3475	1980	Los Altos, California		
		Saint Nicholas Church	I/7	M
3476	1980	Baltimore, Maryland		
		First Presbyterian Church	III/32	
3477	1980	Columbia, South Carolina		
		First Presbyterian Church	III/43	
3478	1979	Trois-Rivières, Québec		
		Conservatoire de Musique	II/7	M
3479	1980	Bloomington, Minnesota		
		Lutheran Church		
		of the Redemption	II/9	M
3480	1980	Bloomington, Illinois		
		First Church of Christ, Scientist	II/10	

SELECTED ORGANS

The following are Casavant organs that show the influence of Gerhard Brunzema. All these instruments have mechanical key action. A letter in parenthesis after a stop name indicates the note on which a short-compass stop begins.

Queen's University Kingston, Ontario
Opus 3223, 1974

HAUPTWERK		BRUSTWERK		PEDAL	
8	Praestant	8	Gedackt	16	Subbass
8	Hohlflöte	4	Rohrflöte	8	Prinzipal
4	Oktave	2	Flöte	4	Oktave
2⅔	Nasat	½	Scharf II	16	Fagott
2	Oktave	8	Regal		
1⅓	Mixtur IV				
8	Trompete				

1–5 of Praestant from Hohlflöte
Technical and artistic direction, specification, and scaling: Gerhard Brunzema
Factory superintendent: Roger Delisle
Departmental foremen and assistants: Georges Chicoine, Paul Demers, Jean-Paul Frenière, Gilles Lemonde, Roger Lemonde, Germain Ledoux, Paul Lemieux, Germain Petit, Paul-Emile Phaneuf
Artistic conception and case design: Jean-Claude Gauthier
Chest layout and action design: Gaston Bonin and Jean-Guy Dupont
Keyboards and console action: Normand Giard
Windchests: Guy Danserault, Guy Roy
Case: Rosaire Bourgault, Jean-Paul Lemonde, David Beaudoin
Pipes: Guy Godbout, Jean-Guy Beauchamp, Laval Lemaire, Georges Lusignant, Jean-Paul Tanguay
Voicing: Paul Roy, Gaetan Robert, Gilles Chabot, Gerald Archambault, Raymond Duguay
Installation: Denis Campbell, Denis Mailhot, Jean Robichaud
Final finishing: Paul Roy, Gerald Archambault
Sources: *The Diapason* 66 (December 1974): 9; *Music* 9 (January 1975): 14

United Presbyterian Church   **Newton, Iowa**
Opus 3241, 1975

HAUPTWERK		BRUSTWERK (expressive)		PEDAL	
8	Prinzipal	8	Gedackt	16	Subbass
8	Hohlflöte	8	Salizional	8	Prinzipal
4	Oktav	4	Rohrflöte	4	Oktav
2	Waldflöte	2	Prinzipal		Mixtur III
	Mixtur IV		Sesquialtera II (c)	16	Fagott
8	Trompete		Scharf III		

Tremulant
Couplers: BW→HW   HW→P   BW→P
Dedication recital: 13 April 1975 by Davis Folkerts
Drawknob layout:

	Left				Right		
	Tremulant	2	Prinzipal	8	Trompete		Mixtur
	Scharf	4	Rohrflöte	2	Waldflöte	4	Oktav
	Sesquialtera	8	Gedackt	8	Hohlflöte	8	Prinzipal
8	Salizional		HW→BW		HW→P		
16	Fagott		BW→P	8	Prinzipal	16	Subbass
	Mixtur	4	Oktav				

Source: Jeannette Campbell, letter, 13 June 1996

Grace Lutheran Church   **Champaign, Illinois**
Opus 3246, 1975

HAUPTWERK		BRUSTWERK		PEDAL	
8	Prinzipal	8	Gedackt	16	Subbass
8	Hohlflöte	4	Rohrflöte	8	Prinzipal
4	Oktave	2	Prinzipal	4	Oktave
2	Flöte	1⅓	Quinte	2	Mixtur III
2⅔	Sesquialtera II	8	Regal	16	Fagott
1⅓	Mixtur IV				
8	Trompete				

Case: oak
1–5 of Praestant from Hohlflöte
Design: Gerhard Brunzema
Installation: Carroll Hanson and Martin Ott
Consultant: Gerhard Krapf

Dedication recital: 4 May 1975 by Gerhard Krapf
Source: *The Diapason* 67 (January 1976): 15

***Wilfrid Laurier University*   Waterloo, Ontario**

Opus 3256, 1975

HAUPTWERK		BRUSTWERK		PEDAL	
8	Hohlflöte	8	Gedackt	16	Subbass
4	Prinzipal	4	Rohrflöte	8	Prinzipal
2	Waldflöte	2	Prinzipal	4	Oktave
2⅔	Sesquialtera II	1⅓	Quinte	8	Trompete
1⅓	Mixtur IV	8	Regal		

Source: *Music* 9 (April 1975): 8

***Dordt College*   Sioux Center, Iowa**

Opus 3258, 1974

MANUAL I		MANUAL II		PEDAL	
8	Holpijp	8	Regal	16	Bordun
4	Roerfluit			8	Holpijp
2	Octaaf				
1⅓	Quint				

Coupler: I→P
Drawknob layout:

	Left		*Right*
4	Roerfluit	8	Holpijp
1⅓	Quint	2	Octaaf
	I→P		Key switch
8	Holpijp	16	Bordun

Source: Joan Ringerwole, letter, 17 May 1996

***Saint Mark's Lutheran Church*   Cedar Rapids, Iowa**

Opus 3262, 1975

HAUPTWERK		BRUSTWERK		PEDAL	
8	Prinzipal	8	Gedackt	16	Subbass
8	Hohlflöte	4	Rohrflöte	8	Oktave
4	Oktave	2	Flöte	8	Trompete
2	Oktave		Terzian II		
	Mixtur III-IV				
8	Dulzian				

Tremulant to the whole organ
Couplers: BW→HW   HW→P
1-12 of Prinzipal from Hohlflöte
Dedication recitals: 25 April 1975 by Randolph Foy; 27 April 1975
by David Boe
Source: Organ dedication program, editor's personal collection

Oakland University   Rochester, Michigan

Opus 3265, 1975

HAUPTWERK		BRUSTWERK (expressive)		PEDAL	
8	Praestant	8	Holzgedackt	16	Subbass
8	Hohlflöte	4	Rohrflöte	8	Oktave
4	Oktave	2	Klein Prinzipal	4	Oktave
4	Spitzflöte		Zimbel IV		Mixtur IV
2⅔	Sesquialtera II (c)	8	Regal	16	Fagott
2	Oktave	4	Rohr Shalmei	8	Trompete
2	Waldflöte		Tremulant		
	Mixtur V				
8	Trompete				

Cymbelstern
Couplers: BW→HW   HW→P   BW→P
1-5 of Praestant from Hohlflöte
Sources: *Music* 9 (October 1975): 12; Worden, 13

Williamsburg Presbyterian Church   Williamsburg, Virginia

Opus 3275, 1975

HAUPTWERK		RÜCKPOSITIV		PEDAL	
8	Prinzipal	8	Gedackt	16	Subbass
8	Hohlflöte	4	Prinzipal	8	Prinzipal
4	Oktave	4	Rohrflöte	4	Oktave
2⅔	Nasat	2	Oktave	8	Trompete
2	Waldflöte		Sesquialtera II		
	Mixtur III		Scharf III		
8	Dulzian		Tremulant		

Zimbelstern
Couplers: RP→HW   HW→P   RP→P

Hauptwerk is upper manual keyboard; Rückpositiv is lower
Drawknob layout:

	Left			*Right*	
	RP		HW	HW	RP
	Tremulant	2	Waldflöte	8 Dulzian	Scharf
	Sesquialtera	2⅔	Nasat	Mixtur	2 Oktave
4	Rohrflöte	8	Hohlflöte	4 Oktave	4 Prinzipal
			RP→HW	8 Prinzipal	8 Gedackt
	RP→P		HW→P		
16	Subbass	8	Trompete	4 Oktave	8 Prinzipal

Source: Instrument

Carthage College Kenosha, Wisconsin

Opus 3276, 1975

HAUPTWERK		OBERWERK		SCHWELLWERK	
16	Praestant (f)	8	Praestant (f)	16	Gedackt
8	Oktave	8	Gedackt	8	Rohrflöte
8	Hohlflöte	4	Oktave	8	Spitzgamba
4	Oktave	4	Spitzflöte	4	Querflöte
2⅔	Quinte	2⅔	Nasat	2	Flachflöte
2	Oktave	2	Flöte	2⅔	Kornett III (c)
	Mixtur V	1⅗	Terz		Mixtur V
	Scharf IV		Scharf IV	8	Oboe
16	Trompete	8	Dulzian		Tremulant
8	Spanische		Tremulant		
	Trompete				

BRUSTWERK		PEDAL	
8	Holzgedackt	16	Praestant
4	Rohrflöte	8	Oktave
2	Oktave	8	Gedacktflöte
1⅓	Nasat	4	Oktave
	Zimbel II		Mixtur IV
8	Regal	16	Posaune
		8	Trompete
		4	Trompete

Sources: *The Diapason* 65 (May 1974): 8; *Music* 10 (June 1976): 3

McMaster University   Hamilton, Ontario, Canada
Opus 3286, 1975

MANUAL I	MANUAL II	PEDAL
8 Hohlflöte	8 Gedackt	16 Sordun
2 Prinzipal	4 Rohrflöte	8 Gedacktflöte
	1⅓ Quinte	

Source: *The American Organist* 23 (May 1989): 127

Ronald Burmeister residence   Rockford, Illinois
Opus 3295, 1975

MANUAL I	MANUAL II	PEDAL
8 Hohlflöte	8 Gedackt	8 Gedacktflöte
2 Prinzipal	4 Rohrflöte	4 Dulzian
	1⅓ Quinte	

Couplers: I→P   II→P
1–12 of Gedackt and Gedacktflöte from Hohlflöte
Source: Thomas Erickson, letter, 5 July 1995

Church of the Maternity of the Blessed Virgin   St. Paul, Minnesota
Opus 3302, 1976

HAUPTWERK	BRUSTWERK (expressive)	PEDAL
16 Bordun	8 Gedackt	16 Subbass
8 Praestant	4 Spitzgedackt	8 Oktave
8 Hohlflöte	2 Flöte	4 Oktave
4 Oktave	Terzian II	16 Posaune
2⅔ Quinte	8 Regal	8 Trompete
2 Oktave		
Mixtur IV		
8 Trompete		

Tremulant
Coupler: HW→P
1–5 of Praestant from Hohlflöte
Source: Thomas Erickson, letter, 11 August 1995

Fox Point Evangelical Lutheran Church   **Milwaukee,**
Wisconsin

Opus 3306, 1976

GREAT		SWELL		PEDAL	
8	Prinzipal	8	Gedackt	16	Subbass
8	Hohlflöte	8	Gemshorn	8	Prinzipal
4	Oktave	8	Schwebung (c)	4	Oktave
2	Waldflöte	4	Spitzflöte	16	Fagott
	Mixtur IV	2	Prinzipal		
		8	Trompete		

Tremulant
Couplers: SW→GR   GR→P   SW→P
1-5 of HW Prinzipal from Hohlflöte
Dedication recital: 12 September 1976 by William P. Roth
Drawknob layout:

Left			*Right*
8 Trompete	Tremulant	Mixtur IV	2 Prinzipal
8 Gemshorn	2 Waldflöte	4 Oktave	4 Spitzflote
8 Schwebung	8 Hohlflöte	8 Prinzipal	8 Gedackt
	SW→GR	GR→P	16 Fagott
	SW→P		4 Oktave 8 Prinzipal 16 Subbass

Source: Organ dedication program, editor's personal collection

First United Methodist Church   **Casper, Wyoming**

Opus 3316, 1976

HAUPTWERK		SCHWELLWERK	
8	Prinzipal	8	Bourdon
8	Hohlflöte	8	Gemshorn
4	Oktave	8	Schwebung (c)
2⅔	Nasat	4	Spitzflöte
2	Waldflöte	2	Weitprinzipal
	Mixtur IV		Zimbel III
16	Dulzian	8	Oboe
8	Trompete		

OBERWERK		PEDAL	
8	Gedackt	16	Subbass
4	Prinzipal	8	Prinzipal
4	Rohrflöte	4	Oktave
2	Oktave		Mixtur III
1⅓	Quintflöte	16	Posaune
	Sesquialtera II (c)	8	Trompete
	Scharf III	4	Schalmei
8	Krummhorn		

Source: Copy of original specification, 5 May 1975, editor's personal collection

Saint Peter's Lutheran Church   Ottawa, Ontario

Opus 3328, 1976

HAUPTWERK		BRUSTWERK		PEDAL	
8	Praestant	8	Gedackt	16	Subbass
8	Hohlflöte	4	Rohrflöte	8	Prinzipal
4	Oktave	2	Prinzipal	4	Oktave
2	Flöte	1⅓	Quinte	16	Fagott
	Mixtur IV		Sesquialtera II		
8	Trompete		Tremulant		

Source: Royal Canadian College of Organists National Convention, *The American Organist* 17 (May 1983): 68

Saints Peter and Paul Church   Omaha, Nebraska

Opus 3335, 1977

HAUPTWERK		BRUSTWERK (expressive)		PEDAL	
8	Prinzipal	8	Gedackt	16	Subbass
8	Hohlflöte	4	Rohrflöte	8	Oktave
4	Oktave	2	Flöte	4	Oktave
2	Oktave		Terzian II	16	Posaune
	Mixtur V	8	Regal	8	Trompete
8	Trompete				

Tremulant to the whole organ
Couplers: BW→HW   HW→P
Installation supervised by Irenée Létourneau
Dedication recital: 26 June 1977 by Thomas Brantigan
Drawknob layout:

	Left			Right		
	HW		BW	BW		HW
8	Trompete		Tremulant	Terzian II		Mixtur V
2	Oktave	8	Regal	4 Rohrflöte	4	Oktave
8	Hohlflöte	2	Flöte	8 Gedackt	8	Prinzipal
8	Trompete		BW→HW	4 Oktave	16	Subbass
16	Posaune		HW→P	8 Oktave		

Source: Mary Alice Kubovy, letter, 5 May 1996

Fergusson Presbyterian Church   **St. Louis, Missouri**

Opus 3340, 1977

GRAND ORGUE	RÉCIT	PEDALE
8 Montre	8 Bourdon	16 Soubasse
8 Flûte à Cheminée	8 Viola de Gamba	8 Octavebasse
4 Prestant	8 Voix céleste (prepared)	4 Octave
2 Quarte de Nasard	4 Flûte Octaviente	16 Basson
Cornet II (prepared)	2 Doublette	
Fourniture IV	Cymbale III	
	8 Trompette de Récit	

1-5 of Montre from Flûte à Cheminée
Scaling, layout, and voicing supervision: Gerhard Brunzema
Specification: Stephen McKersie
Installation and final voicing: Martin Ott
Dedication recital: 24 July 1977 by Stephen McKersie
Source: *The Diapason* 69 (December 1977): 20

University of Alberta   **Edmonton, Alberta**

Opus 3358, 1978

HAUPTWERK		SCHWELLWERK	
16	Bordun	8	Offenflöte
8	Praestant	8	Gemshorn
8	Hohlflöte	8	Schwebung (g)
4	Oktave	4	Oktave
4	Spitzflöte	4	Querflöte
2⅔	Nasat	2	Waldflöte
2	Oktave		Mixtur V
2	Blockflöte	16	Fagott
1¾	Terz	8	Trompete
	Mixtur V		Tremulant
8	Trompete		

RÜCKPOSITIV		PEDAL	
8	Gedackt	16	Subbass
4	Praestant	8	Oktave
4	Rohrflöte	8	Gedacktbass
2	Oktave	4	Oktave
1⅓	Quinte		Mixtur IV
	Sesquialtera II	16	Posaune
	Scharf IV	8	Trompete
8	Krummhorn	4	Schalmei
	Tremulant		

Couplers: RP→HW   SW→HW   HW→P   SW→P
Stop action: electropneumatic
Case: mahogany
Dedication recital: 1 October 1978 by Gerhard Krapf
Drawknob layout:

Left

PEDAL				SCHWELLWERK		
4 Schalmei		Mixtur IV		8 Trompete		Tremulant
8 Trompete		4 Oktave		16 Fagott		Mixtur V
16 Posaune		8 Oktave		2 Waldflöte		4 Oktave
8 Gedacktbass		16 Subbass		4 Querflöte		8 Offenflöte
SW→P		HW→P		8 Gemshorn		8 Schwebung

Right

HAUPTWERK		RÜCKPOSITIV	
8 Trompete	Mixtur V		
1⅗ Terz	2 Oktave	Tremulant	Scharf IV
2 Blockflöte	4 Oktave	8 Krummhorn	2 Oktave
2⅔ Nasat	8 Praestant	1⅓ Quint	4 Praestant
4 Spitzflöte	16 Bourdon	Sesquialtera	8 Gedackt
8 Hohlflöte		4 Rohrflöte	
SW→HW	RP→HW		

Sources: Marnie Giesbrecht, letter, 14 June 1996; *The American Organist* 13 (January 1979): 48; *The Diapason* 70 (December 1978): 14

Dordt College Sioux Center, Iowa

Opus 3360, 1978

HOOFDWERK		BOVENWERK (expressive)	
16	Praestant	8	Praestant
8	Octaaf	8	Voix céleste
8	Holpijp	8	Baarpijp
4	Octaaf	4	Dwarsfluit
2⅔	Quint	2⅔	Nasard
2	Octaaf	2	Fluit
	Mixtuur VI	1⅗	Terts
	Scherp IV		Cymbel III
16	Trompet	8	Hobo
8	Spaanse Trompet		Tremulant
8	Vox Humana		

RUGWERK		PEDAAL	
8	Praestant	16	Praestant
8	Gedeckt	8	Octaaf
4	Octaaf	4	Octaaf
4	Roerfluit		Mixtuur IV
2	Octaaf	32	Bazuin
1⅓	Quint	16	Bazuin
	Sexquialter II	8	Trompet
	Scherp V	2	Cornet
8	Dulciaan		
	Tremulant		

Cymbelster
Couplers: BVW→HW   RW→HW   HW→P   BVW→P   RW→P
Stop action: electric
Case: oak
Case height: 33 feet
Pedal division is located in two side towers
Order of manual keyboards from top: Bovenwerk, Hoofdwerk,
Rugwerk
Spaanse Trompet is *en chamade*
Vox Humana is based on the stop in the Müller organ in the
Waalse Kerk, Amsterdam, Netherlands
Dedication recital: Joan Ringerwole
Drawknob layout:

Left

PEDAAL		BOVENWERK	
	Mixtuur VI		
2 Cornet	4 Octaaf	1⅗ Terts	Tremulant
8 Trompet	8 Octaaf	2 Fluit	8 Hobo
16 Bazuin	16 Praestant	2⅔ Nasard	Cymbel III
32 Bazuin	HW→P	4 Dwarsfluit	8 Praestant
BW→P	RW→P	8 Baarpijp	8 Voix céleste

Right

HOOFDWERK		RUGWERK	
Scherp IV	Mixtuur VI		
Cymbelster	2 Octaaf	Tremulant	Scherp V
8 Vox Humana	2⅔ Quint	8 Dulciaan	1⅓ Quint
8 Spaanse Trompet	4 Octaaf	Sexquialter II	2 Octaaf
16 Trompet	8 Octaaf	4 Roerfluit	4 Octaaf
8 Holpijp	16 Praestant	8 Gedekt	8 Praestant
BW→HW	RW→HW		

Sources: Joan Ringerwole, letter, 25 September 1995; *The American Organist* 14 (February 1980): 53; *The Diapason* 70 (November 1979): 1, 3

First Lutheran Church   **Mabel, Minnesota**

Opus 3363, 1977

HAUPTWERK		SCHWELLWERK		PEDAL	
8	Praestant	8	Spitzflöte	16	Subbass
8	Hohlflöte	4	Rohrflöte		
4	Oktave	2	Prinzipal		
	Mixtur IV	1⅓	Quinte		
		8	Dulzian		

Couplers: SW→HW   HW→P   SW→P
Case: oak
Installation: Thomas Erickson and Carroll Hanson
Principal voicer: Gerhard Brunzema
Dedication recital: 1978 by William Kuhlman
Sources: *The American Organist* 13 (July 1979): 42; *The Diapason* 70 (December 1979): 16

Trinity Church (Episcopal)   **Princeton, New Jersey**

Opus 3364, 1978

GRAND ORGUE		RÉCIT	
16	Bourdon	8	Bourdon
8	Montre	8	Viole de gambe
8	Bourdon	8	Voix céleste (G)
5⅓	Gros nasard	4	Flûte conique
4	Prestant	2	Octavin
3⅕	Grosse tierce		Cornet V (f)
2⅔	Quinte		Plein Jeu IV
2	Doublette	16	Basson
	Cornet V (c)	8	Trompette
	Fourniture V–VI	8	Hautbois
8	Trompette		
8	Voix humaine		CHAMADE
4	Clairon	8	Trompette en chamade

POSITIF DE DOS
8	Montre
8	Bourdon
4	Prestant
4	Flûte
2⅔	Nasard
2	Doublette
1⅗	Tierce
1⅓	Larigot
	Cymbale IV
8	Cromorne
8	Hautbois (c)

PEDALE
16	Contrebasse
8	Octave
4	Octave
	Fourniture IV
16	Bombarde
8	Trompette
4	Clairon

Tremblant fort, Tremblant doux
Clochettes
Stop action: electropneumatic
Pedal keyboard: flat/parallel
Tonal design: Gerhard Brunzema, Donald Corbett, André Isoir, James Litton, Ronald Miller
Dedication recitals: 17 October 1978 by James Litton; 2 November 1978 by André Isoir; 27 March 1979 by Joan Lippincott; 24 April 1979 by Harold Pyscher
Source: Litton, 44–45

First Presbyterian Church **Boulder, Colorado**

Opus 3372, 1978

HAUPTWERK
16	Bordun
8	Praestant
8	Rohrflöte
4	Oktave
2⅔	Quinte
2	Oktave
	Mixtur V
16	Dulzian
8	Trompete

RÜCKPOSITIV
8	Gedackt
4	Praestant
4	Koppelflöte
2	Waldflöte
	Sesquialtera II
	Scharf IV
8	Trichterregal

SCHWELLWERK		PEDAL	
8	Holzgedackt	16	Subbass
8	Gemshorn	8	Oktave
8	Schwebung (c)	4	Oktave
4	Spitzprinzipal		Mixtur IV
4	Gedacktflöte	16	Posaune
2	Oktave	8	Trompete
	Mixtur III	4	Schalmei
8	Oboe		

Dedication recital: 25 February 1979
Source: Organ dedication program, editor's personal collection

Church of Saint Mary the Virgin   **Falmouth, Maine**

Opus 3384, 1978

HAUPTWERK		RÜCKPOSITIV		PEDAL	
8	Praestant	8	Gedackt	16	Subbass
8	Hohlflöte	4	Praestant	8	Prinzipal
8	Spitzgamba	4	Rohrflöte	4	Oktave
4	Oktave	2	Gemshorn	16	Fagott
2⅔	Nasat		Sesquialtera II	8	Trompete
2	Oktave		Scharf III		
	Mixtur IV	8	Krummhornregal		
8	Dulzian				

Tremulant
Couplers: RP→HW   HW→P   RP→P
Pedal keyboard: flat/parallel
1-7 of HW Praestant from Hohlflöte
1-14 of Spitzgamba from Hohlflöte
1-4 of RP Praestant from Rohrflöte
Hauptwerk is upper manual keyboard; Rückpositiv is lower
Date on opus list is 1978; date on organ is 1979

Drawknob layout:

Left		Right	
RP	HW	HW	RP
Tremulant	8 Dulzian	Mixtur	Sesquialtera
8 Krummhornregal	2⅔ Nasat	2 Oktave	Scharf
2 Gemshorn	8 Hohlflöte	4 Oktave	4 Praestant
4 Rohrflöte	8 Spitzgamba	8 Praestant	8 Gedackt
	RP→HW		
RP→P	HW→P	4 Oktave	16 Subbass
16 Fagott	8 Trompete	8 Prinzipal	Key switch

Source: Instrument; John Corrie, letter, 18 August, 1995

Zion Lutheran Church **Kalamazoo, Michigan**
Opus 3386, 1978

HAUPTWERK
16   Bordun
 8   Praestant
 8   Hohlflöte
 4   Oktave
 4   Spitzflöte
2⅔   Quinte
 2   Oktave
      Kornett V (c')
      Mixtur IV-VI
 8   Trompete

RÜCKPOSITIV
 8   Gedackt
 4   Praestant
 4   Rohrflöte
2⅔   Nasat
 2   Gemshorn
1⅗   Terz
1⅓   Quintflöte
      Scharf IV
 8   Krummhorn

BRUSTWERK (enclosed)
 8   Holzgedackt
 8   Spitzgamba
 4   Spitzgedackt
 2   Waldflöte
 8   Vox Humana

PEDAL
16   Holzprincipal
16   Subbass
 8   Oktave
 4   Oktave
      Mixtur V
16   Posaune
 8   Trompete

Tremulant
Wind pressure: 71 mm (2¾ inches)
Built under the direction of Gerhard Brunzema
Installation: Normand Giard

Tonal finishing: Yves Champagne and Gilles Charest
Dedication recital: 10 June 1979 by Kathryn Loew, Western
Michigan University
Source: *The Diapason* 71 (September 1980): 20

Saint Peter's Cathedral   Scranton, Pennsylvania

Opus 3414, 1979

HAUPTWERK		OBERWERK	
16	Bourdon	8	Gedackt
8	Praestant	4	Praestant
8	Schwebung (c)	4	Rohrflöte
8	Hohlflöte	2⅔	Nasat
4	Oktave	2	Flöte
4	Spitzflöte	1⅗	Terz
2⅔	Quinte	1	Sifflöte
2	Oktave		Scharf IV
	Mixtur V	8	Dulzian
	Scharf IV	4	Trompete
8	Trompete		Tremulant

BRUSTWERK		PEDAL	
8	Holzgedackt (oak)	16	Prinzipal (oak)
4	Flöte	16	Subbass (oak)
2	Prinzipal	8	Oktave
2	Blockflöte	4	Oktave
1⅓	Quinte	2	Flöte
	Terzian II		Mixtur V
8	Regal	16	Posaune
	Tremulant	8	Trompete
		2	Kornett

Couplers: OW→HW   HW→P   OW→P
Stop action: mechanical
Pedal keyboard: flat/parallel
Case: painted oak
Order of manual keyboards from top: Brustwerk, Hauptwerk,
Oberwerk
Tonal design: Gerhard Brunzema

Visual design: Jean-Claude Gauthier
Drawknob layout:

Left

PEDAL	OBERWERK	HAUPTWERK	BRUSTWERK
2 Kornett	1 Sifflöte	8 Trompete	
8 Trompete	1⅗ Terz	4 Spitzflöte	8 Regal
16 Posaune	2 Flöte	8 Hohlflöte	
2 Flöte	2⅔ Nasat	8 Schwebung	2 Blockflöte
OW→P	4 Rohrflöte	16 Bourdon	4 Flöte
HW→P		OW→HW	

Right

BRUSTWERK	HAUPTWERK	OBERWERK	PEDAL
Tremulant	Scharf IV	Tremulant	
Terzian II	Mixtur V	4 Trompete	Mixtur V
1⅓ Quinte	2 Oktave	8 Dulzian	4 Oktave
2 Prinzipal	2⅔ Quinte	Scharf IV	8 Oktave
8 Holzgedackt	4 Oktave	4 Praestant	16 Prinzipal
Key switch	8 Praestant	8 Gedackt	16 Subbass

Source: Instrument; Larry Hoey, personal conversation, 19 October, 1995; *The Diapason* 69 (October 1978): 16

Our Savior's Lutheran Church **Menomonie, Wisconsin**

Opus 3433, 1980

HAUPTWERK	BRUSTWERK	PEDAL
16 Bordun	8 Gedackt	16 Subbass
8 Praestant	4 Spitzgedackt	8 Oktave
8 Hohlflöte	2 Flöte	16 Posaune
4 Oktave	1⅓ Quinte	8 Trompete
2⅔ Quinte	8 Regal	
2 Oktave		
1⅗ Terz		
Mixtur IV		
8 Trompete		

Tremulant
Coupler: HW→P
Stop action: mechanical

Pedal keyboard: flat/parallel
Source: Thomas Erickson, letter, 5 July 1995

Covenant Lutheran Church Stoughton, Wisconsin

Opus 3462, 1980

HAUPTWERK		BRUSTWERK		PEDAL	
8	Praestant	8	Holzgedackt	16	Subbass
4	Oktave	4	Rohrflöte		
	Mixtur IV	2	Flöte		
8	Trompete		Kornet II (c)		

Tremulant
Couplers: BW→HW HW→P BW→P
Source: Thomas Erickson, letter, 5 July 1995

Lutheran Church of the Redemption Bloomington, Minnesota

Opus 3479, 1980

MANUAL I		MANUAL II		PEDAL	
8	Praestant	8	Gedackt	16	Subbass
4	Oktave	4	Rohrflöte		
	Mixtur IV	2	Prinzipal		
8	Trompete		Sesquialtera II		

Tremulant
Couplers: II→I I→P II→P
Source: Thomas Erickson, letter, 5 July 1995

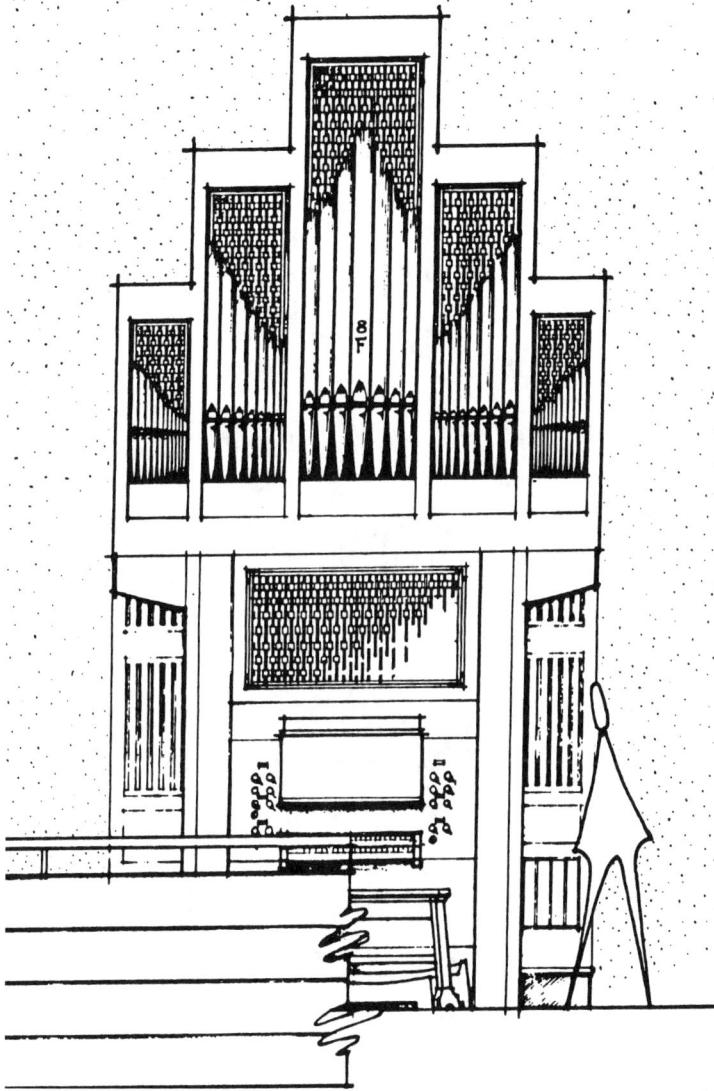

Figure 9
Grace Lutheran Church
Champaign, Illinois
Casavant Frères Opus 3246, 1975

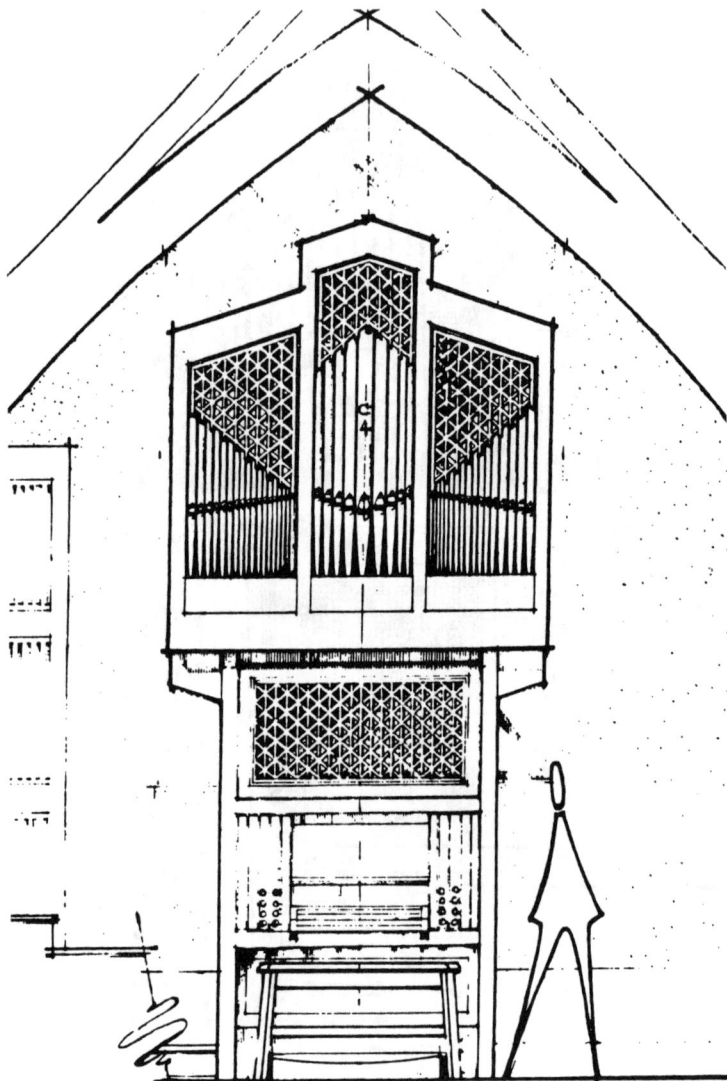

Figure 10
Saint Mark's Lutheran Church
Cedar Rapids, Iowa
Casavant Frères Opus 3262, 1975

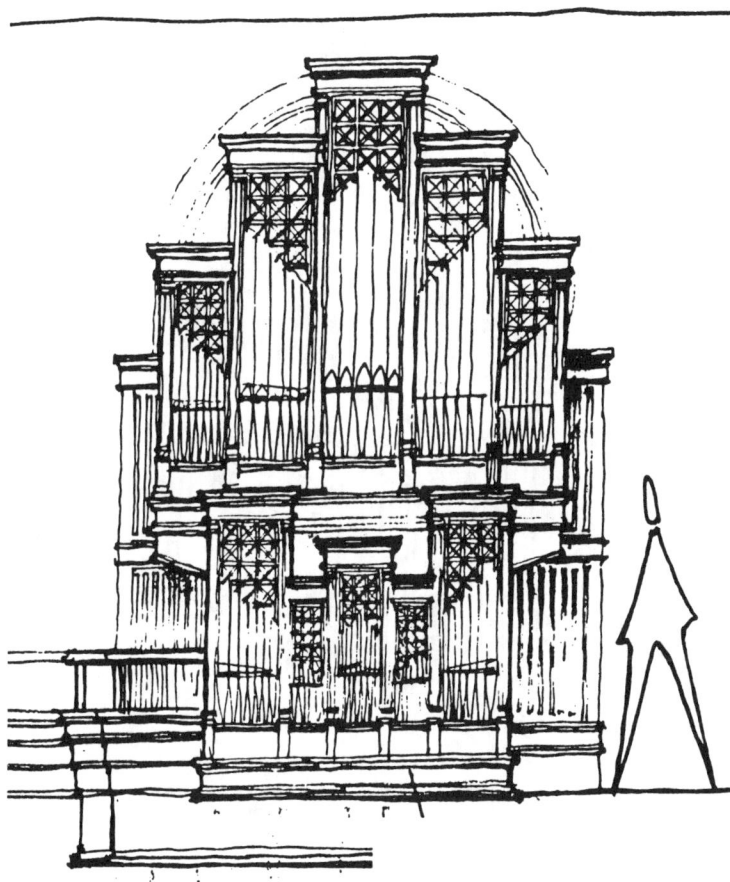

Figure 11
Williamsburg Presbyterian Church
Williamsburg, Virginia
Casavant Frères Opus 3275, 1975

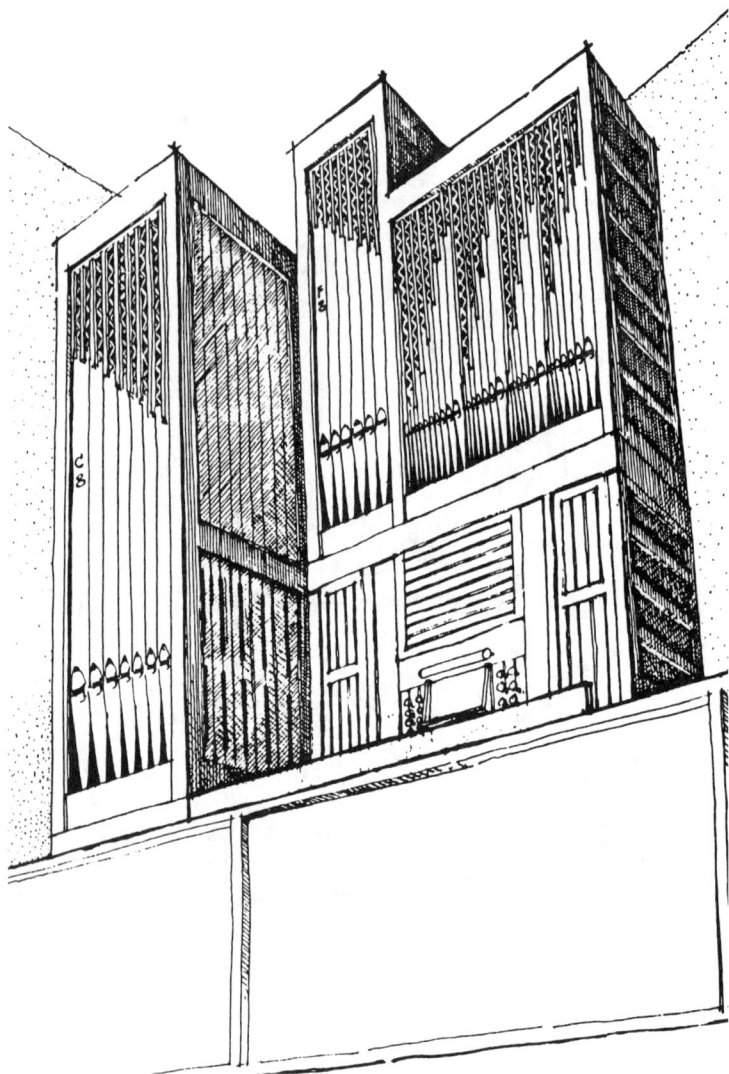

Figure 12
Church of the Maternity of the Blessed Virgin
St. Paul, Minnesota
Casavant Frères Opus 3302, 1976

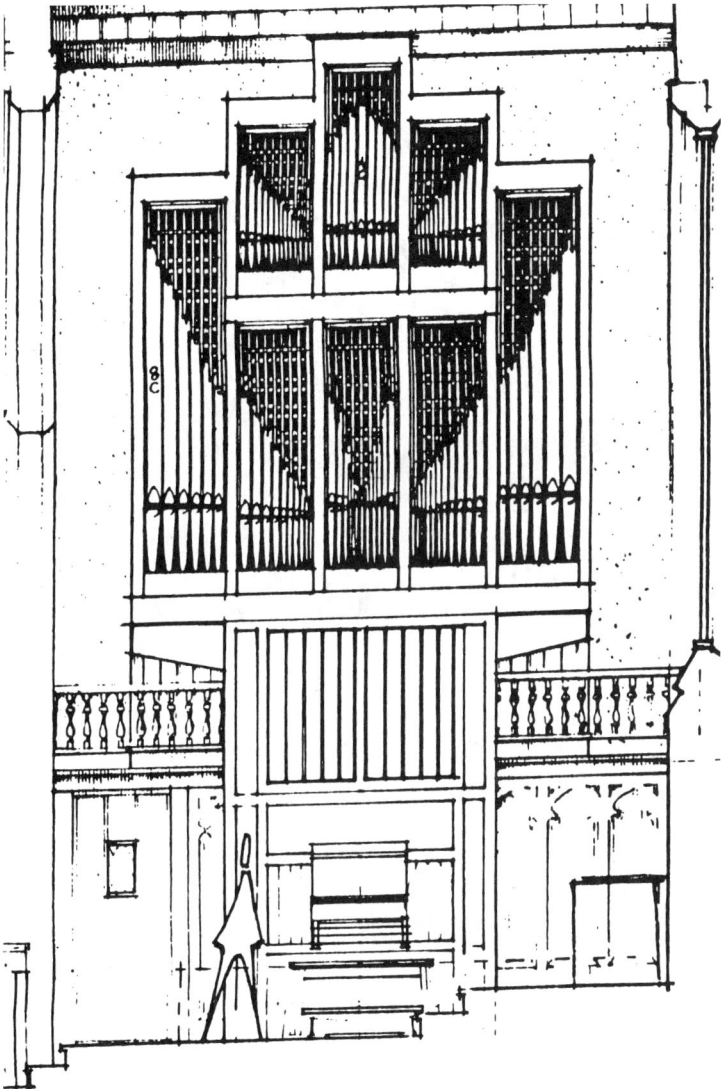

Figure 13
First United Methodist Church
Casper, Wyoming
Casavant Frères Opus 3316, 1976

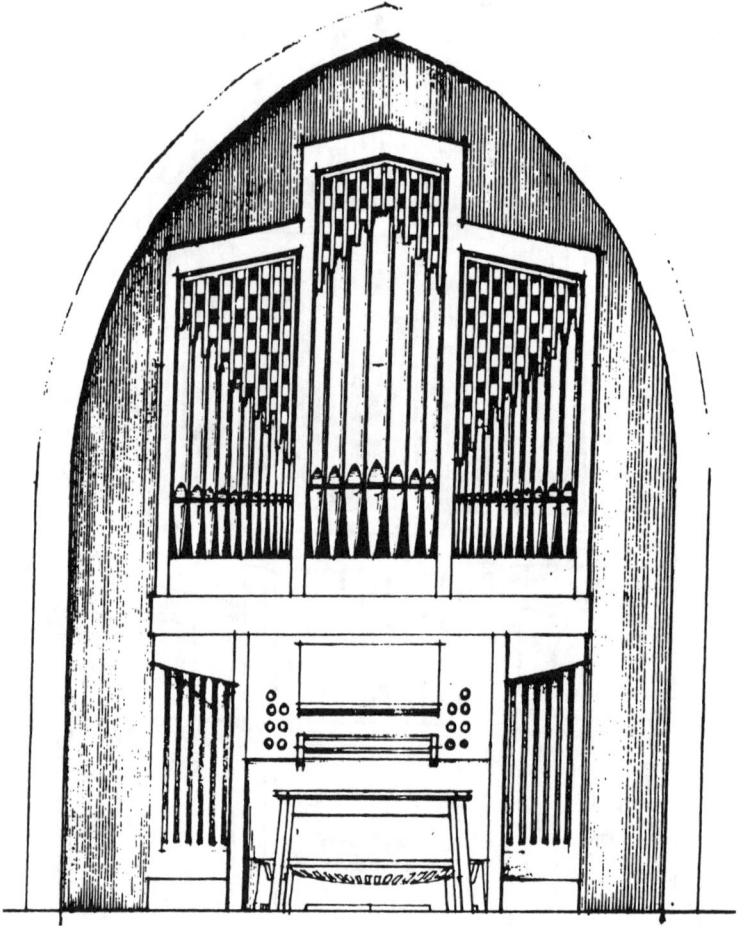

Figure 14
Saint Peter's Lutheran Church
Ottawa, Ontario
Casavant Frères Opus 3328, 1976

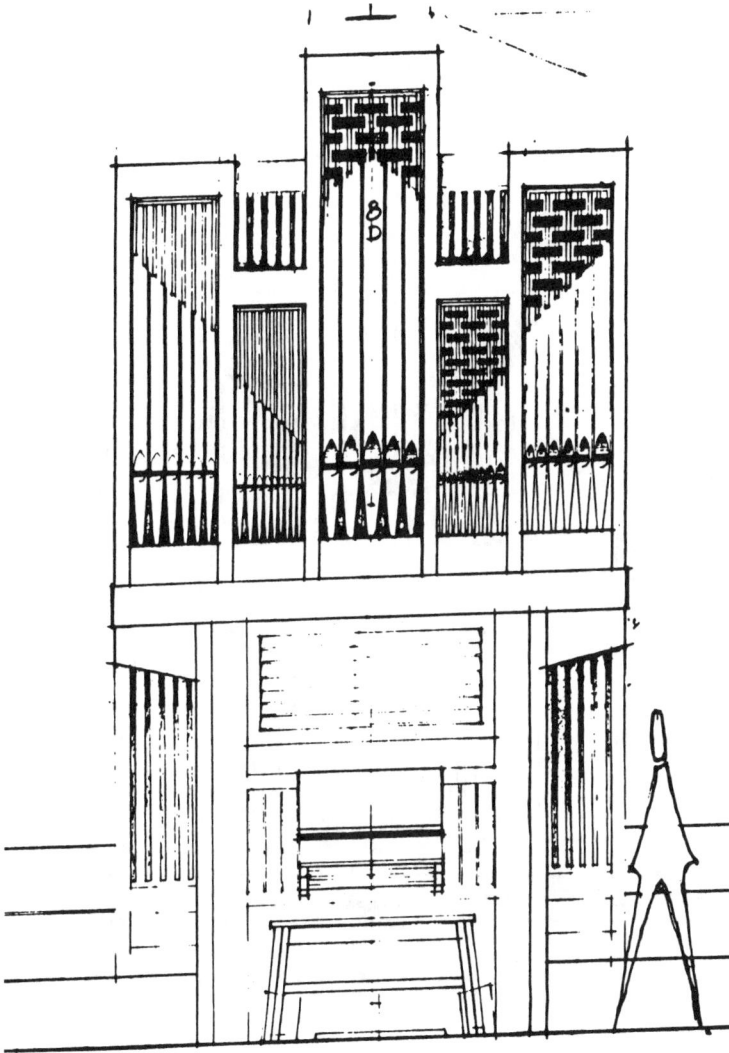

Figure 15
Saints Peter and Paul Church
Omaha, Nebraska
Casavant Frères Opus 3335, 1977

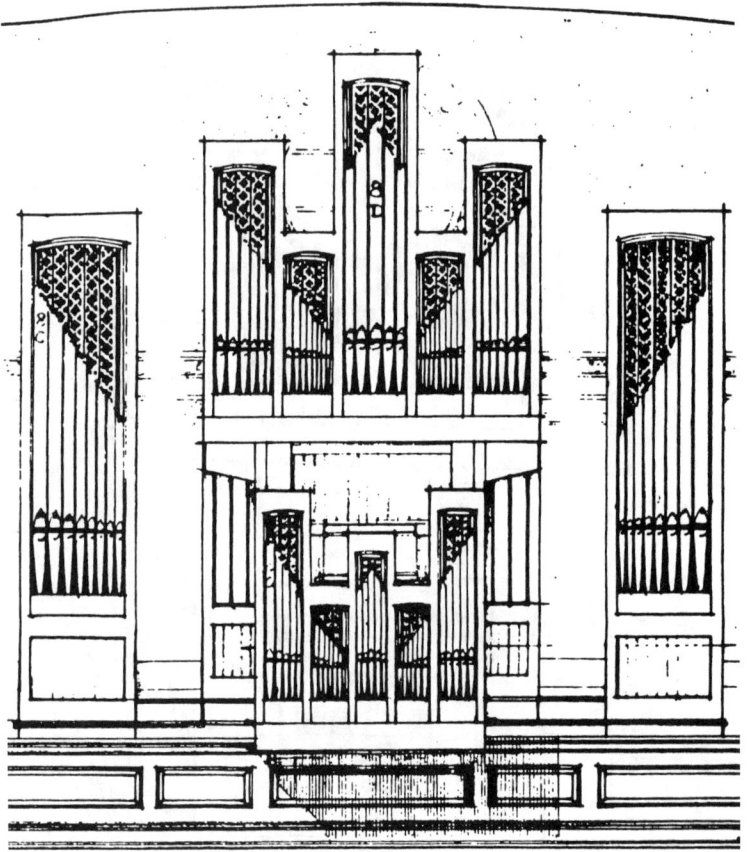

Figure 16
University of Alberta
Edmonton, Alberta
Casavant Frères Opus 3358, 1978

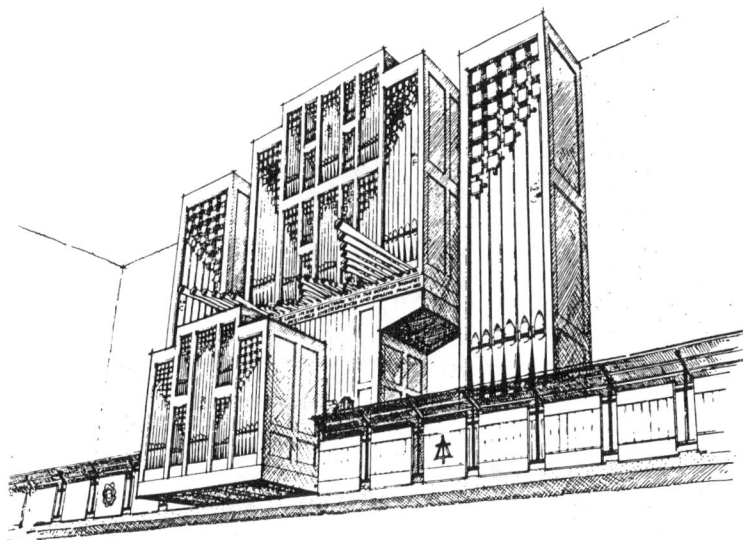

Figure 17
Dordt College
Sioux Center, Iowa
Casavant Frères Opus 3360, 1978

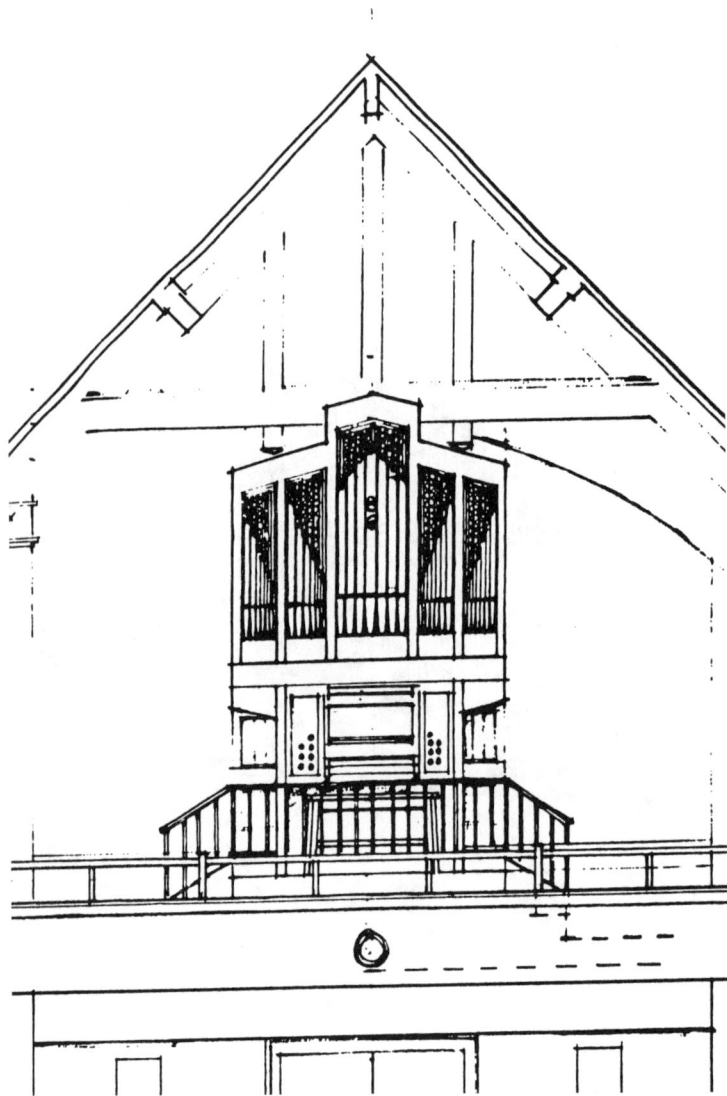

Figure 18
First Lutheran Church
Mabel, Minnesota
Casavant Frères Opus 3363, 1977

Figure 19
Trinity Church
Princeton, New Jersey
Casavant Frères Opus 3364, 1978

Figure 20
First Presbyterian Church
Boulder, Colorado
Casavant Frères Opus 3372, 1978

Figure 21
Church of Saint Mary the Virgin
Falmouth, Maine
Casavant Frères Opus 3384, 1978

Figure 22
Saint Peter's Cathedral
Scranton, Pennsylvania
Casavant Frères Opus 3414, 1979

✣ 24

1980-1992: Brunzema Organs, Incorporated, Fergus, Ontario, Canada

OPUS LIST

Roman numerals indicate the number of manual keyboards. Arabic numerals followed by the letter *s* indicate the number of stops; those followed by the letter *r* indicate the number of ranks. The absence of an *s* or an *r* means the number of ranks equals the number of stops. The uppercase letter *P* indicates the presence of a pedal division with independent stops; the lowercase letter *p* indicates the presence of a pedal keyboard but no pedal division (a "pulldown" pedal). (Source: Brunzema Archives)

Opus	Year	Location, Size, and Type
1	1980	Montréal, Québec *McGill University*
		I/3 (8 Holzgedackt, 4 Holzgedackt, 2 Prinzipal)
2	1981	Kitchener, Ontario *Saint Peter's Lutheran Church*
		I/3 (same stoplist as Opus 1)
3	1981	LaGrange, Illinois *First Presbyterian Church*
		I/4 Kisten Orgel

Opus	Year	Location, Size, and Type
4	1981	Guelph, Ontario *University of Guelph*
		I/4 Kisten Orgel
5	1982	Pella, Iowa *Central College*
		II/P/18s/21r
6	1982	Waterloo, Ontario *Conrad Graebel Institute*
		I/4 Kisten Orgel
7	1982	Waterloo, Ontario *Saint John's Lutheran Church*
		I/4 Kisten Orgel
8	1982	Pella, Iowa *Central College*
		I/4 Kisten Orgel
9	1982	Regina, Saskatchewan *Luther College*
		I/4 Kisten Orgel
10	1982	Winnipeg, Manitoba *Saint James Lutheran Church*
		I/P/10s/13r
11	1982	Edmonton, Alberta *University of Alberta*
		II/P/6 (prepared as II/P/9)
12	1983	Kitchener, Ontario
		Blessed Sacrament Parish
		I/P/10s/13r (1991: II/P/13s/16r)
13	1983	Wolfville, Nova Scotia *Saint Andrew's United Church*
		I/P/11s/15r
14	1983	San Antonio, Texas *Saint Luke's Episcopal Church*
		I/4 Kisten Orgel
15	1984	Waterloo, Ontario *Wilfrid Laurier University*
		I/4 Kisten Orgel
16	1984	Sewanee, Tennessee *School of Theology, University of the South*
		I/4 Kisten Orgel
17	1985	Manila, Philippines *Chapel of the Commercial & Industrial Bank*
		I/4 Kisten Orgel
18	1985	Annville, Pennsylvania *Lebanon Valley College*
		I/4 Kisten Orgel
19	1985	Bloomington, Indiana *Indiana University*
		I/4 Kisten Orgel

Opus	Year	Location, Size, and Type
20	1986	Brantford, Ontario *Mohawk Chapel* I/4 Kisten Orgel
21	1987	Bethlehem, Pennsylvania *Bach Choir* I/4 Kisten Orgel
22	1985	Brussels, Belgium *Michel Roy residence* I/1
23	1985	Fergus, Ontario *Residence organ* I/4
24	1985	Akron, Ohio *Hans Zbinden residence* II/p/8½
25	1986	Glace Bay, Nova Scotia *Saint Anne's* *Roman Catholic Church* II/P/22s/26r
26	1986	West Hartford, Connecticut *Edward Wagner residence* I/p/5
27	1987	Toronto, Ontario *Holy Family Church* II/P/20s/24r
28	1988	Charlotte, North Carolina *Saint John's* *Episcopal Church* II/P/25s/33r
29	1987	New York, New York *William Humphries residence* II/p/8½
30	1987	Solon, Ohio *George Hoffman residence* II/P/9½
31	1987	Toronto, Ontario *Chinese Methodist Church* I/4 Kisten Orgel
32	1987	Evansville, Indiana *First Presbyterian Church* I/4 Kisten Orgel
33	1988	Ann Arbor, Michigan *Marilyn Mason* I/4 Kisten Orgel
34	1989	Bryn Mawr, Pennsylvania *Bryn Mawr* *Presbyterian Church* I/4 Kisten Orgel
35	1989	Ottawa, Ontario *Karen Holmes* I/4 Kisten Orgel
36	1989	Winnipeg, Manitoba *Peter Letkemann* I/4 Kisten Orgel

Opus	Year	Location, Size, and Type
37	1990	Springfield, Illinois *First Presbyterian Church* I/4 Kisten Orgel
38	1990	Seoul, South Korea *Dong Presbyterian Church* II/P/16s/20r
39	1991	London, Ontario *University of Western Ontario* I/4 Kisten Orgel
40	1992	Bielefeld, Germany *Daniel Brunzema* I/4 Kisten Orgel
41	1992	Fergus, Ontario *Brunzema family* I/4 Kisten Orgel

THE ORGANS

The instruments built in the Fergus workshop have a manual keyboard compass of C-g′′′ (56 notes) and a pedal keyboard compass of C-f′ (30 notes); exceptions are noted below for Opuses 22, 23, 26, and the Kisten Orgel. Flat/parallel pedal keyboards are standard. Unless indicated, cases are made from quartersawn white oak with an oil finish. A letter in parentheses after a stop name indicates the note on which a short-compass stop begins.

Kisten Orgel

Opuses 3, 4, 6-9, 14-21, 31-37, 39-41
(Opuses 1 and 2 are three-stop versions of the Kisten Orgel)

8	Gedackt	oak and walnut
4	Flöte	oak and walnut; stopped
2	Prinzipal	metal, 70% tin; C-B are stopped
1⅓	Quinte	metal, 70% tin; C-B are ⅔′ pitch

Compass: CD-d′′′ (50 notes)
Carved pipeshades designed by Meta Brunzema
Pitch: a′ = 440 Hz at 21°C (70°F)
Height
   Total height: 92 cm (36 inches)
   Upper section: 61 cm (24 inches)
   Lower section: 31 cm (12 inches)

Width: 92 cm (36 inches)
Depth: 49 cm (19 inches)
Upper section contains pipes, windchest, and keyboard
   Weight: 60-64 kg (133-141 pounds)
Lower section contains electric blower with regulators
   Weight: 39-45 kg (86-100 pounds)
Source: Company brochure

The following text, written by Gerhard Brunzema, would have been sent as a letter to prospective buyers along with the Kisten Orgel brochure.

Why we designed the *Kisten Orgel* the way we did

Our instrument is designed to provide the highest musical qualities. We build the wooden pipes from white oak (two stops), the metal pipes are from 70% tin alloy. All pipes are made professionally and have a high degree of tuning stability. The instrument has openings for sound egress on three sides. This makes it much easier to achieve a precise tuning. The 8' stop and the 4' are meant to be played together with a perfect blend. We do not build the 4' as a solo stop. The pipes of our organ are, in general, voiced strongly and the organ can therefore be used in larger rooms. The wind supply is generously dimensioned and is incorporated into the instrument when the two parts are superimposed. This allows us to have a well regulated wind pressure as well as a practically noiseless operation. The noise level of the blower is so low that the instrument can be used for high quality recording sessions. The blower has been installed with an incorporated cooling system to avoid heat build up in the organ wind. This keeps the organ in tune even when used for a prolonged period of time during rehearsals and performances.

Our instrument is designed to be a TRULY transportable organ

The name of the *Kisten Orgel* comes from the Germanic word *Kiste* which literally means a wooden box or crate. The organ pipes are contained in such a box and are protected when in use and also during transportation. This means that the instrument may not be too large or too heavy. Two persons should be able to carry the parts. It should not be necessary to hire a moving company for transportation. We have achieved this goal by building the organ in two parts: the upper section contains the windchest with the pipes, the lower section houses only the bellows and the electric blower. The critical dimension for ease of transportation is the depth of the larger part. Our instrument is only 48.5 cm (19⅛ inches) and therefore fits through any door, and can even be moved around narrow corners and hallways. The instrument also fits into most passenger cars, through side doors. The two-part construction means that the weight of the wind supply is carried separately. A truly transportable instrument should have no protruding elements. Those have a tendency to get damaged while being moved. Our keyboard usually protrudes from the instrument, but rests within the instrument during transport. The organ has carrying handles which fold in when not in use. A transportable organ should also be built ruggedly. We chose white oak for the case and avoided metal façade pipes, protruding moldings or gold leaf decor. We finish our organ without lacquer, which has the advantage that small transport damages can be touched up easily. Additional protection is provided by a vinyl cover for the upper part, supplied with each instrument.

Our instrument is built to last

The instruments are made on the North American continent with the construction details corresponding to the climate. All materials are of the best quality. The organ pipes are very solidly installed, so that the tuning is kept stable even after extensive moving. The open metal pipes are cone tuned, the metal stopped pipes have soldered-on caps. The tuning stability of the wooden pipes is enhanced by using first-class material for the pipe walls and stoppers. The keyboard is made on our premises using selected sugar pine, ebony and bone covered sharps. The key action (suspended) is of the highest quality and is light and responsive. We use a first-rate blower, which needs no lubricating. The organ comes with a matching bench. The keyboard can be folded upwards to give access to the pipes. The height of our instrument is such that only one person is necessary for tuning.

The *Kisten Orgel* is a good buy

The instrument is the result of more than 30 years of experience in making transportable organs. We deliver our instruments personally to insure the good function. Since you are dealing with us directly and we are able to do maintenance on short notice, our five year warranty is thus meaningful to our customers. The instruments has a lovely sound and an attractive appearance. The value of a *Kisten Orgel* increases from year to year.

Central College Pella, Iowa

Opus 5, 1982

HAUPTWERK		BRUSTWERK		PEDAL	
8	Praestant	8	Gedackt	16	Subbass
8	Schwebung (c)	4	Rohrflöte	8	Oktave
8	Hohlflöte	2	Prinzipal	4	Oktave
4	Oktave	1⅓	Quinte	8	Trompete
2⅔	Nasat	16	Rankett		
2	Waldflöte				
1⅗	Terz				
1⅓	Mixtur IV				
8	Trompete				

Mixtur:	C	1⅓	1	⅔	½
	B	2	1⅓	1	⅔
	a♯	2⅔	2	1⅓	1
	a♯'	4	2⅔	2	1⅓
	a''	8	4	2⅔	2

Tremulant
Couplers: BW→HW   HW→P   BW→P
Naturals: rosewood
Sharps: ebony
1–12 of Pedal Oktave from Praestant
Drawknob layout:

	Left				*Right*		
8	Trompete				Tremulant	8	Praestant
8	Hohlflöte	16	Rankett			8	Schwebung
2⅔	Nasat	4	Rohrflöte	8	Gedackt	4	Oktave
2	Waldflöte	1⅓	Quinte	2	Prinzipal		Mixtur
1⅗	Terz		BW→HW				Key switch
	HW→P		BW→P				
16	Subbass	8	Trompete	8	Oktave	4	Oktave

Source: Davis Folkerts, telephone conversation, 8 January 1994;
The American Organist 16 (October 1982): 65; *The Diapason* 73
(October 1982): 14; Overduin, 127

Saint James Lutheran Church   **Winnipeg, Manitoba**

Opus 10, 1982

MANUAL   PEDAL
8 Hohlflöte (bass/treble)   16   Subbass
8 Gedackt
4 Praestant
4 Rohrflöte (bass/treble)
2 Oktave
2 Flöte (treble)
   Sesquialtera II (treble)
   Mixtur III
8 Dulzian (bass/treble)

Divided stops may be adjusted to divide at either b-c′ or c′-c#′
Coupler: Manual→Pedal
Naturals: ebony
Sharps: rosewood
Wind pressure: 55 mm (2⅛ inches)
Drawknob layout:

	Left			*Right*	
Order of Stops		Drawknob Layout	Order of Stops		Drawknob Layout
8	Gedackt	O	8	Hohlflöte	O O
4	Rohrflöte	O O	4	Praestant	O
2	Flöte	O		Sesquialtera	O
8	Dulzian	O O	2	Oktave	O
	M→P	O		Mixtur	O
16	Subbass	O			

Sources: Shirley Wildeman, letter, 2 June 1996; *The Diapason* 73
(November 1982): 3

University of Alberta   **Edmonton, Alberta**

Opus 11, 1982

MANUAL I   MANUAL II   PEDAL
8   Hohlflöte   8   Gedackt   16   Subbass
4   Rohrflöte   4   Spitzgedackt
2⅔ Quinte* (g)   2   Spitzflöte*
2   Prinzipal   1⅗ Terz*

*prepared for

Couplers: II→I   I→P
Naturals: rosewood
Sharps: ebony
Dimensions (height × width): 240 × 145 cm (94 × 57 inches)
1–14 of the Hohlflöte and the Gedackt from the Subbass
1–12 of the Subbass are located behind the case
Gerhard Krapf collaborated on the specification
Drawknob layout:
(proposed drawknob positions of prepared-for stops in brackets)

Left		Right	
4 Rohrflöte	4 Spitzgedackt	8 Gedackt	8 Hohlflöte
[2⅔ Quinte]	[1⅗ Terz]	[2 Spitzflöte]	2 Prinzipal
I→P		II→I	16 Subbass

Sources: Marnie Giesbrecht, letter, 14 June 1996; *The American Organist* 17 (June 1983): 47; *The Diapason* 74 (February 1983): 11

***Blessed Sacrament Parish*   Kitchener, Ontario**

Opus 12, 1983

HAUPTWERK   PEDAL
 8 Praestant   16   Subbass
 8 Schwebung (c)
 8 Gedackt (bass/treble)
 4 Oktave
 4 Rohrflöte (bass/treble)
2⅔ Quinte (bass/treble)
 2 Oktave
1⅓ Mixtur IV (bass/treble)
 8 Trompete (bass/treble)

BRUSTWERK, expressive (added in 1991)
 8 Holzgedackt
 4 Holzflöte
 2 Flöte

Mixtur:	C	1⅓	1	⅔	½
	B	2	1⅓	1	⅔
	a♮	2⅔	2	1⅓	1
	a♮′	4	2⅔	2	1⅓
	a″	8	4	2⅔	2

Divided stops may be adjusted to divide at either b–c′ or c′–c♯′
Tremulant (1991)
Couplers: HW→P   BW→P
1983—Naturals: ebony; Sharps: rosewood
1991—Naturals: ebony; Sharps: bone-covered walnut
Wind pressure: 64 mm (2½ inches)
1–6 of Praestant from Gedackt
Subbass pipes are behind the case in two rows, in an A layout
Drawknob layout:

Extreme Left		*Left*		*Right*
	Tremulant	8	Schwebung	8	Praestant
8	Holzgedackt	8	Gedackt	4	Oktave
4	Holzflöte	4	Rohrflöte	2⅔	Quinte
2	Flöte	8	Trompete	2	Oktave
	BW→P		HW→P		Mixtur
		16	Subbass		

The drawknobs at the extreme left were installed when the Brustwerk was added in 1991; the other drawknobs are original from
1983. For divided stops, the two drawknobs are placed next to
each other rather than on opposite sides of the keyboards.
Sources: Instrument; Brunzema Archives; *The American Organist* 18 (March 1984): 54; *The Diapason* 75 (January 1984): 12;
Overduin, 127–129

Saint Andrew's United Church   Wolfville, Nova Scotia

Opus 13, 1983

MANUAL		PEDAL	
8	Praestant	16	Subbass
8	Bordun (bass/treble)	8	Trompete
4	Oktave		
4	Rohrflöte (bass/treble)		
2	Oktave		
2	Flöte		
	Sesquialtera II (treble)		
	Mixtur IV		
8	Trompete (bass/treble)		

Tremulant
Coupler: Manual→Pedal

Naturals: ebony
Sharps: rosewood
Wind pressure: 64 mm (2½ inches)
Dedication recital: William H. Wright
Drawknob layout:

	Left			*Right*	
Order of Stops		**Drawknob Layout**	**Order of Stops**		**Drawknob Layout**
8	Bordun	O O	8	Praestant	O
4	Rohrflöte	O O	4	Oktave	O
2	Flöte	O	2	Oktave	O
	Sesquialtera	O		Mixtur	O
8	Trompete	O O		Tremulant	O
	M→P	O	16	Subbass	O
8	Trompete	O		Key switch	

Sources: Truth Cavanagh, letter, 14 November 1996; *The American Organist* 19 (January 1985): 52; *The Diapason* 75 (February 1984): 11

Michel Roy residence   **Brussels, Belgium**

Opus 22, 1985

MANUAL
  8   Quintadena

Compass: C–d‴ (51 notes)
Pipes of oak, with 17 pipes in façade
Dimensions (height × width × depth): 186 × 82 × 36 cm (73 × 32 × 14 inches); keyboard protudes 20 cm (8 inches)
Source: Brunzema Archives

Residence organ   **Fergus, Ontario**

Opus 23, 1985

MANUAL
  8   Rankett
  4   Flöte
  2   Quintadena
  1   Oktave

Compass: C–d‴ (51 notes)
Oktave extends to the top of compass without breaks

A sliding shutter just above the keyboard varies the sound of the Rankett

Sliders protrude from the left side of the case

Dimensions (height × width × depth): 186 × 82 × 36 cm (73 × 32 × 14 inches); keyboard protudes 20 cm (8 inches)

Sources: Instrument; Brunzema Archives

Hans Zbinden residence   Akron, Ohio

Opus 24, 1985

MANUAL I	MANUAL II	PEDAL
8 Gedackt	8 Spitzflöte	(no stops)
4 Praestant	4 Rohrflöte	
2 Flöte	2⅔ Quinte (treble)	
1⅓ Quinte	2 Oktave	
	8 Regal	

Couplers: II→I   I→P   II→P

Wind pressure: 64 mm (2½ inches)

Dimensions (height × width × depth): 238 × 133 × 71 cm (94 × 52 × 28 inches); pedal keyboard protrudes 71 cm (28 inches) from case

Reservoir and blower in organ case

Instrument can be disassembled into three case parts which fit through standard doors

Sources: *The American Organist* 19 (November 1985): 88; *The Diapason* 76 (November 1985): 1, 15

Saint Anne's Roman Catholic Church   Glace Bay, Nova Scotia

Opus 25, 1986

HAUPTWERK	BRUSTWERK (expressive)	PEDAL
16 Bordun	8 Gedackt	16 Subbass
8 Praestant	8 Salizional	8 Oktave
8 Hohlflöte	4 Rohrflöte	4 Oktave
4 Oktave	2 Flöte	16 Posaune
4 Spitzflöte	1⅓ Quinte	8 Trompete
2⅔ Nasat	Scharff II	
2 Oktave	8 Krummhorn	
1⅗ Terz		
Mixtur IV		
8 Trompete		

Mixtur:	C	1⅓	1	⅔	½
	B	2	1⅓	1	⅔
	a♯	2⅔	2	1⅓	1
	a♯′	4	2⅔	2	1⅓
	a″	8	4	2⅔	2

Scharff:	C	½	⅓
	c	1	⅔
	f′	1⅓	1
	f″	2⅔	2

Tremulant
Couplers: BW→HW   HW→P   BW→P
Wind pressure: 71 mm (2¾ inches); single reservoir
Façade pipes, mixtures, and reeds are 70% tin
1-9 of Bordun has the pipes of the Hohlflöte sounding with
a 5⅓′
1-17 of Salizional from Gedackt
The Posaune has full-length resonators from F
Consultant: Craig Cramer
Dedication recital: 15 June 1986 by Craig Cramer
Drawknob layout:*

Left				Right		
8	Hohlflöte	8	Salizional	Tremulant	16	Bordun
4	Spitzflöte	2	Flöte	8 Gedackt	8	Praestant
2⅔	Nazat	1⅓	Quinte	4 Rohrflöte	4	Octave
1⅗	Tierce	8	Krummhorn	Scharf	2	Octave
8	Trompete		BW→HW			Mixtur
	HW→P		BW→P	8 Octave	16	Subbass
8	Trompete	16	Posaune	4 Octave		

Sources: James McNeil, telephone conversation, 1 September
1995; letter, Gerhard Brunzema to Saint Anne's Church, 26 December 1984; *The American Organist* 21 (April 1987): 85; *The
Diapason* 77 (November 1986): 13

*The spellings are those found on the instrument

Edward Wagner residence   West Hartford, Connecticut
Opus 26, 1986

MANUAL		PEDAL
8	Quintade	permanently coupled to manual
8	Gedackt	
4	Rohrflöte	
2	Praestant	
1⅓	Quinte	

All stops divided, selectable at b-c′ or c′-c♯′
The order of the stop names above represents the layout of the
drawknobs, duplicated on each side of the keyboard
Manual compass: C-d‴ (51 notes)
Pedal compass: C-d′ (27 notes)
Naturals: ebony
Sharps: rosewood
Praestant pipes are 70% tin
Case: painted oak; case design and coloring by Meta Brunzema
Dimensions (height × width × depth): 236 × 121 × 70 cm (93
× 48 × 28 inches)
1-17 of Quintade from Gedackt
Dedication recital: November 8 and 9, 1986 by Edward Wagner,
with Barbara Riihimaki, piano, and Susan Casper, flute
Sources: Instrument; *The American Organist* 22 (June 1988): 60;
The Diapason 79 (June 1988): 14

Holy Family Church   Toronto, Ontario
Opus 27, 1987

HAUPTWERK		SCHWELLWERK		PEDAL	
8	Praestant	8	Gedackt	16	Subbass
8	Schwebung (d♯)	8	Quintade	8	Oktave
8	Hohlflöte	4	Rohrflöte	4	Oktave
4	Oktave	2	Spitzflöte	8	Trompete
4	Spitzflöte		Scharff II		
2⅔	Quinte	8	(Trichter) Regal		
2	Oktave				
1⅗	Terz				
	Mixtur IV				
8	Trompete				

Tremulant
Couplers: SW→HW   HW→P   SW→P
Naturals: ebony
Sharps: rosewood
Schwellwerk is in the Brustwerk position
1-6 of Praestant from Hohlflöte
1-12 of Quintade from Gedackt
Drawknob layout:

	Left				*Right*		
8	Hohlflöte	8	Quintade	8	Gedackt	8	Schwebung
4	Spitzflöte	2	Flöte	4	Rohrflöte	8	Praestant
2⅔	Quinte	8	Regal		Scharff	4	Oktave
1⅗	Terz					2	Oktave
8	Trompete		SW→HW		Tremulant		Mixtur
	HW→P		SW→P	8	Oktave	16	Subbass
8	Trompete			4	Oktave		

Source: Instrument; letter, Gerhard Brunzema to Craig Cramer, 9 June 1987
Note: This organ and the church were destroyed in a fire on 13 June 1997.

Saint John's Episcopal Church   **Charlotte, North Carolina**

Opus 28, 1988

HAUPTWERK		RÜCKPOSITIV		PEDAL	
16	Bordun	8	Gedackt	16	Subbass
8	Praestant (II from g′)	4	Praestant	8	Oktave
8	Schwebung (f)	4	Rohrflöte	4	Oktave
8	Hohlflöte	2	Oktave	16	Posaune
4	Oktave	2	Waldflöte	8	Trompete
4	Spitzflöte	1⅓	Nasat		
2⅔	Nasat		Sesquialtera II		
2	Oktave		Scharff III		
	Mixtur V	8	Krummhorn		
8	Trompete				
8	Spanische Trompete				

Mixtur:	C	1⅓	1	⅔	½	½
	c	2	1⅓	1	⅔	⅔
	c′	2	1⅓	1⅓	1	1
	f♯′	2⅔	2	1⅓	1⅓	1
	c″	4	2⅔	2	2	1⅓
	a♯″	4	4	2⅔	2⅔	2

Sesquialtera:	C	1⅓	⅘
	d	2⅔	1⅗
	d♯‴	3⅕	2⅔

Scharff:	C	½	⅓	¼
	c	⅔	½	⅓
	g	1	⅔	½
	c′	1⅓	1	⅔
	g′	2	1⅓	1
	c″	2⅔	2	1⅓
	a♯″	4	2⅔	2

Tremulant
Zimbelstern
Couplers: RP→HW   HW→P   RP→P
Naturals: ebony
Sharps: bone-covered walnut
Hauptwerk is upper manual keyboard; Rückpositiv is lower
Pedal case behind the main case measures 20 feet, 4 inches high
to accommodate the full-length resonators of the Posaune
Pipe shades decorated with gold leaf
Two wedge-shaped bellows
Consultant: Peter Williams
Dedication recital: 16 April 1989 by Peter Williams

Drawknob layout:

Left				Right	
	16	Bordun	8	Schwebung	
4 Rohrflöte				8	Gedackt
	8	Hohlflöte	8	Praestant	
2 Waldflöte				4	Praestant
	4	Spitzflöte	4	Oktave	
1⅓ Nasat				2	Oktave
	2⅔	Nasat	2	Oktave	
Sesquialtera					Scharff
	8	Spanische Trompete		Mixtur	
8 Krummhorn					Tremulant
		RP→HW	8	Trompete	
RP→P				16	Subbass
		HW→P	8	Oktave	
16 Posaune					
	8	Trompete	4	Oktave	

Sources: Instrument; Brunzema Archives; Charles Crutchfield, letter, 14 November 1995; *The American Organist* 24 (February 1990): 78; *The Diapason* 80 (June 1989): 11

William Humphries residence New York, New York

Opus 29, 1987

MANUAL I		MANUAL II		PEDAL
8	Gedackt	8 Spitzflöte		(no stops)
4	Praestant	4 Rohrflöte		
2	Flöte	2⅔ Quinte (aⁱ)		
1⅓	Quinte	2 Oktave		
		8 Regal		

Couplers: II→I   I→P   II→P
Naturals: ebony
Sharps: rosewood

Case: bleached white oak
Dimensions (height × width × depth): 238 × 133 × 71 cm (94
× 52 × 28 inches); pedal keyboard protrudes 71 cm (28 inches)
from case
1–8 of Praestant from Rohrflöte
1–19 of Spitzflöte from Gedackt
Sources: *The American Organist* 22 (August 1988): 53; *The Diapason* 79 (November 1988): 11

George Hoffman residence   Solon, Ohio

Opus 30, 1987

MANUAL I		MANUAL II		PEDAL	
8	Gedackt	8	Spitzflöte	16	Subbass
4	Praestant	4	Rohrflöte		
2	Flöte	2⅔	Quinte (treble)		
1⅓	Quinte	2	Oktave		
		8	Regal		

Zimbelstern
Couplers: II→I   I→P   II→P
1–8 of Praestant from Rohrflöte
1–19 of Spitzflöte from Gedackt
Source: Brunzema Archives

Dong Presbyterian Church   Seoul, South Korea

Opus 38, 1990

HAUPTWERK		BRUSTWERK (expressive)		PEDAL	
8	Praestant	8	Gedackt	16	Subbass
8	Hohlflöte	4	Rohrflöte	8	Prinzipal
4	Oktave	2	Flöte	4	Oktave
2	Oktave	1⅓	Quinte	16	Posaune
	Sesquialtera II	8	Schalmey	8	Trompete
	Mixtur IV				

Sesquialtera:	C	$\frac{2}{5}$	$\frac{2}{5}$		
	B	$1\frac{1}{3}$	$\frac{4}{5}$		
	a	$2\frac{2}{3}$	$1\frac{3}{5}$		
	d♯'''	$3\frac{1}{5}$	$2\frac{2}{3}$		

Mixtur:	C	$1\frac{1}{3}$	1	$\frac{2}{3}$	$\frac{1}{2}$
	B	2	$1\frac{1}{3}$	1	$\frac{2}{3}$
	a♯	$2\frac{2}{3}$	2	$1\frac{1}{3}$	1
	a♯'	4	$2\frac{2}{3}$	2	$1\frac{1}{3}$
	a♯''	4	$2\frac{2}{3}$	2	2

Tremulant
Couplers: BW→HW   HW→P   BW→P
1–6 of Praestant from Hohlflöte
1–12 of Posaune have half-length resonators
Source: Brunzema Archives

Figure 23
Gerhard Brunzema

Figure 24
Kisten Orgel
Brunzema Organs, Inc.

Figure 25
Central College
Pella, Iowa
Brunzema Organs Opus 5, 1982

Figure 26
Saint James Lutheran Church
Winnipeg, Manitoba
Brunzema Organs Opus 10, 1982

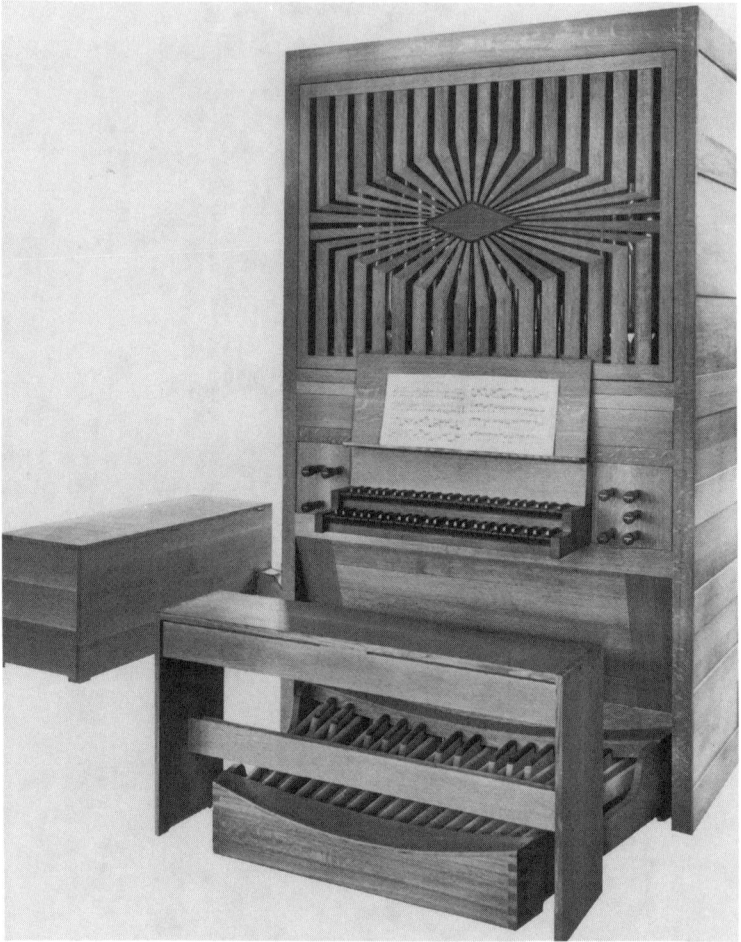

Figure 27
University of Alberta
Edmonton, Alberta
Brunzema Organs Opus 11, 1982

Figure 28
Blessed Sacrament Parish
Kitchener, Ontario
Brunzema Organs Opus 12, 1983

Figure 29
Saint Andrew's United Church
Wolfville, Nova Scotia
Brunzema Organs Opus 13, 1983

Figure 30
Residence organ
Fergus, Ontario
Brunzema Organs Opus 23, 1985

Figure 31
Hans Zbinden residence
Akron, Ohio
Brunzema Organs Opus 24, 1985

Figure 32
Saint Anne's Roman Catholic Church
Glace Bay, Nova Scotia
Brunzema Organs Opus 25, 1986

Figure 33
Edward Wagner residence
West Hartford, Connecticut
Brunzema Organs Opus 26, 1986

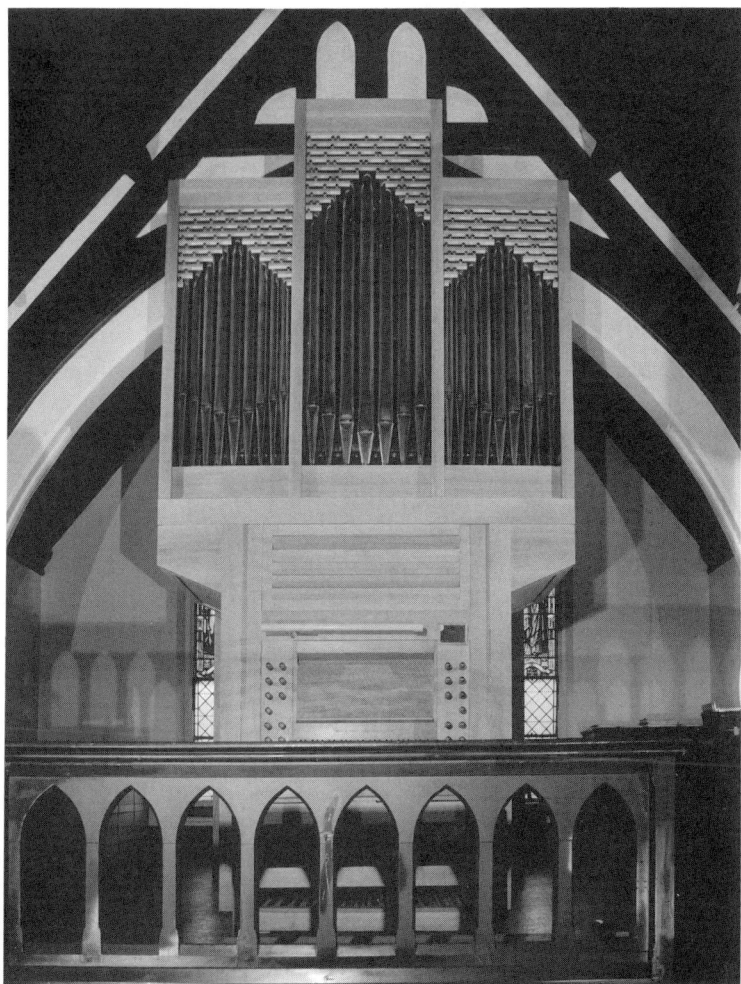

Figure 34
Holy Family Church
Toronto, Ontario
Brunzema Organs Opus 27, 1987

Figure 35
Saint John's Episcopal Church
Charlotte, North Carolina
Brunzema Organs Opus 28, 1988

Figure 36
William Humphries residence
New York, New York
Brunzema Organs Opus 29, 1987

Figure 37
George Hoffman residence
Solon, Ohio
Brunzema Organs Opus 30, 1987

Figure 38
Dong Presbyterian Church
Seoul, South Korea
Brunzema Organs Opus 38, 1990

❖ 25

Description of the Organ for Blessed Sacrament Parish, Kitchener, Ontario, Canada

Brunzema Organs, Inc., Opus 12 (1983, 1991) with reference to other building practices in the Fergus workshop

DISPOSITION

HAUPTWERK (1983)		BRUSTWERK, expressive (1991)		PEDAL (1983)
8	Praestant	8	Holzgedackt	16 Subbass
8	Schwebung (c)	4	Holzflöte	
8	Gedackt	2	Flöte	
4	Oktave			
4	Rohrflöte			
2⅔	Quinte			
2	Oktave			
1⅓	Mixtur IV			
8	Trompete			

Mixtur:	C	1⅓	1	⅔	½
	B	2	1⅓	1	⅔
	a♯	2⅔	2	1⅓	1
	a♯'	4	2⅔	2	1⅓
	a″	8	4	2⅔	2

Tremulant (1991)
Couplers: Hauptwerk to Pedal   Brustwerk to Pedal
Date on opus list is 1983; dates on organ are 1982 and 1991
The Gedackt, Rohrflöte, Quinte, Mixtur, and Trompete are divided stops; they may be adjusted to divide at either b–c' or c'–c♯'

ROOM

Volume: approximately 145,000 cubic feet
Reverberation of empty room:
    at 65 Hz, 3 seconds
    at 131 Hz, 2.5 seconds
    at 262 Hz and up, 2 seconds

CASE

Material: Quartersawn white oak with Watco® Danish oil finish
Height at highest point: 4916 mm
Height at lowest point: 3590 mm
Height from floor to impost: 2100 mm
Height of impost: 140 mm
Height from impost to highest point: 2676 mm
Height from impost to lowest point: 1350 mm
Width of upper case: 2500 mm
Width of lower case: 1530 mm
Depth of organ, excluding pedal keyboard: 2050 mm
Depth of main case: 1080 mm
Thicknesses
    Impost: 60 mm
    Main supports
        Upper case: 25 mm
        Lower case: 28 mm

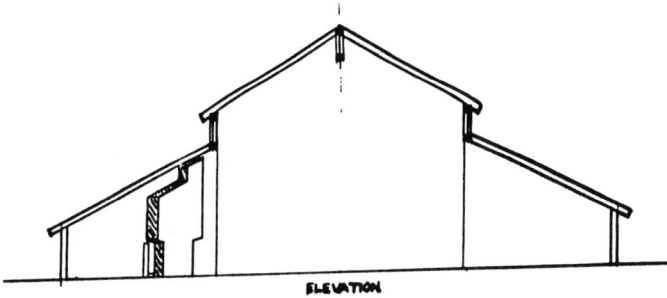

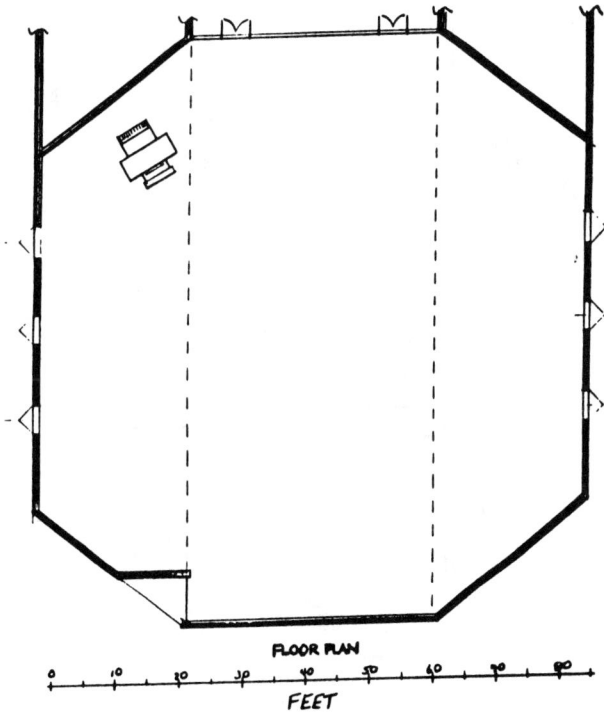

Figure 39
Kitchener: Elevation and floor plan of the church,
showing the location of the organ

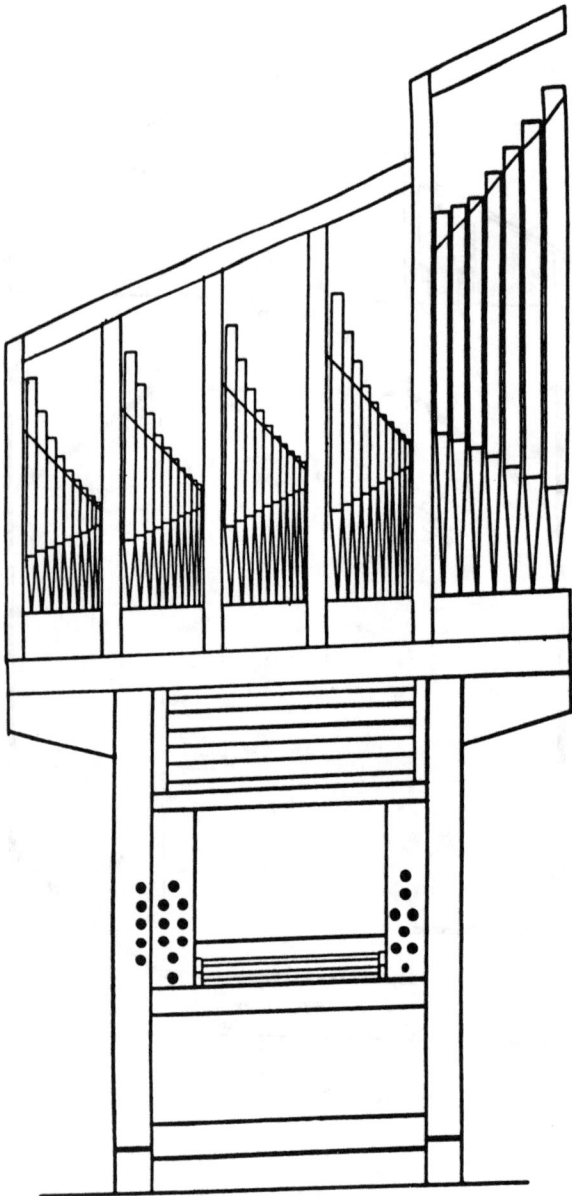

Figure 40
Kitchener: Front elevation

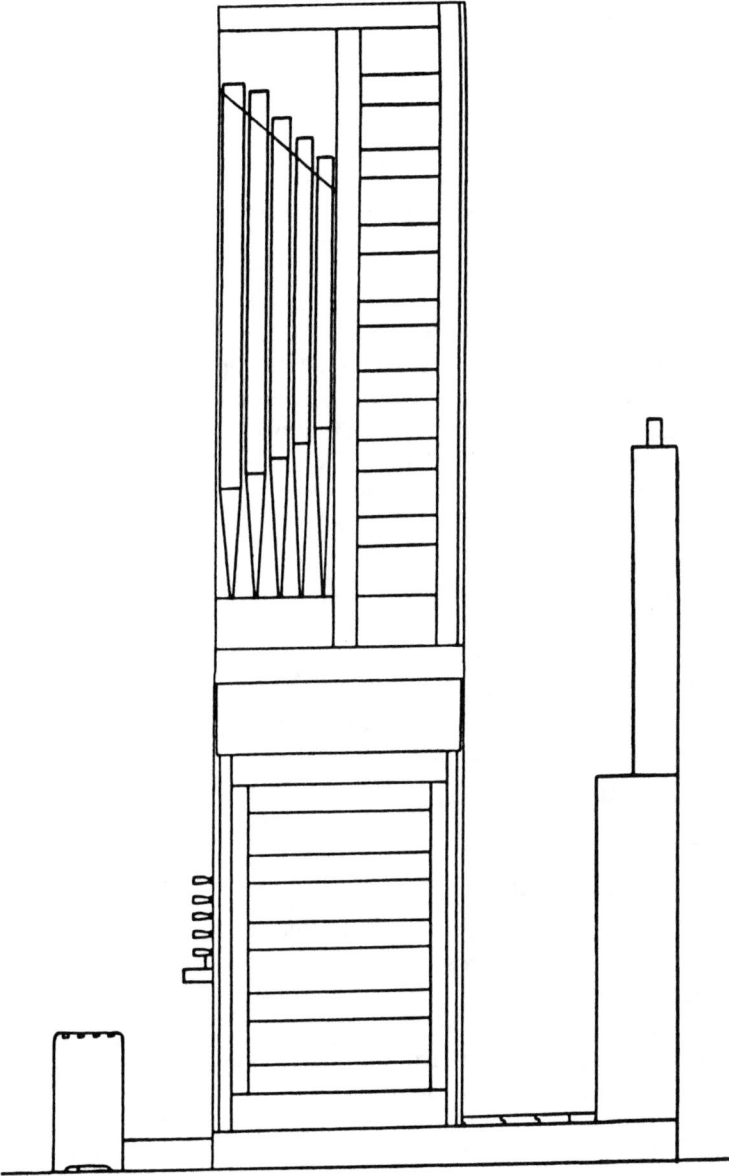

Figure 41
Kitchener: Side elevation

Rails and stiles
  Upper case: 20 mm
  Lower case: 18 mm
  Back: 16 mm
Panels
  Upper case: 6 mm
  Lower case: 8 mm
In front of the Brustwerk division are five horizontal louvers opening upward, operated by a foot pedal.

FAÇADE

The façade is divided into five fields in the front of the case and one field in the right side. It contains all the pipes of the HW Praestant 8′ from F♯ to g‴ plus a silent g♯‴. The pipe layout from left to right (as one faces the organ) is as follows:
  1. g♯, c′, e′, g♯′, c″, e″, g♯″, c‴, e‴, silent g♯‴
  2. g, b, d♯′, g′, b′, d♯″, g″, b″, d♯‴, g‴
  3. f♯, a♯, d′, f♯′, a♯′, d″, f♯″, a♯″, d‴, f♯‴
  4. f, a, c♯′, f′, a′, c♯″, f″, a″, c♯‴, f‴
  5. e, d♯, d, c, A♯, G♯, F♯ // G, A, B, c♯
F♯ pipe is the last pipe in the front of the case; the pipes G, A, B, and c♯ are placed exposed in the right side of the case. The F♯ pipe may be seen from both the front and the side.

Width of front fields: 346, 357, 375, 385, 630 mm
Width of side field: 518 mm
Width of stiles between fields: 80 mm

KEYBOARDS

Manual Keyboards

Suspended keys (class II levers, rear fulcrum)
Compass: C–g‴ (56 notes)
Octave span: 165.2 mm

	HW	BW
Distance from fulcrum to front of natural key:	515 mm	415 mm
Distance from fulcrum to attachment of action:	275	280
Natural key head length:	43	40
Sharp length:	76	66
Sharp height above naturals:	12	11
Keyfall:	10	9

Vertical distance between manual keyboards: 60 mm
Upper manual keyboard overlaps lower by 25 mm
Key covers: 1983—ebony naturals, rosewood sharps
            1991—ebony naturals, bone-covered walnut sharps
A new Hauptwerk manual keyboard was made in 1991

The standard dimensions used for the lengths of naturals and sharps was 43 and 76 mm, respectively, as illustrated by the Hauptwerk keyboard. The Brustwerk keys of Opus 12 are shorter than this because of the restraints imposed by the existing action of the lower manual keyboard.

The following list is Brunzema's schedule of typical keyfalls (in mm).

	Normal				Very large organs	
BW	9	9	9.5	9.5	10	10
HW	10.5	11	11.5	12	12.5	13
RP	10	10	10.5	10.5	11	11

The height of the sharps keys is designated as 2 mm higher than the keyfall. The actual keyfalls of several instruments are shown below.

Pella, Opus 5	BW	9
	HW	10.5
Winnipeg, Opus 10		10
Edmonton, Opus 11	II	8
	I	9
Kitchener, Opus 12	BW	9
	HW	10
Wolfville, Opus 13		10
Akron, Opus 24	II	8
	I	9
Glace Bay, Opus 25	BW	9
	HW	11.5
Toronto, Opus 27	SW	9
	HW	10.5
Charlotte, Opus 28	HW	10.5
	RP	10
Seoul, Opus 38	II	9
	I	10

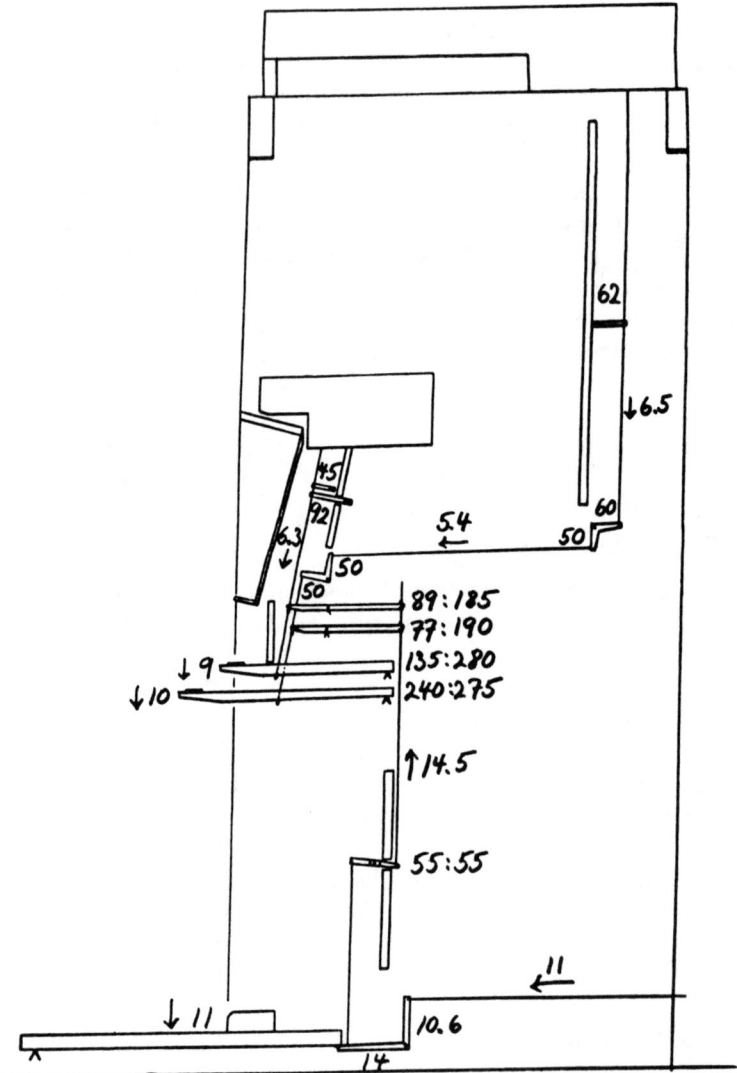

Figure 42
Kitchener: Diagram of key action and couplers, showing
keyfalls, the travel of the trackers, and the lengths of lever arms.
All measurements are in millimeters

Pedal Keyboard
Type: Flat/parallel
Compass: C–f' (30 notes)
Octave span: 469 mm (33.5 mm between semitones)
Length of naturals in front of sharps: 495 mm
Length of sharps: 130 mm
Height of sharps above naturals: 31 mm
Height between lowest manual keyboard and pedal keyboard: 750 mm
Set-back of pedal sharps from lowest manual keyboard: 140 mm
Distance between top of bench and naturals: 505 mm
Keyfall of naturals in front of sharps: 11 mm
Material of naturals and sharps: fumed oak

KEY ACTION AND COUPLERS

Most instruments from the Fergus workshop employed suspended keys (rear fulcrum). The two-manual residence/practice organs and the organ in Glace Bay, Opus 25, employ balanced keys (middle fulcrum); for the organ in Charlotte, Opus 28, suspended keys were used for the Hauptwerk and balanced keys for the Rückpositiv. Gerhard Brunzema was very particular that the key levers always be as short as possible. Balanced keys were used if it meant gaining the advantage of shorter key lengths and/or fewer connections in the action. Standard action construction consisted of wooden rollers of pine or fir with bushed maple arms, and trackers with wire hooks. Some of the later rollerboards were made in metal; for example, for Seoul (Opus 38), 8-mm brass tubing with soldered brass arms was used because the vertical distance between the manual keyboards and the windchests was at a premium. The action squares at Kitchener are maple with bushed eyelets, mounted in a wire beam. Couplers were always connected to drawknobs rather than hitch-down pedals.

STOP ACTION

The stop action is made in black-painted iron with welded-on arms; trundles are made of oak. While there were several drawknob styles, that at Kitchener is the style Brunzema preferred; he was not particularly concerned with the ability to pull out two or more drawknobs at once.

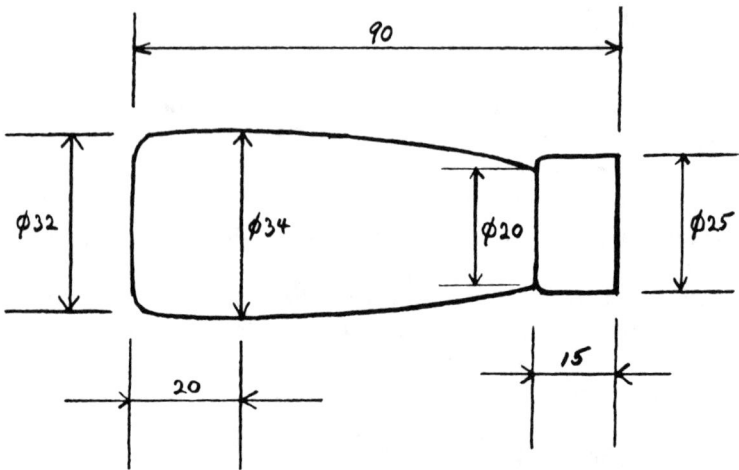

Figure 43
Kitchener: Drawknob. This is the style preferred by
Gerhard Brunzema. Measurements are in millimeters

WINDCHESTS

Dimensions		HW		BW
Total length:		2305 mm		1245 mm
Total depth:		1008		420
Height, excluding rackboards:		191		170
Note channel length:		938		370
Note channel height:		45		32
Note channel widths:	C:	18	C:	16
	c:	17	c:	14
	f♯:	15	f♯:	13
	c′:	14	c′:	12
	f♯′:	13	c‴:	10
	c″:	12		
	c‴:	11		
Pallet box height:		70		60
Pallet box depth:		315		260
Pallet opening length:		220		185
Pallet opening width:	C:	14	C:	13
	c:	12	c:	12
	c′:	10	f♯:	11
	c″:	9	c′:	10

Pallet movement:	↖	7		6.3
Pluck, in Newtons	C:	0.82 N	C:	0.65 N
(1 ounce = 0.278 N)	c:	0.73	c:	0.61
	c′:	0.63	c′:	0.53
	c″:	0.58	c″:	0.53
	c‴:	0.58	c‴:	0.53
Travel of sliders:		?20 mm		20 mm
Travel of drawknobs:		60		60

Layout of stops on Hauptwerk windchest, back to front

Back   8   Trompete (C, D, E, F♯, and G♯ are offset, inside right)
             Mixtur:
                  ½
                ⅔
                    1
                 1⅓
       2   Oktave
       4   Rohrflöte
      2⅔   Quinte
       8   Schwebung c-g‴; 8 Gedackt C♯, D♯, F, G, A, B
       4   Oktave
       8   Gedackt C, D, E, F♯, G♯, A♯, c-g‴
Front   8   Praestant (in façade)

Note sequence of Hauptwerk windchest, left to right (as viewer faces the organ)

g♯, c′, e′, g♯′, c″, e″, g♯″, c‴, e‴, g, b, d♯′, g′, b′, d♯″, g″, b″, d♯‴, g‴, f♯, a♯, d′, f♯′, a♯′, d″, f♯″, a♯″, d‴, f♯‴, f, a, c♯′, f′, a′, c♯″, f″, a″, c♯‴, f‴, e, d♯, d, c♯, c, B, A♯, A, G♯, G, F♯, F, E, D♯, D, C♯, C

Layout of stops on Brustwerk windchest, back to front

Back   8   Holzgedackt; C-B placed horizontally behind windchest
       4   Holzflöte
Front   2   Flöte

Note sequence of Brustwerk windchest, left to right

C, D, E, F♯, G♯, A♯, c→g‴, B, A, G, F, D♯, C♯

Construction details

Pallets are covered with two layers of leather. Foam-plastic slider seals were used above sliders and stand-off rings below. Generally, the windchest layouts were conceived to avoid grooving wherever possible.

WIND SYSTEM

Wind pressure: 630 Pascals (N/m²) = 64 mm = 2½ inches
Reservoir: parallel rise, 1 m × 2 m
Two Hauptwerk windlines, internal dimensions 75 × 100 mm and 100 × 110 mm; one Brustwerk windline, internal dimensions 49 × 100 mm

Most large instruments had single-fold wedge bellows connected to a curtain valve. Smaller residence organs and the Kisten Orgel had schwimmer regulators. Brunzema carefully calculated wind consumption and designed windline dimensions to achieve stable wind without having to resort to extensive use of concussion bellows. All pedal windchests had integrated winkers. Windlines were always in wood; for rectangular windlines, plywood was used for the wide dimension and oak or poplar for the narrow dimension. Tremulants were a pneumatically operated exhaust motor supplied by Laukhuff.

MATERIALS

Quartersawn white oak: case, wood pipes
Poplar: Hauptwerk windchest
Mahogany: Brustwerk windchest, Hauptwerk and Brustwerk sliders
Plywood: windchest tables
Pine or fir: rollers
Hard maple: squares, roller arms
Yellow cedar: trackers
Sugar pine: key bodies, pallets, coupler levers, backfalls
Rosewood: drawknobs

Gerhard Brunzema normally used poplar for windchests, but the Opus 12 Brustwerk windchest was made of mahogany. The reason for this was that there was a supply of mahogany in the workshop that was to be used originally for sliders, but it turned out to be unacceptable for this purpose. It was this lumber that was used for the windchest. Sliders in some of the early instruments were made of Pertinax®, a plastic difficult to work. The material eventually settled on for later instruments was 4.5-mm Honduras mahogany.

LAYOUT OF DRAWKNOBS
Order of Stops:

Extreme Left (1991)		Left Stop Jamb (1983)		Right Stop Jamb (1983)	
	Tremulant	8	Schwebung	8	Praestant
8	Holzgedackt	8	Gedackt, b/tr	4	Oktave
4	Holzflöte	4	Rohrflöte, b/tr	2⅔	Quinte, b/tr
2	Flöte	8	Trompete, b/tr	2	Oktave
	BW→P		HW→P		Mixtur, b/tr
		16	Subbass		Key switch

Arrangement of Drawknobs:

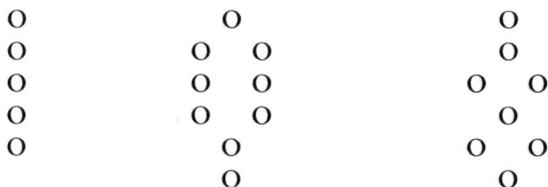

```
O          O              O
O        O  O             O
O        O  O          O  O
O        O  O             O
O          O           O  O
           O              O
```

Vertical distance between drawknob centers: 80 mm
Horizontal distance between drawknob centers (divided stops): 80 mm
Maximum diameter of drawknobs: 34 mm

TEMPERAMENT

This temperament was described in 1970 by J. van Biezen and is the same as that used by Francesco Vallotti in the eighteenth century. The fifths F–C, C–G, G–D, D–A, A–E, and E–B are tuned narrow by one-sixth of the Pythagorean comma (approximately four cents) and all other fifths are tuned pure.

Deviation of notes from equal temperament in cents

C: +5.9	F♯: −2.1
G: +4.0	C♯: 0.0
D: +1.9	G♯: +1.8
A: 0.0	D♯: +4.0
E: −2.0	A♯: +5.4
B: −4.1	F: +7.8

Size of major 3rd intervals, in cents
(Pure = 386; Equal temperament = 400; Pythagorean = 408)

392:	F–A, C–E, G–B
396:	B♭–D, D–F♯
400:	E♭–G, A–C♯
404:	A♭–C, E–G♯
408:	D♭–F, F♯–A♯, B–D♯

PIPE SCALES

All measurements are in millimeters. Diameters are related to the *Normalmensur* scale (C = 155.5 mm; c = 92.4; c′ = 54.9; c″ = 32.6; c‴ = 19.3). The numerical relationships of mouth width (MW) to circumference (Circum.) and mouth height (MH) to mouth width are included here in the manner computed by Brunzema. Since mouth width and mouth height are sometimes understood as a percentage or a fraction of the circumference and mouth width, respectively, the following table may be used for converting the numbers.

Circum./MW or MW/MH	Percentage	Fraction
5.0	20	⅕
4.5	22	²⁄₉
4.0	25	¼
3.5	29	²⁄₇
3.0	33	⅓
2.5	40	²⁄₅
2.0	50	½

HW PRAESTANT 8′

70% tin; 1-6 (C-F) from Gedackt 8′; all pipes (F♯-g‴) in façade

	F♯	c	c′	c″	c‴
Diameter (C=136 mm)	103	78	46	26.3	16.9
(NM relation)	(−3.5)	(−3.9)	(−4.1)	(−5.0)	(−3.2)
Mouth Width	80.9	61.3	38	21.7	14
(Circum./MW)	(4.0)	(4.0)	(3.8)	(3.8)	(3.8)
Mouth Height	20.9	17.4	9.1	6.3	3.8
(MW/MH)	(3.9)	(3.5)	(4.2)	(3.4)	(3.7)
Flue Width	.65	.58	.50	.42	.32
(% of MW)	(.80)	(.95)	(1.3)	(1.9)	(2.3)

	F♯	c	f♯	c′	f♯′	c″	f♯″	c‴
Toeboard Hole	11.0	10.0	9.0	8.5	7.0	6.0	5.5	5.0

HW SCHWEBUNG 8′ (from c)

40% tin; 13-32 (c-g′) with ears; tuned sharp to Praestant 8′

	C	c	c′	c″	c‴
Diameter	—	70	44	25.2	16.3
(NM relation)		(−6.4)	(−5.1)	(−6.0)	(−4.1)
Mouth Width	—	52.4	32.9	18.8	12.2
(Circum./MW)		(4.2)	(4.2)	(4.2)	(4.2)
Mouth Height	—	20.2	11.2	6.7	3.8
(MW/MH)		(2.6)	(2.9)	(2.8)	(3.2)

HW GEDACKT 8′

25% tin; with ears

	C	c	c′	c″	c‴
Diameter	95	62	41	26.5	16.8
(NM relation)	(−11.4)	(−9.2)	(−6.5)	(−4.8)	(−3.3)
Mouth Width	80.7	49.9	32.2	20.8	13.2
(Circum./MW)	(3.7)	(3.9)	(4.0)	(4.0)	(4.0)

Mouth Height	33.7	21.4	12.7	7.9	5.2
(MW/MH)	(2.4)	(2.3)	(2.5)	(2.6)	(2.5)

HW OKTAVE 4′

25% tin; 1-20 (C-g) with ears

	C	c	c′	c″	c‴
Diameter	76	44	25	17	10.5
(NM relation)	(−4.5)	(−5.1)	(−6.2)	(−3.1)	(−2.2)
Mouth Width	59.7	34.6	19.6	13.4	8.2
(Circum./MW)	(4)	(4)	(4)	(4)	(4)
Mouth Height	18.0	11.0	7.2	4.1	2.3
(MW/MH)	(3.3)	(3.2)	(2.7)	(3.3)	(3.6)

HW ROHRFLÖTE 4′

25% tin; 1-12 (C-B) stopped without chimneys; with ears

	C	c	c′	c″	c‴
Diameter	63	43.9	30.2	18	12.2
(NM relation)	(−8.9)	(−5.2)	(−1.8)	(−1.8)	(+1.3)
Mouth Width	49.5	34.5	23.7	14.1	9.6
(Circum./MW)	(4)	(4)	(4)	(4)	(4)
Mouth Height	21	16	8.4	5.4	3
(MW/MH)	(2.4)	(2.2)	(2.8)	(2.6)	(3.2)
Chimney Length	—	82	48	24	12
Chimney Diameter	—	10.0	8.4	6.3	4.8

HW QUINTE 2 ⅔′

25% tin; 1-12 (C-B) with ears

	C	c	c′	c″	c‴
Diameter	60	34	19.3	12.2	7.4
(NM relation)	(−3.0)	(−4.0)	(−5.0)	(−3.7)	(−3.0)
Mouth Width	47.1	26.7	14.4	9.1	5.5
(Circum./MW)	(4.0)	(4.0)	(4.2)	(4.2)	(4.2)
Mouth Height	11.4	6.8	4.5	2.8	1.6
(MW/MH)	(4.1)	(3.9)	(3.2)	(3.3)	(3.4)

HW OKTAVE 2′

25% tin; 1–10 (C–A) with ears

	C	c	c′	c″	c‴
Diameter	44	24	14.9	9.3	6.3
(NM relation)	(−5.1)	(−7.1)	(−6.1)	(−5.0)	(−2.0)
Mouth Width	34.6	18.8	11.7	7.3	4.9
(Circum./MW)	(4)	(4)	(4)	(4)	(4)
Mouth Height	8.0	5.3	3.4	2.1	1.2
(MW/MH)	(4.3)	(3.5)	(3.4)	(3.5)	(4.1)

HW MIXTUR IV

The scales for the Mixtur resemble the Oktave 2′.

HW TROMPETE 8′

Resonators: 70% tin; 1–49 full-length, 50–56 double-length
Shallots: cylindrical *Schiffenkehle;* 45° ends; 1–20 with brass facings under the tongues, 21–56 open throughout
Blocks: 1-18 plain with sockets, 19–56 nut-and-ring (French blocks)

	C	c	c′	c″	c‴
Resonator Length	2180	1066	523	248	115
Upper Diameter	108	83	61	53	49
Lower Diameter	14.5	12.1	9.0	7.6	6.5

	C	c	g	g♯	c′	c″	c‴
Shallot Diameter	12	9.2	8.0	7.4	6.9	5.8	4.7
Shallot Depth	8.7	7.0	6.2	5.5	5.0	4.7	3.9
Shallot Length	114	75	61	58	50	37	27.4
Opening Width	7.8	7.4	7.3	—	—	—	—
Opening Length	61	40	35.5	—	—	—	—
Tongue Width	12.7	10.2	8.9	8.9	8.2	6.4	5.0
Tongue Thickness	0.5	0.3	0.23	0.23	0.2	0.17	0.09
Tongue Rise	1.5	1.5	1.1	0.9	0.8	0.5	0.4

BW HOLZGEDACKT 8′

Quartersawn white oak

	C	c	c′	c″	c‴
Inside					
Depth × Width	95 × 60	63 × 39	45 × 28	27 × 18	16 × 13
Corresponding					
Diameter	85.2	55.9	40.1	25.0	16.3
(NM relation)	(−13.9)	(−11.6)	(−7.3)	(−6.2)	(−4.1)
Mouth Width	60	39	28	18	13
(Circum./MW)	(4.5)	(4.5)	(4.5)	(4.4)	(3.9)
Mouth Height	32.0	20.9	12.2	6.8	3.3
(MW/MH)	(2.5)	(1.9)	(2.3)	(2.6)	(3.9)
Flue Width	.48	.47	.41	.39	.24
(% of MW)	(.6)	(1.2)	(1.5)	(2.2)	(1.8)
Toe Hole Diameter	9.4	9.7	7.3	5.7	3.8
Wall Thickness	8	6	4	3	3

BW HOLZFLÖTE 4′

Quartersawn white oak; 1-12 (C-B) stopped, remainder open

	C	c	c′	c″	c‴
Inside					
Depth × Width	57.4 × 45.1	39.1 × 27.8	23.7 × 17.7	14.4 × 11.3	9.7 × 7.6
Corresponding					
Diameter	57.4	37.2	23.1	14.4	9.7
(NM relation)	(−11)	(−9)	(−8)	(−7)	(−4)
Mouth Width	45.1	27.8	17.7	11.3	7.6
(Circum./MW)	(4.0)	(4.2)	(4.1)	(4.0)	(4.0)
Mouth Height	19.9	10.9	6.6	4.1	2.6
(MW/MH)	(2.3)	(2.6)	(2.7)	(2.8)	(2.9)
Flue Width	.40	.35	.35	.33	.31
(% of MW)	(.9)	(1.3)	(2.0)	(2.9)	(4.1)

Toe Hole Diameter	8.3	9.3	7.5	5.8	5.0
Wall Thickness	6.0	4.0	3.5	3.5	3.5

BW FLÖTE 2'

40% tin; 1-12 (C-B) stopped; 70° languid

	C	c	c'	c''	c'''
Diameter	50.4	40.6	25.2	15.7	9.7
(NM relation)	(−2.0)	(+5.0)	(+6.0)	(+7.1)	(+8.0)
Mouth Width	35.2	30.4	18.5	11.7	7.3
(Circum./MW)	(4.5)	(4.2)	(4.3)	(4.2)	(4.2)
Mouth Height	9.6	7.3	4.9	3.2	2.0
(MW/MH)	(3.7)	(4.2)	(3.8)	(3.7)	(3.7)
Flue Width	.39	.28	.32	.33	.33
(% of MW)	(1.1)	(.92)	(1.7)	(2.8)	(4.5)
Toe Hole Diameter	6.9	8.0	6.7	6.0	4.7
Wall Thickness	.93	.86	.72	.61	.51

PEDAL SUBBASS 16'

Quartersawn white oak; located unenclosed behind main case, in two rows, in an A layout

	C	c	c'
Inside Depth × Width	166	107.1	68.9
	× 119.5	× 74.5	× 46.7
Corresponding Diameter	158.9	100.8	64.0
(NM relation)	(−11.5)	(−10.0)	(−8.5)
Mouth Width	119.5	74.5	46.7
(Circum./MW)	(4.2)	(4.3)	(4.3)
Mouth Height	59.3	31.3	19.4
(MW/MH)	(2.0)	(2.4)	(2.4)
Flue Width	1.7	.87	.69
(% of MW)	(1.4)	(1.2)	(1.5)
Toe Hole Diameter	Not available		
Wall Thickness	15.3	11.2	8.0

DECIBEL VALUES

The following lists the decibel values for the Principal chorus of Opus 12, as computed by Brunzema.

		C	c	c′	c″	c‴
8	Praestant	79.0 (F♯)	78.5	77.5	76.5	74.5
4	Oktave	78.0	77.0	75.0	73.5	69.5
2⅔	Quinte	76.0	74.0	72.0	69.0	67.0
2	Oktave	73.0	72.0	70.5	67.0	67.0
	Mixtur					
4		—	—	—	72.0	69.0
2⅔		—	—	72.0	70.5	69.0
2		—	72.0	71.0	68.5	69.0
1⅓		73.0	72.0	70.5	68.0	—
1		73.0	72.0	69.5	—	—
⅔		73.0	72.0	—	—	—
½		71.5	—	—	—	—

APPENDIXES

Appendix A

Three Articles by Gerhard Brunzema

THE COVERING OF ORGAN PIPES WITH PURE TIN FOIL BY USING EPOXY RESIN CEMENT

Front pipes which are of a high-lead content alloy do not have a natural metallic luster but rather are dull and grey. (Of course, the following is also valid for pipes of zinc or copper.) If such pipes should be bright, it is possible to cover them with a polished foil of pure tin. Generally speaking, egg white (chicken or goose eggs) was used as cement. However, it is probable that shellac (see Karl Bormann, *Die gotische Orgel von Halberstadt,* p. 116) or *Mixion* was also used. Inasmuch as these "cements" contain solvents, it is very possible, especially in the case of new pipes, that the foil will blister with time. Older, heavily oxidized pipes can, however, be covered using egg whites quite effectively. It is necessary that the egg white be spread very thin and that all the excess be rubbed away. Nevertheless, this method is not completely reliable against blistering. For this reason the process of covering pipes using epoxy resin will be explained.

Materials

- Pure tin foil 0.03 mm (0.001 inch) thick, or thicker, up to 0.06 mm (0.002 inch)
- Cement: AGOMET U1 & hardener
- Solvent: ATLAS-AGO
- Two mixing trays of polyethylene to be obtained from: DE-GUSSA, Atlas-AGO, Chemische Fabrik GmbH, 6451 Wolfgang bei Hanau.

Tools

- Soft, lint-free rags for spreading the cement on the foil
- Sharp knife (scalpel) and straight edge
- Cutting board
- Two pairs of rollers to use as bearings for the pipes
- Several small soft rags to rub the foil onto the pipes

Procedure

1. New pipes should be washed in the usual manner. Old pipes should be cleaned and free from any lacquer or coating. Voicing of front pipes first is recommended to avoid the possibility of fingerprints.
2. The surface must be dry and dust-free. Complicated procedures for the removal of grease (et cetera) are not necessary.
3. Inasmuch as the cement hardens faster at higher temperatures, it is advisable to work in a room at approximately 15°C, maximum 20°C (59–68°F).
4. AGOMET U1 binder is mixed with 1.5% hardener (by weight). Most useful are the above mentioned mixing trays of polyethylene. Stir 10 grams U1 together with .15 gram hardener, mixing them completely. The hardener is available in tubes of 7 grams each. When using this small tube, you must squeeze out a 5 cm (2-inch) long strip of hardener for the weighed-out 10 grams amount of U1.
5. For best results, two people should complete the work: the first cuts the foil to size and spreads the cement, the second rubs the foil onto the pipes.
6. Cutting the foil to size:
   width = twice the diameter of the pipe
   length = width of the roll of foil = 400 mm (15¾ inches).

7. The cement is spread very thin and evenly onto the ready-cut piece of foil. One begins covering at the top of the pipe body. The second piece of foil overlaps the first by approximately 5 mm (⅗ inch). A following piece is then so cut that it ends at the top of the mouth. Then one covers to the languid seam. A further piece is cut tapered for the lower part of the mouth. Other tapered pieces are also necessary for the foot. One covers up to approximately 1 cm (½ inch) from the toe. Rubbing the foil with small, soft rags, one begins in the middle and works towards both sides. The overlapping foil pieces are not further treated as the joint is almost invisible from a distance.
8. The solvent ATLAS-AGO is used to clean the tools and bench after finishing.

(Section reprinted from *ISO Information* 1 [February 1969]: 55–56)

UNIT ORGANS?

In the article "Your Church Can Afford a Pipe Organ" (*The American Organist,* September 1984, p. 57), [the author] suggests unit organs for small churches with limited funds. I feel, however, that churches with less than 500 seats are also entitled to have pipe organs of high artistic value and integrity. Superb tonal quality, directness of action and an attractive appearance characterize even small mechanical organs. When we speak of one-manual instruments, prices can be kept within reasonable limits. That a proper pipe organ should absolutely have two manuals and free pedal seems to be a widespread belief. I, however, feel that a one-manual instrument can very beautifully serve a congregation and enhance the musical life of a community. In an expert's report of 1723, J. S. Bach described the newly built one-manual organ in Störmthal near Leipzig with the words "qualified, durable and praiseworthy." He composed Cantata 194, *Höchsterwünschtes Freudenfest,* for the inauguration of this organ.

(Section reprinted from *The American Organist* 19 [January 1985]: 12)

KARL SCHUKE: A TRIBUTE

Karl Schuke, who died last May at the age of 80, will be remembered by those who knew his work as a gifted builder of modern mechanical pipe organs. His firm, the *Karl Schuke Berliner Orgelbauwerkstatt*, built over 400 instruments since its founding in 1952. The firm began by building smaller organs in the Berlin area, but soon expanded with contracts for large, modern trackers in Europe, Japan, Korea, and the U.S. Schuke was also a teacher. At the time of his death, he had been a professor at the *Berliner Musikhochschule* since 1962. His firm carries on under the guidance of his longstanding associates Wolfgang Theer, Ernst Bittcher, and Wolfgang Kobischke.

For many years before starting his own firm in West Germany, Schuke worked in his father's organ building workshop in Potsdam, which, from 1933 onwards, he ran in partnership with his brother. In the thirties, Schuke did much original research into structural and acoustical principles of historic organs of the classical period. In particular, he studied the 18th-century instruments of Joachim Wagner and Gottfried Silbermann. This work enabled him to construct a 25-stop mechanical organ in Berlin-Zehlendorf in 1935, at a time when most large modern organs were designed with electric action and voiced in the romantic style. Around this time, he also designed several smaller positiv organs based on historic organs in the Berlin Musical Instrument Collection. All this led him to be considered something of a pioneer of the modern mechanical organ, along with Paul Ott and Rudolf von Beckerath.

I regularly came into contact with Karl Schuke through annual meetings of the *Altenbrucher Kreis,* a small group of organ builders and musicologists interested in high quality restorations of historic organs. Schuke was responsible for a contribution to the art of organ restoration with his 1969 reconstruction of a 26-stop Schnitger organ in Berlin's Eosander-Kapelle. This organ had been completely destroyed in World War II.

Karl Schuke believed the pipe organ could advance the musical aspirations of the 20th century. To this end, he established close contact with a range of contemporary composers, such as Hugo Distler, Siegfried Reda, Gerd Zacher, and others, and built instruments responsive to their work.

I knew Schuke as a refined, soft-spoken gentleman with a strongly humanistic and philosophical outlook on life. He was of the same generation as Rudolf von Beckerath, and the two were good friends and close colleagues. Their use of early organbuilding techniques in their modern instruments inspired a new generation of builders.

Schuke's life was rooted in the world of a well-known 19th-century German writer, Theodor Fontane, whose descriptions of German society, Schuke liked to say, mirrored his own early perceptions. Indeed, in Fontane may be found the following passage, which sums up Schuke's own philosophy: "All that is Old, if it is relevant, should be cherished; but it is for the New that we must nevertheless live; and above all, we may never forget the Great Interconnectedness of things."

(Section reprinted from *The Diapason* 78 [November 1987]: 2)

Appendix B

Selected Organ Proposals

The following are excerpts from proposals by Gerhard Brunzema of organs that were never built. The information given for the 12-stop organ is typical of what was sent to potential clients.

**A HOUSE ORGAN OF 10 STOPS ON TWO
MANUALS AND PEDAL**

MANUAL I		MANUAL II		PEDAL	
8	Gedackt	8	Spitzgedackt	16	Subbass
4	Praestant	4	Rohrflöte	8	Subbass (extension)
2	Flöte	2	Oktave		
1⅓	Quinte	1	Sifflöte		Three couplers

Dimensions: 2330 mm (91.7 inches) high, 1560 mm (61.4 inches) wide
The pipes for the two manuals are on a combined windchest
The pedal windchest is located in the lower case
1–12 of Gedackt and 1–42 of Subbass made from white oak
1–12 of Spitzgedackt from Gedackt
1–12 of Subbass are outside the case

AN ORGAN OF 12 STOPS ON TWO MANUALS AND PEDAL

HAUPTWERK	BRUSTWERK	PEDAL
8 Praestant	(expressive)	16 Subbass
8 Hohlflöte	8 Holzgedackt	
4 Oktave	4 Rohrflöte	
4 Spitzflöte	2 Flöte	
2 Oktave	8 Regal	
Sesquialtera II		
Mixtur IV		

Couplers: BW→HW   HW→P   BW→P

The organ shall be free-standing and encased. The case shall be built from white oak and finished with Watco® oil natural. The placement for this organ is in the back of the church as shown on the enclosed line drawings. The façade pipes (HW Praestant 8′ from F♯) shall be made from polished tin (70% Sn). There shall be pipe shades above the façade pipes. The first six notes are in common with the stop Hohlflöte 8′. The first 12 pipes of the stop Subbass 16′ shall be placed at the back of the lower case and shall be made from white oak. The rest of the Subbass pipes shall be placed inside the lower part of the case. Most open pipes are cut to length and cone tuned; the stopped metal pipes have soldered-on caps.

The console shall be attached to the organ; key and stop action shall be mechanical. The Brustwerk division shall be expressive through horizontal louvers operated by a balanced foot pedal. The stops and couplers shall be controlled by drawknobs. The naturals of the keyboards are covered with ebony, the sharps consist of walnut overlaid with selected bone. The pedalboard is of the straight and parallel type with 30 keys.

There will be a blower and a wedge-shaped reservoir built into a box located as shown on the floor plan. The platform around the lower part of the case is included in this project.

There will also be a bench as well as lights for the music rack
and for the pedalboard.

AN ORGAN OF 14 STOPS ON TWO MANUALS AND PEDAL

HAUPTWERK		BRUSTWERK		PEDAL	
8	Praestant	(expressive)		16	Subbass
8	Hohlflöte	8	Gedackt	8	Oktave
4	Oktave	4	Holzflöte	8	Trompete
4	Spitzflöte	2	Flöte		
2⅔	Quinte	1⅓	Quinte		
2	Oktave				
	Mixtur IV				

Tremulant
Couplers: BW→HW   HW→P   BW→P
1-12 of Pedal Oktave from Praestant
1-14 of Subbass placed behind the lower case

AN ORGAN OF 16 STOPS ON TWO MANUALS AND PEDAL

MANUAL I		MANUAL II		PEDAL	
8	Praestant	8	Gedackt	16	Subbass
8	Hohlflöte	4	Rohrflöte	8	Prinzipal
4	Oktave	2	Flöte	4	Oktave
2	Oktave	1⅓	Quinte	16	Posaune
	Sesquialtera II (a)	8	Schalmey	8	Trompete
	Mixtur IV				

Tremulant
Couplers: II→I   I→P   II→P
The pipes for the two manuals are on a combined windchest
The pedal division is located on both sides of the manual divisions
1-6 of Praestant is stopped, made from white oak, and placed inside the case
1-15 of Gedackt from Hohlflöte

AN ORGAN WITH 19 STOPS ON TWO
MANUALS AND PEDAL

This and the 28-stop proposal were alternatives for the same location.

HAUPTWERK		BRUSTWERK		PEDAL	
16	Bourdon	(expressive)		16	Subbass
8	Praestant	8	Holzgedackt	8	Oktave
8	Hohlflöte	4	Rohrflöte	4	Oktave
4	Oktave	2	Flöte	16	Posaune
4	Spitzflöte		Terzian II	8	Trompete
2⅔	Quinte	8	Regal		
2	Oktave				
	Mixtur IV				
8	Trompete				

Tremulant
Couplers: BW→HW   HW→P   BW→P

The pedal is located in a separate case behind the main case
Holzgedackt and Subbass made from oak
1–4 of Posaune have half-length resonators

AN ORGAN WITH 23 STOPS ON TWO
MANUALS AND PEDAL

HAUPTWERK		BRUSTWERK		PEDAL	
16	Bourdon	(expressive)		16	Subbass
8	Praestant	8	Holzgedackt	8	Oktave
8	Hohlflöte	4	Holzprinzipal	4	Oktave
8	Spitzflöte	4	Rohrflöte		Mixtur IV
4	Oktave	2	Flöte	16	Posaune
4	Gemshorn	1	Oktave	8	Trompete
2⅔	Quinte		Terzian II		
2	Oktave	8	Regal		
	Mixtur V				
8	Trompete				

Tremulant
Couplers: BW→HW   HW→P   BW→P
1-12 of Spitzflöte from Hohlflöte
1-12 of Holzprinzipal stopped
Holzgedackt, Holzprinzipal, and Subbass made from oak

AN ORGAN OF 25 STOPS ON TWO MANUALS AND PEDAL

This and the 35-stop proposal were alternatives for the same location.

HAUPTWERK		BRUSTWERK		PEDAL	
8	Praestant	(expressive)		16	Subbass
8	Hohlflöte	8	Holzgedackt	8	Oktave
8	Spitzflöte	4	Holzprinzipal	4	Oktave
4	Oktave	4	Rohrflöte	2	Flöte
4	Spitzflöte	2	Flöte		Mixtur V
2⅔	Quinte		Terzian II	16	Posaune
	Sesquialtera II	1	Oktave	8	Trompete
2	Oktave	8	Regal	2	Kornett
	Mixtur V				
8	Trompete				

Tremulant
Couplers: BW→HW   HW→P   BW→P

AN ORGAN WITH 27 STOPS ON TWO MANUALS AND PEDAL

HAUPTWERK		HINTERWERK		PEDAL	
16	Bordun	(expressive)		16	Subbass
8	Praestant	8	Gedackt	8	Oktave
8	Hohlflöte	8	Gambe	4	Oktave
4	Oktave	8	Schwebung (c)	16	Posaune
4	Spitzflöte	4	Prinzipal	8	Trompete
2⅔	Quinte	4	Nachthorn	2	Trompete
2	Oktave	2	Oktave		
2	Flöte		Kornett III		
	Mixtur V		Mixtur IV		
8	Trompete	8	Schalmey		
		8	Trompete		
		4	Klarine		

Tremulant for Hinterwerk and Pedal
Couplers: Hinterwerk→Hauptwerk Hauptwerk→Pedal Hinterwerk→Pedal
1-4 of the Gambe from Gedackt
Subbass made of metal
Posaune has full-length resonators
Hinterwerk and Pedal in a combined case; the pedal parts of this
combined case shall have grill openings to the front
Hinterwerk has vertical louvers operated by a balanced pedal

AN ORGAN WITH 28 STOPS ON TWO MANUALS AND PEDAL

This and the 19-stop proposal were alternatives for the same location.

HAUPTWERK		SCHWELLWERK		PEDAL	
16	Bordun	(expressive)		16	Subbass
8	Praestant	8	Gedackt	8	Oktave
8	Hohlflöte	8	Gambe	8	Gedacktflöte
4	Oktave	8	Voix céleste	4	Oktave
4	Spitzflöte	4	Prinzipal		Mixtur IV
2⅔	Quinte	4	Rohrflöte	16	Posaune
2⅔	Nasat	2	Flöte	8	Trompete
2	Oktave		Mixtur IV		
2	Flöte	8	Oboe		
1⅗	Terz	4	Trompete		
	Mixtur V				
8	Trompete				

Tremulant
Couplers: SW→HW HW→P SW→P
The pedal is located in two separate cases to left and right of the
Swell case, behind the main case
Subbass made from oak
1-4 of Posaune have half-length resonators

AN ORGAN WITH 35 STOPS ON THREE
MANUALS AND PEDAL

This and the 25-stop proposal were alternatives for the same location.

HAUPTWERK		OBERWERK	
16	Quintadena	(expressive)	
8	Praestant	8	Gedackt
8	Hohlflöte	8	Gambe
8	Spitzflöte	8	Voix céleste (c)
4	Oktave	4	Oktave
4	Spitzflöte	4	Flöte
2⅔	Quinte	2	Oktave
	Sesquialtera II		Kornett III
2	Oktave	16	Dulzian
	Mixtur V	8	Oboe
8	Trompete		

BRUSTWERK		PEDAL	
8	Holzgedackt	16	Subbass
4	Holzprinzipal	8	Oktave
4	Rohrflöte	4	Oktave
2	Flöte	2	Flöte
	Terzian II		Mixtur V
1	Oktave	16	Posaune
8	Regal	8	Trompete
		2	Kornett

Tremulant
Couplers: BW→HW OW→HW HW→P
Hauptwerk, Brustwerk and Oberwerk housed in one case
The pedal division housed in two towers, symmetrically located to the left and right of the main case
The façade pipes from HW Praestant 8', HW Quintadena 16' #1–#7, and Pedal Oktave 8'

Appendix C

Selected Pipe Shade Designs

The following figures show selected pipe shade designs of organs with which Gerhard Brunzema was involved. While not necessarily personally designed by him, they show his influence and they illustrate well his conviction that the organ case should reflect the time in which it was built, that it should not exceed the ornamentation in the room, and that the decoration of an organ should be as simple and straightforward as possible. The Casavant designs are primarily a collaboration between Jean-Claude Gauthier and Gerhard Brunzema. Even though a specific organ is listed for each design, some designs were used on many different organs.

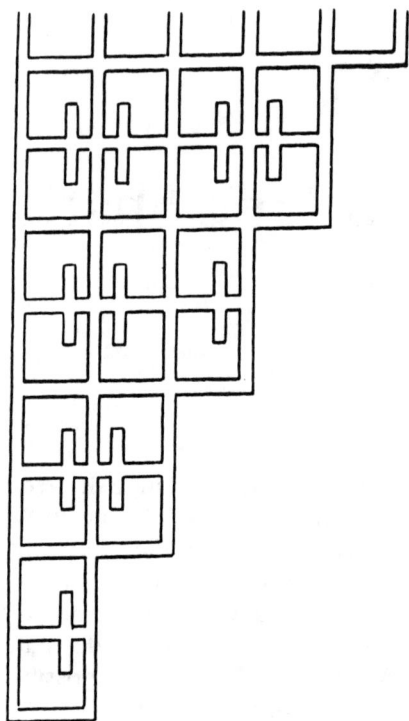

Figure 44
Evangelische Kirche
Bremen-Oberneuland, Germany
Ahrend & Brunzema Opus 45, 1966

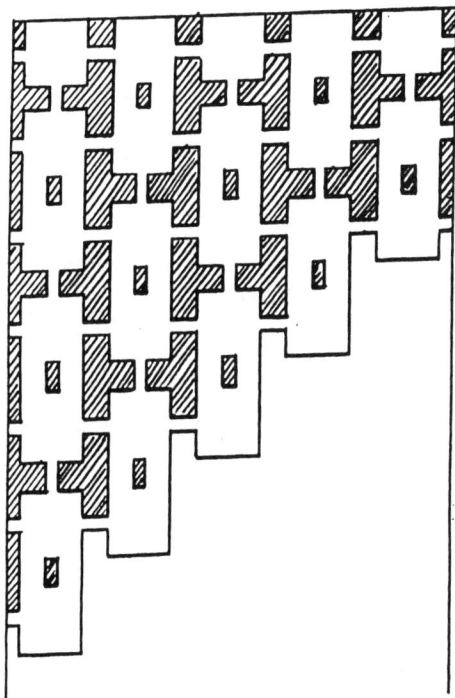

Figure 45
Evangeliumskirche
Gütersloh, Germany
Ahrend & Brunzema Opus 57, 1968

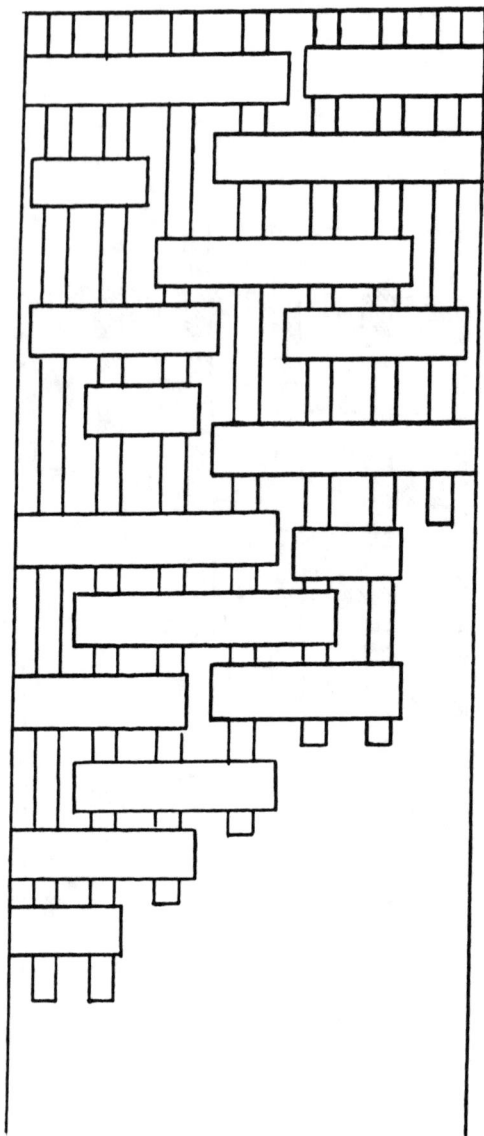

Figure 46
Cantate Domino
Frankfurt/Main, Germany
Ahrend & Brunzema Opus 68, 1970

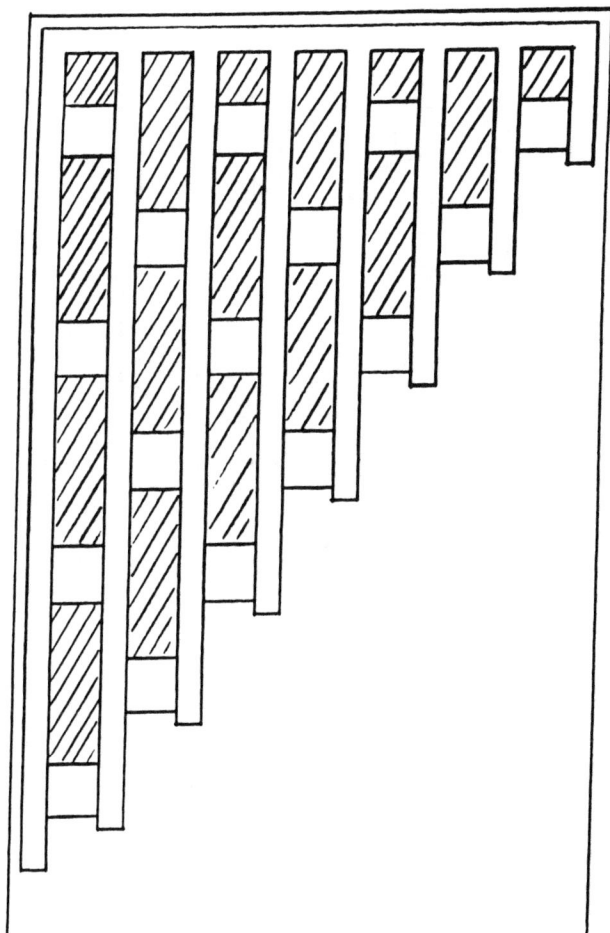

Figure 47
Queen's University
Kingston, Ontario
Casavant Frères Opus 3223, 1974

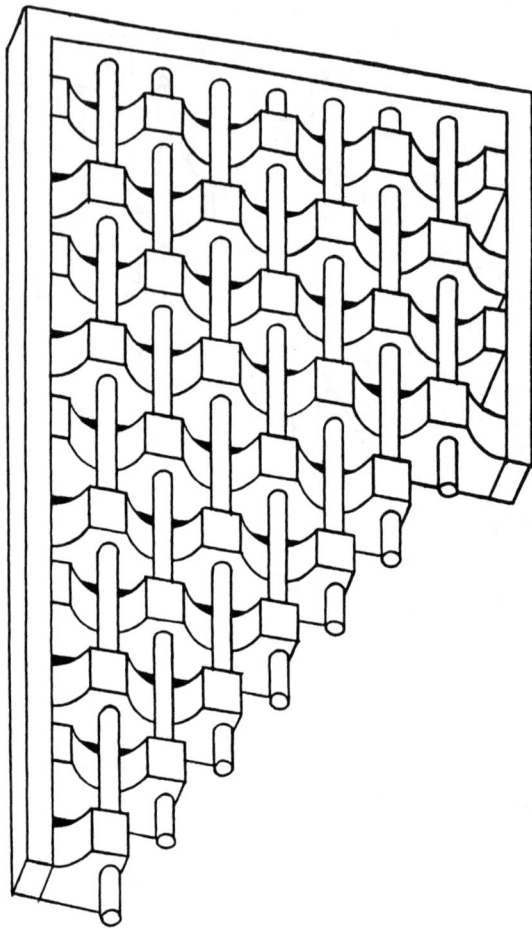

Figure 48
Grace Lutheran Church
Champaign, Illinois
Casavant Frères Opus 3246, 1975

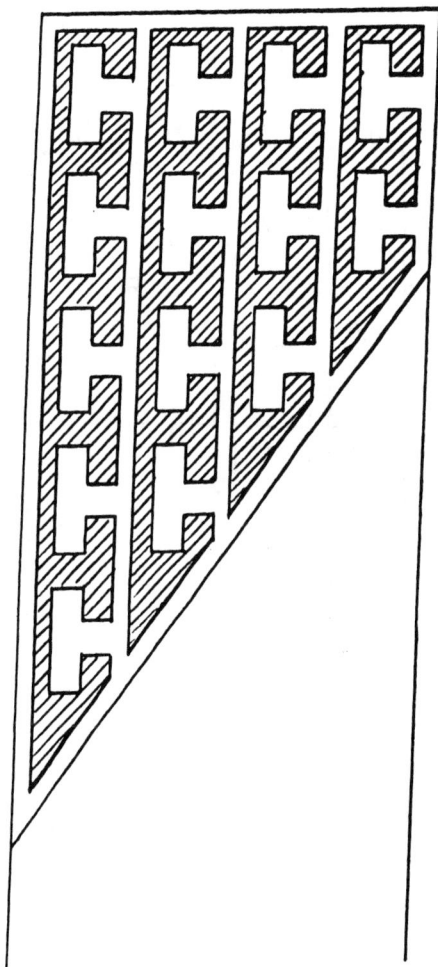

Figure 49
Saints Peter and Paul Church
Omaha, Nebraska
Casavant Frères Opus 3335, 1977

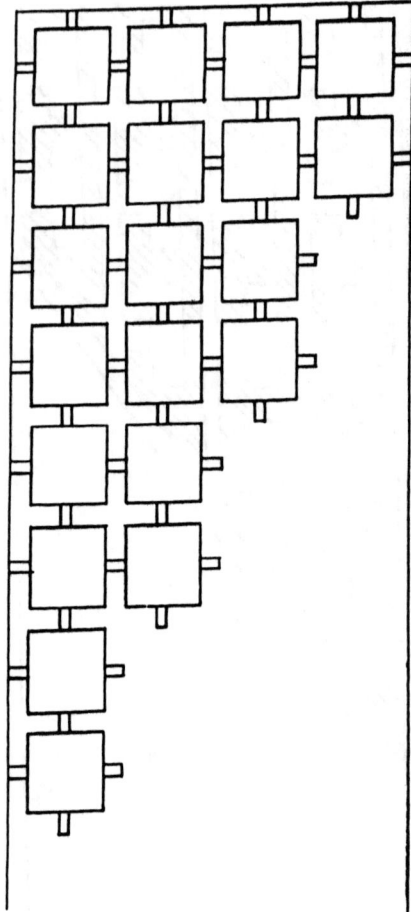

Figure 50
Dordt College
Sioux Center, Iowa
Casavant Frères Opus 3360, 1978

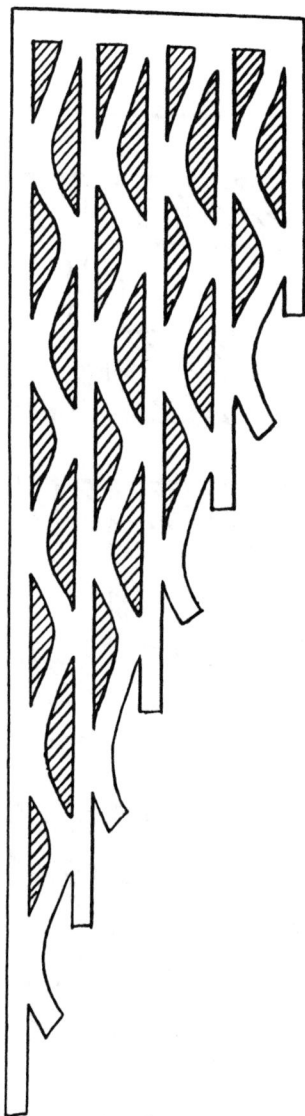

Figure 51
First Lutheran Church
Mabel, Minnesota
Casavant Frères Opus 3363, 1977

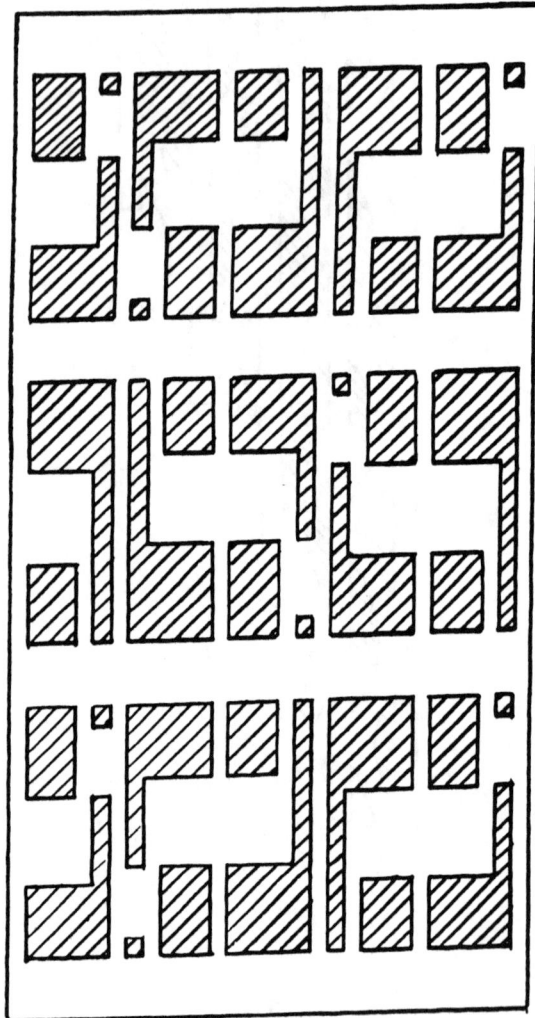

Figure 52
State University of New York at Stony Brook
Stony Brook, New York
Casavant Frères Opus 3397, 1978

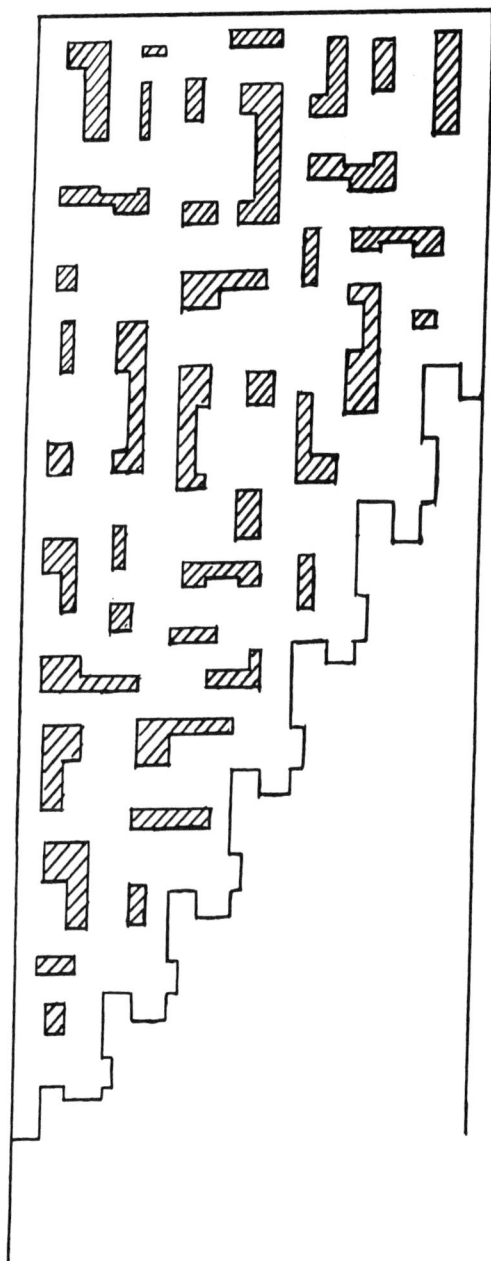

Figure 53
Saint Peter's Cathedral
Scranton, Pennsylvania
Casavant Frères Opus 3414, 1979

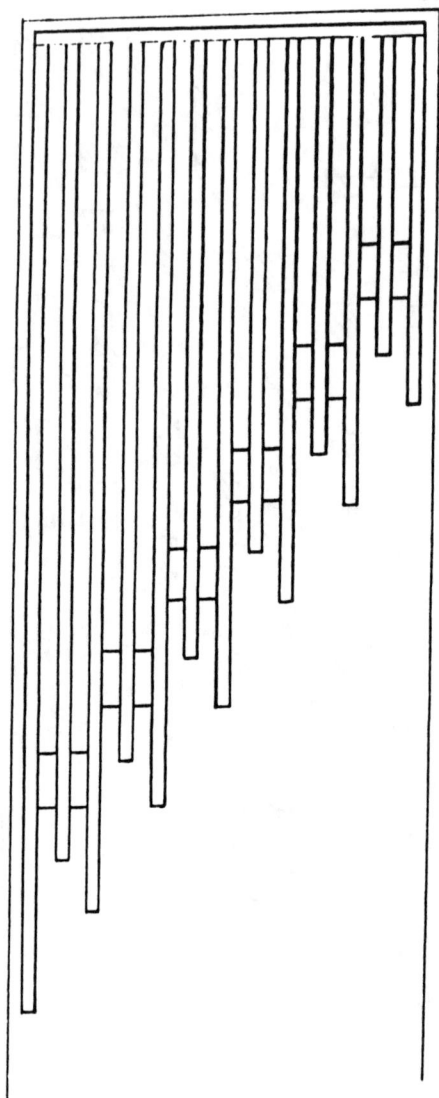

Figure 54
Victoria Arts Centre
Melbourne, Australia
Casavant Frères Opus 3434, 1980

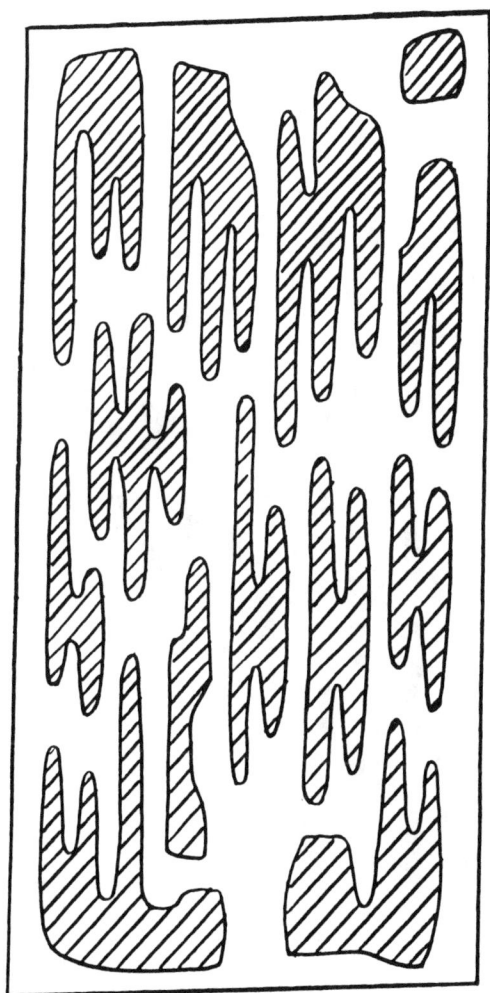

Figure 55
Kisten Orgel
Brunzema Organs, Inc.
Original design by Meta Brunzema

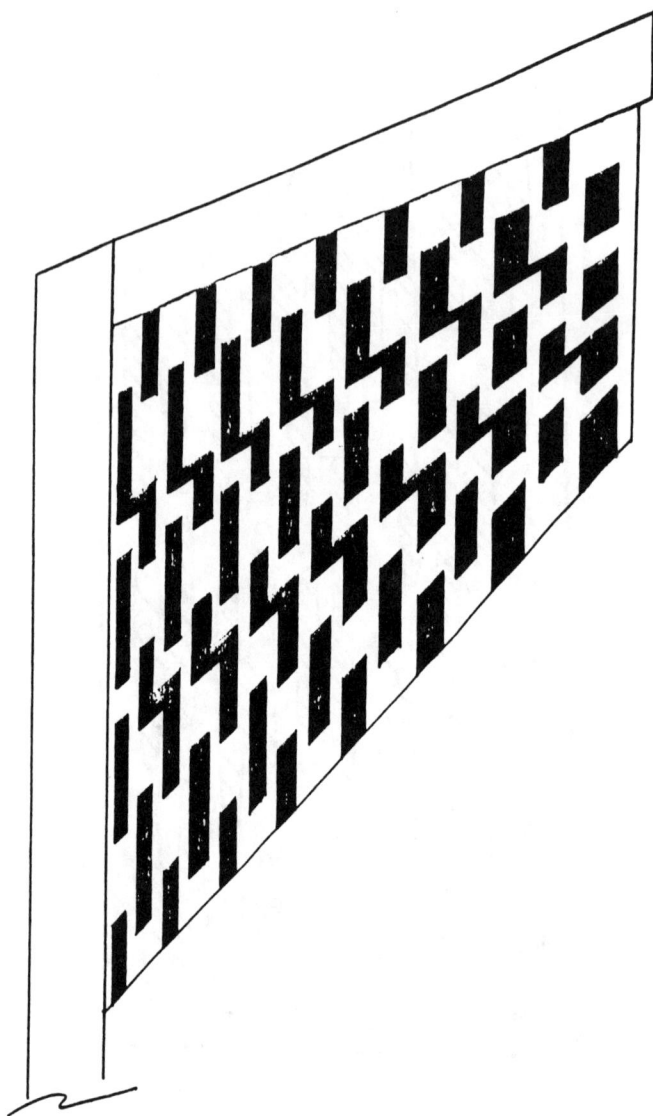

Figure 56
Blessed Sacrament Parish
Kitchener, Ontario
Brunzema Organs Opus 12, 1983

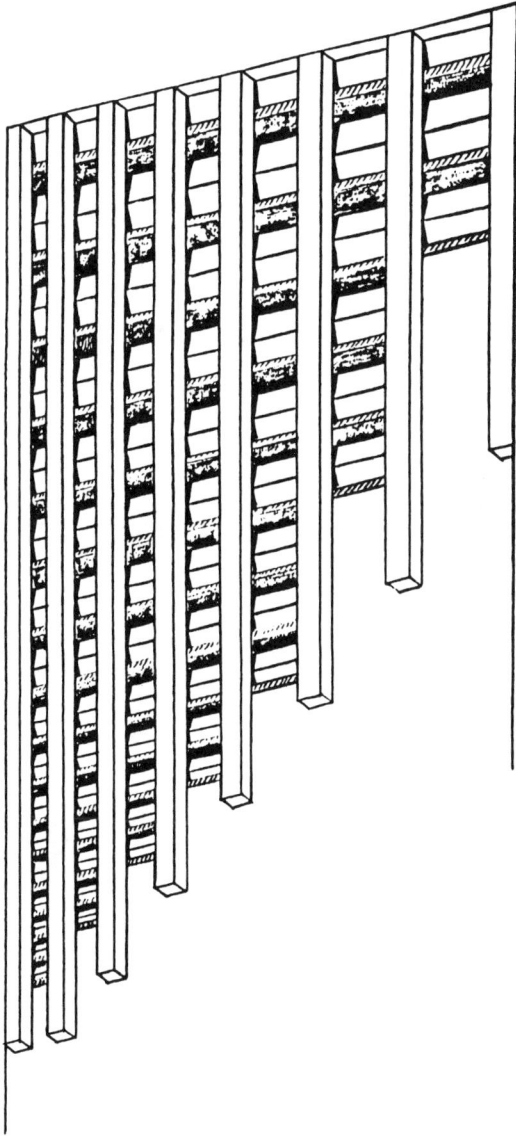

Figure 57
Dong Presbyterian Church
Seoul, South Korea
Brunzema Organs Opus 38, 1990

Appendix D

Discography

Recordings listed here are either long-playing records (LP) or compact discs (CD). Under each instrument, the recordings are listed alphabetically by performer. The names preceded by an asterisk refer to organs with their own separate listing. Sources used were the recordings themselves; Lade; Wallmann and Moe; the review of recordings in *The American Organist, The Diapason,* and *The Organ Yearbook;* and the catalogs of The Organ Literature Foundation, Braintree, Massachusetts.

It is unfortunate that several of these recordings omit Gerhard Brunzema's name, referring to the instruments as "Ahrend organs."

AHREND & BRUNZEMA: RESTORATIONS

Amsterdam: *Waalse Kerk,* Opus 43 (1965)

Kolbein Haga. CD: Simax PSC 1038 (1988). J. S. Bach: BWV 541, 547, 590, 645-650, 659, 660, 661, 769.

Ton Koopman. CD: Novalis 150 005-2 (1986). J. S. Bach: BWV 542, 552, 565, 639, 645, 659, 767; recorded February 1986.

"This is a very convincing record of the Waalse Kerk organ, with its forceful tone, sibilant, rich, and colourful. All frequencies seem to me very well recorded, and the immediacy is welcome amongst so much distantly recorded sound one hears on disc."—Peter Williams, *The Organ Yearbook* 19 (1978): 148.

Ton Koopman. CD: Deutsche Gramophone DG 427801. J. S. Bach: BWV 564, 565, 582, 590, 645–650.

Ton Koopman. "J. S. Bach: Trio Sonatas" (BWV 525–530). CD: Archiv Produktion 447 277-2 (1983).

Includes a short essay by Christoph Wolff about the music in English translation; no stoplist; recorded May 1982.

Gustav Leonhardt. "J. S. Bach: Orgelwerke I." 2 LPs: RCA SEON RL 30382. BWV 533, 544, 547, 548, 656, 658, 659, 668, 733, 769.

Gustav Leonhardt. "J. S. Bach: Orgelwerke II." 2 LPs: RCA SEON RL 30428. BWV 546, 562, 565, 572, 618, 663, 665–666, 710, 736, 766.

Gustav Leonhardt. "J. S. Bach: Toccata & Fuge d-moll BWV 565. . . ." LP: RCA SEON GL 71051; CD: RD 71051 (1986).

Music of Bach, Böhm, Buxtehude, Froberger, Krebs, Pachelbel, and Scheidemann; includes stoplists and registrations; Waalse Kerk organ recorded January 1972 and March 1973; also includes performances on the organs at Compatsch, *Marienhafe (recorded May 1976), Ochtersum, Stade, Stams, and Wilten.

Gustav Leonhardt. LP (17 cm): Disco-Nederland. Music of Bach, Couperin, Grigny, von Ritter, and Weber.

Jacques van Oortmerssen. CD: Denon C37-7376. J. S. Bach: BWV 528, 532, 568, 768.

Innsbruck: *Hofkirche*, Opus 70 (1970)

Reinhard Jaud. "Christian Erbach Orgelwerke." LP: Motette M 10770 (1985).

Includes a stoplist, registrations, and notes on the composer and the organ by Friedrich W. Riedel in German with an English translation; recorded April 1983.

Reinhard Jaud. "Historische Orgeln: Ebert-Orgel (1558) in der Hofkircke zu Innsbruck." LP: Calig Cal 30 449 (1977).

Music of Bull, Byrd, Hassler, Isaac, Kotter, Schlick, Schmidt, Sweelinck, and Tallis; includes a stoplist, registrations, pipe scales, mixture compositions, a diagram of the organ in cross-section, several photographs, and notes in German about the organ, the organbuilder, and the performer; also includes the musical editions used and a bibliography; recorded August 1977.

"Every registration in the 14 pieces gives a lesson to the careful listener—the marvellously breathy 4′ Prinzipal, the dazzling flutes, the winsome distance achieved by closing the case doors, the varying effect of the tremulant, the completely satisfactory effect produced by playing a Sweelinck Echo Fantasia on the two manuals' 4′ Prinzipals only, and so on. The reeds and mixtures are relatively conventional—which, given the original builder and his restorer, says much about the virtues of the chorus flues. The recording conveys the breathy quality very well."—Peter Williams, *The Organ Yearbook* 10 (1979): 176–177.

Karl Maureen. "Johann Ulrich Steigleder: Tabulaturbuch 'Dass Vater unser' (1627)." 2 LPs: Coronata COR 1011 (no date); 2 CDs: Coronata COR 1211.

Includes extensive program notes in German and English, a description of the organ and its restoration, and cross-sectional drawings of the organ.

Michael Radulescu. 2 LPs: Pape Orgeldokumente OD 1002. Music of Brumann, Buchner, Hofhaimer, Kotter, Nachtigall, Schlick.

"This is a model 'organ document': an organ of prime, almost unique importance; good, close recording; fully appropriate repertory of music; a reasonably full booklet of documentation; and good, suitable playing, with a careful and sensitively chosen array of registrations showing as fully as possible the sounds that result from the permutations possible when a builder understands robust voicing."—Peter Williams, *The Organ Yearbook* 16 (1986): 182.

Herbert Tachezi. "Orgelmusik: Renaissance." CD: TELDEC 8.42587. Music of Cabezon, Erbach, Hofhaimer, Kotter, Merulo, Praetorius, and Tomas de Santa Maria.

Marienhafe, Opus 65 (1969)

Martin Böcker. "Denkmäler Barocker Orgelbaukunst: Die Holy-Orgel zu Marienhafe." LP: Ambitus 68 829; CD: Ambitus 97 829 (1988).

Music of Bach, Böhm, Buxtehude, Scheidemann, and Scheidt; includes a stoplist, registrations, and notes by Martin Böcker about the music and by Reinhard Ruge about the organ, in German with English and French translations; recorded May 1988.

Rupert Gottfried Frieberger. "Historische Orgeln: Ostfriesland." LP: Christophorus SCGLX 74035.

Music of Buxtehude, Scheidemann, Sweelinck, and selections from various tablature books; also includes performances on the organs at Hohenkirchen, *Rysum, *Uttum, and *Westerhusen.

Gustav Leonhardt. "Die authentischen Orgeln aus Renaissance und Barock: Norddeutschland." 2 LPs: RCA SEON RL 30765 (1981).

Music of Attaingnant, Böhm, Buxtehude, Hofhaimer, Scheidemann, Schildt, Sicher, Siefert, and Tallis; includes stoplists, registrations, and notes by Jürgen Ahrend in German about the organs, with English and French translations; recorded March and May 1976; also includes performances on the organs at Ochtersum, *Rysum, Stade, and *Uttum.

Gustav Leonhardt. "J. S. Bach: Toccata & Fuge d-moll BWV 565. . . ." See *Amsterdam: Waalse Kerk*.

Harald Vogel. "Orgelland Ostfriesland: Gotick—Renaissance—Barock." CD: Deutsche Harmonia Mundi HM 939-2 (1989).

Music of Bach, Böhm, Buxtehude, Goudimel, Hassler, Hofhaimer, Ileborgh, Isaac, Paumann, Scheidt, Schlick, and Sweelinck; includes registrations and extensive notes by Harald Vogel in German about the organs and the repertoire, with some English translations; recorded May and June 1989; also includes performances on the organs at Norden-Ludgerikirche, *Rysum, *Uttum, Weener, and *Westerhusen.

Rysum, Opus 25 (1961)

Antoine Bouchard. "Les plus belles orgues." 2 CDs: Analekta AN 2 8216-7.

Music of Bach, Buxtehude, Dunstable, Kleber, Pachelbel, Paumann, Scheidemann, Susato, Sweelinck, Weckmann, plus anonymous works; includes stoplists and registrations, with notes in French and English; recorded 1974; also includes performances on the organs at Osteel, Dedesdorf, Ganderkesee, Mittelnkirchen, Steinkirchen, and *Westerhusen.

"Even the two seven-stop one-manuals [at Rysum and Westerhusen] are provided with mixtures, but, to my ears, there are no examples of screaming upperwork to be heard. The Principal 8' on the late-15th-century organ at Rysum is as sweet-toned as any I have ever heard."—W. G. Marigold, *The Diapason* 87 (March 1996): 9.

Rupert Gottfried Frieberger. "Historische Orgeln: Ostfriesland." See *Marienhafe*.

Gustav Leonhardt. "Die authentischen Orgeln aus Renaissance und Barock: Norddeutschland." See *Marienhafe*.

Harald Vogel. "Orgelland Ostfriesland: Gotick—Renaissance—Barock." See *Marienhafe*.

Harald Vogel. "Die Spätgotische Orgelkunst: Harald Vogel spielt an der Orgel zu Rysum (1457)." LP: Organa ORA 3001 (?1982).

Music of Attaingnant, Hofhaimer, Kleber, Kotter, Paumann, Schlick, and selections from the Buxheimer Orgelbuch, Adam Ileborgh tabulature, Lochamer Liederbuch, and Wisener Tabulature.

Uttum, Opus 9 (1957)

Rupert Gottfried Frieberger. "Historische Orgeln: Ostfriesland." See *Marienhafe*.

Gustav Leonhardt. "Die authentischen Orgeln aus Renaissance und Barock: Norddeutschland." See *Marienhafe*.

Harald Vogel. "Die niederländische Orgelkunst: J. P. Sweelinck und seine Zeit." LP: Organa ORA 3006 (?1984).

Harald Vogel. "Orgelland Ostfriesland: Gotick—Renaissance—Barock." See *Marienhafe*.

Westerhusen, Opus 4 (1955)

Antoine Bouchard. "Les plus belles orgues." See *Rysum*.

Rupert Gottfried Frieberger. "Historische Orgeln: Ostfriesland." See *Marienhafe*.

Harald Vogel. "Orgelland Ostfriesland: Gotick—Renaissance—Barock." See *Marienhafe*.

AHREND & BRUNZEMA: NEW ORGANS

Amsterdam: *Oude Kerk,* Opus 41 (1965)

Addie de Jong. "J. S. Bach: Koraalbewerkingen uit Cantates." LP: Festivo FES 102 (no date).

Transcriptions from Cantatas 4, 12, 13, 22, 28, 75, 79, 80, 95, 107, 137, 143, 166, and 180; four selections are performed on the Ahrend & Brunzema organ, and ten selections are performed on the Vater/Müller organ; stoplists included; brief program notes in Dutch, German, and English.

Gustav Leonhardt. "Gustav Leonhardt bespeelt het koororgel in de Oude Kerk te Amsterdam." LP: O.K. 101. Music of Bach, Couperin, Pachelbel, Scheidemann, Sweelinck, and Weber.

Aurich, Opus 27 (1961)

Michel Chapuis. "Dietrich Buxtehude: L'Œuvre d'Orgue." LPs: Vol. 5, Valois MB 1475 (1974); Vol. 6, Valois MB 1476 (1974). CD: Vol. 2, Valois V 4432 (1989).

BuxWV 136, 140, 141, 148, 152, 156, 162, 164, 170, 172–74, 176, 194, 195, 208, 209, 212. The CD is a re-issue of material previously released on LP.

André Isoir. "L'Œuvre d'Orgue de Jean-Sébastien Bach." LP: Vol. 8, Calliope CAL 1708 (1976)—BWV 538, 540, 564, 565; Vol. 15, Calliope CAL 1715 (1977)—BWV 536, 542, 546, 547, 583, 1027a; Vol. 16, Calliope CAL 1716 (1977)—BWV 541, 544, 545, 548. CD: Vol. 6, Calliope CAL 9708 (1986)—BWV 538, 540, 542, 564, 565; Vol. 10, Calliope CAL 9712 (1987)—BWV 541, 544, 545, 547, 548, 583; Vol. 12, Calliope CAL 9714—BWV 530, 536, 546, 727, 728, 736, 943, 1027a.

The LPs include a stoplist and extensive program notes by Gilles Cantagrel in French only; volume 8 recorded November 1975; volumes 15 and 16 recorded September 1976. CD volume 12 also contains performances on the Westenfelder organ in Esch-sur-Alzette. The CDs are re-issues of material previously released on the LPs.

Bremen-Oberneuland, Opus 45 (1966)

Michel Chapuis. "Dietrich Buxtehude: L'Œuvre d'Orgue." LP: Vol. 3, Valois MB 1473 (1974); Vol. 4, Valois MB 1474 (1974). CD: Vol. 1, Valois V 4431 (1988).

282   Appendix D

BuxWV 139, 144–146, 150, 153, 154, 159, 166, 167–69, 177, 178, 198–200, 218, 219. The CD includes program notes in French by Harry Halbreich, with English and German translations; a stoplist is provided; recorded May 1973. The CD is a re-issue of material previously released on LP.
Herbert Tachezi. "J. S. Bach: Die Kunst der Fuge, BWV 1080." CD: TELDEC 8.43771 (1977, 1987).
    Includes a stoplist, registrations, and an essay by Herbert Tachezi in German with English and French translations.

Frankfurt/Main: *Cantate Domino,* Opus 68 (1970)

Michel Chapuis. "Dietrich Buxtehude: L'Œuvre d'Orgue." LP: Vol. 7, Valois MB 1477 (1974); CD: Vol. 3, Valois V 4433 (1989).
    BuxWV 75, 138, 143, 147, 155, 163, 165, 188, 196, 221, 222. The CD is a re-issue of material previously released on LP.
André Isoir. "L'Œuvre d'Orgue de Jean-Sébastien Bach." LPs: Vol. 10, Calliope CAL 1710 (1977)—Orgelbüchlein (Part I), BWV 599–620; Vol. 11, Calliope CAL 1711 (1977)—Orgelbüchlein (Part II), BWV 621–644. CD: Vol. 9, Calliope CAL 9711 (1987)—Orgelbüchlein, BWV 599–644.
    The LPs contain extensive program notes by Gilles Cantagrel in French only; there is no stoplist; volumes 10 and 11 recorded November 1977. The CD is a re-issue of material previously released on the LPs.
Jean-Pierre Leguay. "Beethoven, Mozart: L'Œuvre d'Orgue." LP: Calliope CAL 1730.
Jean-Pierre Leguay. "Musiques pour Orgue Mecanique." CD: Euromuses EURM 2016 (?1995).
    Music of Beethoven, Haydn, and Mozart; also includes the Rabiny/Callinet/Delanoye organ at Notre-Dame à Semur en Auxois; the Beethoven and Mozart pieces, recorded in December 1976, are probably re-issues from the preceding LP; the Haydn pieces were recorded September 1994 on the Rabiny organ (although the notes do not specify which pieces are played on which organ); includes stoplists; notes in French, English, and German.

Haarlem: *Doopsgezinde Kerk,* Opus 58 (1968)

Marco bij de Vaate. LP: Intersound 6818.228. Music of Bach and Buxtehude.
Jean-Luc Jaquenod. LP: Studio S.M. Paris. Music of Bach.

CASAVANT FRÈRES

Carthage College, Opus 3276 (1975)

Elizabeth Paul Chalupka. "Mozart, Dupré, Reubke, Bach, D'Aquin: Volume One." LP.

Bach's Passacaglia and Fugue in C minor is performed on the Carthage organ. No record label or catalog number listed.

Dordt College, Opus 3360 (1978)

"Music at Dordt College." CD: Dordt College DCMCD-91 (1991) (privately produced; available from Dordt College, Sioux Center, Iowa, 51250).

Music of Bach, Bagley, Bernstein, Bonnet, Buxtehude, Fasch, Grotenhuis, Holst, Mailman, Mendelssohn, Mollicone, Purday, Schubert, and Vaughan Williams performed by the Concert Band, Chorale, Chamber Orchestra, and Concert Choir of Dordt College, conducted by Henry Duitman and Dale Grotenhuis. Joan Ringerwole performs Joseph Bonnet's *Variations de Concert,* Opus 1, on the organ; includes information about the college, the music department, the conductors, and the organist; the selections were recorded in the Dordt College Chapel between 20 January and 22 August 1991.

Joan Ringerwole. "The Dedicatory Recital at Dordt College." LP (privately produced; available from Dordt College, Sioux Center, Iowa, 51250).

Music of Eben, Krapf, Liszt, Pachelbel, Sweelinck, van Noordt, Walcha, and Widor; includes short program notes with some references to registrations used; also includes a stoplist, information about the organ with a reference to Gerhard Brunzema, a biographical sketch about the organist, and several photographs.

Joan Ringerwole. "Psalms, Hymns and Spiritual Songs." LP (privately produced; available from Dordt College, Sioux Center, Iowa, 51250).

Music of Bingham, Bolcom, Hampton, Hovland, Kee, Parry, Reger, Speuy, van Berg, and Willan; includes short program notes, a stoplist, information about the organ with a reference to Gerhard Brunzema, and a biographical sketch about the organist; recorded March 1983.

BRUNZEMA ORGANS, INC.

Kitchener, Opus 12 (1983/1991)

Thomas Donahue. "Brunzema in Ontario." CD: Calcante Recordings CAL CD 021 (1997). Also available in cassette format (CAL CS 021). Available from Calcante Recordings, 209 Eastern Heights Drive, Ithaca, N.Y., 14850-6303; telephone and fax (607) 273-3675.

Music of Bach, Pepping, and Walther; includes information on Gerhard Brunzema, the organ, and a discussion of the registrations as they relate to the design of the organ; recorded March 1996.

Pella, Opus 5 (1982)

"Dimensions of Praise: Organ and Choral Music Commemorating the Dedication of the Chapel, Central College, Pella, Iowa, May 9, 1982." LP: IPD-
50219 (1982) (privately produced; available from Central College, 812
University, Pella, Iowa, 50219).

Music of Bach, Krapf, Morris, Redford, Sweelinck, and Wood, performed by congregation, choir, brass, and organists Davis Folkerts and
Barbara Boertje. Of the ten selections, three are organ solos, four are
organ-accompanied singing, and three are a cappella singing. Includes information about the performers, the choir, the chapel, the college, and
the organ; no stoplist; the cover is a line drawing showing the interior of
the chapel and the organ.

Appendix E

Photography

The following lists published photographs of the organs of Gerhard Brunzema. Recordings are noted with the performer's last name and the title of the recording; complete information may be found in the discography. Books and journals are noted with the author's last name, identifying year if necessary, and page number(s); complete information may be found in the bibliography. Sources containing just a journal name are either New Organ listings or advertisements.

AHREND & BRUNZEMA

Opus	Location	Source
1	Larrelt, Germany, *Reformierte Kirche*	Lade, 16
3	Hohenlimburg, Germany, *Reformierte Friedhofskapelle*	Lade, 19
4	Westerhusen, Germany, *Reformierte Kirche*	Lade, 19 Vogel, "Orgelland Ostfriesland," 11; Wallmann and Moe, Plate IIb

Opus	Location	Source
9	Uttum, Germany, *Reformierte Kirche*	Lade, 30 Vogel, "Orgelland Ostfriesland," 9; Wallmann and Moe, Plate III
10	Veldhausen, Germany, *Altreformierte Kirche*	Lade, 31
11	Bremen-Farge, Germany, *Reformierte Kirche*	Lade, 19 Pape 1972, 27
18	Scheveningen, Netherlands, *Zorgvlietkerk*	Blanton, 49, back cover Lade, 19 Pape 1972, 25
25	Rysum, Germany, *Reformierte Kirche*	Lade, 32 Leonhardt, "Die authentischen Orgeln . . ." Vogel, "Orgelland Ostfriesland," 7 Wallmann and Moe, Plate IIa
26	Vienna, Austria, *Nikolaus Harnoncourt*	Lade, 19
27	Aurich, Germany, *St. Lamberti*	Lade, 33
29	Espel, Netherlands, *Hervormde Kerk*	Lade, 33
41	Amsterdam, Netherlands, *Oude Kerk* (small organ)	de Jong, "J. S. Bach: Koraalbewerkingen" Lade, 34
42	The Hague, Netherlands, *Johanneskapel*	Lade, 19
43	Amsterdam, Netherlands, *Waalse Kerk*	Lade, 35
44	Leer, Germany, *Große Kirche*	Lade, 19

Opus	Location	Source
45	Bremen, Germany, *Evangelische Kirche Oberneuland*	Lade, 19
49	Castrop-Rauxel, Germany, *Kirche Schwerin-Frolinde*	Jongepier 1974, 336 Pape 1972, 33
51	Aalten, Netherlands, *Gereformeerd Zuiderkerk*	Jongepier 1974, 335
57	Gütersloh, Germany, *Evangeliumskirche*	Jongepier 1974, 336
58	Haarlem, Netherlands, *Doopsgezinde Kerk*	Jongepier 1974, 334, 335 Jongepier 1988, 488-90
64	Schluderns, Italy, *Schloss Churburg*	Krauss, 78-79 Lade, 36
65	Marienhafe, Germany, *St. Marien*	Bocker, "Denkmäler Barocker Orgelbaukunst" Jongepier 1989, 204-206 Lade, 37 Leonhardt, "Die authentischen Orgeln . . ." *The Organ Yearbook* 3 (1972): 84 Vogel, "Orgelland Ostfriesland," 15
68	Frankfurt/Main, Germany, *Cantate Domino*	Lade, 23 Pape 1972, 35
70	Innsbruck, Austria, *Hofkirche*	Jaud, "Christian Erbach Orgelwerke" Jaud, "Ebert-Orgel in der Hofkirche zu Innsbruck" Lade, 38-39 Maureen, "Steigleder: Tablaturbuch" Williams and Owen, 91

Opus	Location	Source
87	Berkeley, California, *University of California*	*The American Organist* 18 (April 1984): 65, 145 Wallmann and Moe, Plate VII

CASAVANT FRÈRES

Opus	Location	Source
3191	New York, New York, *Community of the Holy Spirit*	*Music* 8 (October 1974): 42
3200	Moline, Ilinois, *Trinity Lutheran Church*	*Music* 8 (September 1974): 44
3214	Bay Head, New Jersey, *All Saints Episcopal Church*	*Music* 8 (June 1974): 50
3223	Kingston, Ontario, *Queen's University*	*The Diapason* 66 (December 1974): 9 *Music* 9 (January 1975): 14
3230	Regina, Saskatchewan, *University of Saskatchewan*	*Music* 8 (October 1974): 42
3233	Kenosha, Wisconsin, *Carthage College*	*Music* 9 (February 1975): 8
3235	London, Ontario, *First Saint Andrew's United Church*	*Music* 8 (October 1974): 42
3238	New Haven, Connecticut, *Yale University*	*Music* 8 (October 1974): 42
3247	Mankato, Minnesota, *Bethany Lutheran College*	*Music* 8 (October 1974): 42
3256	Waterloo, Ontario, *Wilfrid Laurier University*	*Music* 9 (April 1975): 8
3258	Sioux Center, Iowa, *Dordt College*	*Music* 8 (October 1974): 42
3259	Montréal, Québec, *McGill University*	*Music* 8 (October 1974): 42
3265	Rochester, Michigan, *Oakland University*	*Music* 9 (October 1975): 12 *The Tracker* 21 (Fall 1976): 13

Opus	Location	Source
3328	Ottawa, Ontario, *Saint Peter's Lutheran Church*	*The American Organist* 17 (May 1983): 68
3340	St. Louis, Missouri, *Fergusson Presbyterian Church*	*The Diapason* 69 (December 1977): 20
3358	Edmonton, Alberta, *University of Alberta*	*The Diapason* 70 (December 1978): 14
3360	Sioux Center, Iowa, *Dordt College*	*The Diapason* 70 (November 1979): 1 Ringerwole, "The Dedicatory Organ Recital at Dordt College"
3363	Mabel, Minnesota, *First Lutheran Church*	*The Diapason* 70 (December 1979): 16
3364	Princeton, New Jersey, *Trinity Church*	*Music* 12 (October 1978): 44-45
3386	Kalamazoo, Michigan, *Zion Lutheran Church*	*The Diapason* 71 (September 1980): 20

BRUNZEMA ORGANS, INC.

Opus	Location	Source
	(various) Kisten Orgel	Cramer, 49 *The Diapason* 75 (January 1984): 14
5	Pella, Iowa, *Central College*	*The American Organist* 16 (October 1982): 65 *The Diapason* 73 (October 1982): 14
10	Winnipeg, Manitoba, *Saint James Lutheran Church*	*The Diapason* 73 (November 1982): 3
11	Edmonton, Alberta, *University of Alberta*	*The American Organist* 17 (June 1983): 47 *The Diapason* 74 (February 1983): 11

Opus	Location	Source
12	Kitchener, Ontario, *Blessed Sacrament Parish*	*The American Organist* 18 (March 1984): 54 Cramer, 47 *The Diapason* 75 (January 1984): 12 Overduin, 128
13	Wolfville, Nova Scotia, *Saint Andrew's United Church*	*The American Organist* 19 (January 1985): 52 *The Diapason* 75 (February 1984): 11
22	Brussels, Belgium, *Michel Roy residence*	*The Diapason* 83 (August 1992): 12
23	Fergus, Ontario, *Residence organ*	*The Diapason* 83 (August 1992): 12
24	Akron, Ohio, *Hans Zbinden residence*	*The American Organist* 19 (November 1985): 88 Cramer, 47 *The Diapason* 76 (November 1985): 1
25	Glace Bay, Nova Scotia, *Saint Anne's Church*	*The American Organist* 21 (April 1987): 85 Cramer, 48 *The Diapason* 77 (November 1986): 13
26	West Hartford, Connecticut, *Edward Wagner residence*	*The American Organist* 22 (June 1988): 60 Cramer, 48 *The Diapason* 79 (June 1988): 14
28	Charlotte, North Carolina, *Saint John's Episcopal Church*	*The American Organist* 24 (February 1990): 78 *The Diapason* 80 (June 1989): 11

Opus	Location	Source
29	New York, New York, *William Humphries residence*	*The American Organist* 22 (August 1988): 53 *The Diapason* 79 (November 1988): 11

Appendix F

Videography

"Castles of the Soul: The Pipe Organs of Gerhard Brunzema." Kitchener, Ontario, Canada: A Rogers Community 20 Production, 1991. 30 minutes. Available from Rogers Community 20, 85 Grand Crest Place, Kitchener, Ontario, Canada, N2G 4A8.

This features interviews with Gerhard Brunzema, his family, and people who knew him; the transcript of these interviews is included in this book. It shows the work done on Brunzema Organs' Opus 12 during the Brustwerk addition. Performances are given on Opus 12 and on two Kisten Orgeln.

"In Search of Bach. The Bach Aria Group at Stony Brook." Stony Brook, New York: The Bach Aria Group Association, Inc., 1983. 60 minutes. Available from The Bach Aria Group Association, Inc., P.O. Box 977, Stony Brook, New York, 11790.

This presents the Bach Aria Festival and Institute, which is held every summer at the State University of New York at Stony Brook (Long Island). It includes rehearsals and concerts performed by the Bach Aria Group and the 40 fellows of the Festival, as well as discussions with the musicians. The continuo organ used is Casavant Frères' Opus 3397 from 1978, designed by Gerhard Brunzema.

Appendix G

The Organs by Location

The following list is organized alphabetically by country. In the third column, the number of manual keyboards and the number of stops are listed. A "P" signifies an independent pedal division, a "p" signifies a "pulldown" pedal (except for Casavant organs: the type of pedal is not differentiated on their master list). The following abbreviations are used for organ type:

   i   = interim organ
   KO = Kisten Orgel ("Box" organ)
   KP = Kneipositiv ("Knee" positive)
   Pos = Positive organ
   R   = Regal
   TO = Truhenorgel ("Cabinet" organ)

The fourth column lists the year, workshop, and opus number. The following abbreviations are used for the workshops:

   AB = Ahrend & Brunzema: new organs only, 1954–1971
   C   = Casavant Frères: mechanical-action organs only, 1973–1981
   B   = Brunzema Organs: all organs, 1980–1992

Note: Small organs are subject to relocation.

AUSTRALIA

Adelaide	University of Adelaide	III/36	1978 C.3405
Melbourne	Victoria Arts Centre	IV/60	1980 C.3434

295

AUSTRIA

| Vienna | Concentus Musicus | I/1 KP | 1959 AB.17 |
| Vienna | Concentus Musicus | I/1 R | 1968 AB.54 |

BELGIUM

| Brussels | Residence organ | I/1 | 1985 B.22 |

CANADA

Alberta

Edmonton	University of Alberta	III/36	1978 C.3358
Edmonton	University of Alberta	I/4	1977 C.3375
Edmonton	Carol Otto residence	II/7	1978 C.3400
Edmonton	Karl Heinz Rose residence	II/7	1979 C.3429
Edmonton	University of Alberta	II/P/6	1982 B.11

Manitoba

| Winnipeg | Saint James Lutheran Church | I/P/10 | 1982 B.10 |
| Winnipeg | Peter Letkemann | I/4 KO | 1989 B.36 |

New Brunswick

| Edmundston | Cathédrale de la Immaculée Conception | I/7 | 1979 C.3441 |
| Sackville | Mount Allison University | I/4 | 1978 C.3398 |

Newfoundland

| Saint John's | Memorial University | II/7 | 1977 C.3351 |

Nova Scotia

Glace Bay	Saint Anne's Church	II/P/22	1986 B.25
Sydney	Westminster		
	Presbyterian Church	I/6	1975 C.3291
Wolfville	Saint Andrew's		
	United Church	I/P/11	1983 B.13

Ontario

Brantford	Mohawk Chapel	I/4 KO	1986 B.20
Fergus	Residence organ	I/4	1985 B.23
Fergus	Brunzema family	I/4 KO	1992 B.41
Guelph	University of	I/4 KO	1981 B.4
	Guelph		
Hamilton	McMaster University	II/7	1975 C.3286
Kingston	Queen's University	II/16	1974 C.3223
Kitchener	Saint Peter's	I/3	1981 B.2
	Lutheran Church		
Kitchener	Blessed Sacrament	II/P/13	1983/1991 B.12
	Parish		
London	First Saint Andrew's	II/7	1974 C.3235
	United Church		
London	University of	I/4 KO	1991 B.39
	Western Ontario		
Ottawa	Saint Peter's	II/15	1976 C.3328
	Lutheran Church		
Ottawa	Karen Holmes	I/4 KO	1989 B.35
St. Catharines	Brock University	I/4	1976 C.3305
Toronto	University of	II/25	1973 C.3185
	Toronto		
Toronto	Festival Singers	I/4	1977 C.3346
	of Canada		
Toronto	Holy Family Church	II/P/20	1987 B.27
Toronto	Chinese Methodist	I/4 KO	1987 B.31
	Church		
Waterloo	Wilfrid Laurier	II/14	1975 C.3256
	University		
Waterloo	Conrad Graebel	I/4 KO	1982 B.6
	Institute		

Waterloo	Saint John's Lutheran Church	I/4 KO	1982 B.7
Waterloo	Wilfrid Laurier University	I/4 KO	1984 B.15

Québec

Mistassini	Les Pères Trappistes	I/4	1980 C.3426
Montréal	McGill University	II/7	1974 C.3259
Montréal	Saint John's Estonian Lutheran Church	II/8	1976 C.3315
Montréal	McGill University	I/3	1980 B.1
Québec	Conservatoire de Musique	II/19	1974 C.3210
Trois-Rivières	Conservatoire de Musique	II/7	1979 C.3478

Saskatchewan

Regina	Luther College	I/4 KO	1982 B.9

GERMANY

Aurich	St. Lamberti	I/4 Pos, i	1956 AB.8
Aurich	St. Lamberti	II/P/25	1961 AB.27
Bielefeld	Daniel Brunzema	I/4 KO	1992 B.40
Bösperde	Evangelische Kirche	II/P/9	1966 AB.46
Bremen	St. Martini	III/P/33	1962 AB.30
Bremen	St. Martini	I/4 TO	1969 AB.60
Bremen	St. Martini	I/1 R	1969 AB.61
Bremen-Farge	Reformierte Kirche	II/P/11	1958 AB.11
Bremen-Oberneuland	Evangelische Kirche	II/P/22	1966 AB.45
Bremerhaven	Reformierte Kirche	I/6	1967 AB.50
Castrop-Rauxel	Kirche Schwerin-Frolinde	III/P/27	1967 AB.49
Emden	Schweizer Kirche	II/p/11	1962 AB.31

Ennepetal-Milspe	Evangelische Kirche	I/4 Pos	1958 AB.12
Frankfurt/Main	Cantate Domino	III/P/32	1970 AB.68
Freren	Reformierte Kirche	I/p/8	1960 AB.23
Gildehaus	Reformierte Kirche	II/P/15	1965 AB.39
Grimersum	Reformierte Kirche	I/4 Pos, i	1958 AB.14
Grimersum	Reformierte Kirche	I/p/8	1958 AB.15
Gütersloh	Evangeliumskirche	II/P/20	1968 AB.57
Hamburg-Altona	Reformierte Kirche	II/P/13	1969 AB.62
Hatzum	Reformierte Kirche	I/p/7	1964 AB.35
Hinte	Reformierte Kirche	I/p/8	1958 AB.16
Hohenlimburg	Reformierte Friedhofskapelle	I/3 Pos	1955 AB.3
Iserlohn	Gemeindehaus *In der Grüne*	I/4 Pos	1956 AB.6
Leer	Kirchsaal Hohe Ellern	I/5	1962 AB.28
Leer-Bingum	St. Matthäi	II/P/13	1969 AB.59
Leer-Heisfelde	Reformierte Kirche	I/4 Pos	1958 AB.13
Leer-Loga	Friedenskirche	II/P/13	1964 AB.36
Leer-Loga	Reformierte Kirche	I/P/9	1969 AB.63
Minden	Altsprachliches Gymnasium	II/P/9	1956 AB.5
Munich	Studio für frühe Musik	I/1 KP	1963 AB.33
Münster	Landesverband der Mission	I/3 Pos	1956 AB.7
Uelsen	Reformierte Kirche	II/P/20	1970 AB.69
Veldhausen	Altreformierte Kirche	I/p/6	1957 AB.10
Westerstede	St. Peter	II/P/23	1971 AB.72
Wybelsum	Reformierte Kirche	I/p/6	1965 AB.38

GREAT BRITAIN

Bath, Somerset	Residence	I/1 KP	1959 AB.21

JAPAN

Gifu City	Holy Spirit Church	II/10	1979 C.3420
Kobe	Kobe College of Music	II/7	1978 C.3399
Kobe	Kobe Women's College	II/7	1978 C.3401
Kumamoto	Junior College of Music	II/4	1979 C.3417
Kyoto	Doshisha Women's College	III/36	1980 C.3456
Nagaro	Nagaro Prefecture's Cultural Hall	II/7	1979 C.3427
Nagoya	Kinjo Gakuin Church	II/19	1980 C.3457
Nagoya	Nagoya Takasagoden	I/5	1979 C.3469
Nishinomiya	Kwansei Gakuin University	II/9	1979 C.3450
Osaka	Soai College	II/7	1979 C.3428
Osaka	Pool College	II/8	1979 C.3439
Setagaya	Holy Ecclesia of Jesus	II/10	1979 C.3419
Takamatsu	Takamatsu Church	I/5	1979 C.3470
Tokyo	Nippon Gakki Company	II/4	1979 C.3472
Toyohashi	Toyohashi Takasagoden	I/5	1979 C.3468
Urawa	Kita-Urawa Catholic Church	II/4	1979 C.3471

NETHERLANDS

Aalten	Gereformeerd Zuiderkerk	II/P/16	1968 AB.51
Amsterdam	Oude Kerk	II/P/17	1965 AB.41
Amsterdam	Private residence	I/1 KP	1968 AB.55
Bant	Hervormde Kerk	I/4 Pos	1959 AB.19
Bath, Zeeland	Hervormde Kerk	I/4 Pos	1960 AB.24
Espel	Hervormde Kerk	I/p/7	1962 AB.29

Groningen	Gereformeerd Kerk	I/6	1960 AB.22
Groningen	Magnaliakerk	II/p/13	1965 AB.40
Haarlem	Doopsgezinde Kerk	III/P/24	1968 AB.58
The Hague	Johanneskapel	II/P/14	1965 AB.42
Rutten	Hervormde Kerk	I/4 Pos	1959 AB.20
Scheveningen	Zorgvlietkerk	III/P/26	1959 AB.18
Wassenaar	Kievitkerk	II/P/21	1963 AB.34

PHILIPPINES

| Manila | Chapel | I/4 KO | 1985 B.17 |

SOUTH KOREA

| Seoul | Dong Presbyterian Church | II/P/16 | 1990 B.38 |

UNITED STATES

California

Berkeley	University of California	I/4 TO	1968 AB.52
Berkeley	University of California	I/1 R	1968 AB.53
Berkeley	University of California	I/1 KP	1968 AB.56
Berkeley	University of California	II/P/12	1975 AB.87
Los Altos	Saint Nicholas Church	I/7	1980 C.3475
Los Angeles	Residence organ	II/P/11	1967 AB.48

Colorado

| Boulder | First Presbyterian Church | III/31 | 1978 C.3372 |
| Denver | Saint John's Catholic Church | I/4 | 1976 C.3298 |

Connecticut

New Haven	Yale University	II/7	1974 C.3238
West Hartford	Edward Wagner residence	I/p/5	1986 B.26
Weston	Norfield Congregational Church	II/12	1973 C.3205

Illinois

Carlinville	Zion Lutheran Church	I/7	1978 C.3373
Champaign	Grace Lutheran Church	II/16	1975 C.3246
Evanston	Saint Matthew's Episcopal Church	II/25	1977 C.3354
LaGrange	First Presbyterian Church	I/4 KO	1981 B.3
Moline	Trinity Lutheran Church	III/32	1973 C.3200
Rockford	Our Savior's Lutheran Church	II/15	1975 C.3245
Rockford	Ronald Burmeister residence	II/7	1975 C.3295
Rockford	Our Savior's Lutheran Church	I/4	1979 C.3423
Rock Island	Augustana College	I/4	1976 C.3242
Springfield	Our Savior's Lutheran Church	II/8	1976 C.3297
Springfield	First Presbyterian Church	I/4 KO	1990 B.37

Indiana

Bloomington	Indiana University	I/4 KO	1985 B.19
Evansville	First Presbyterian Church	I/4 KO	1987 B.32

Iowa

Cedar Falls	University of Northern Iowa	II/7	1978 C.3403

Cedar Rapids	Saint Mark's Lutheran Church	II/13	1975 C.3262
Davenport	Saint Ambrose College	I/5	1977 C.3385
Decorah	First Lutheran Church	II/25	1973 C.3190
Decorah	Good Shepherd Lutheran Church	I/4	1974 C.3333
Iowa City	Sven Hansell residence	I/4	1976 C.3299
Iowa City	Our Redeemer Lutheran Church	II/8	1976 C.3327
Newton	United Presbyterian Church	II/17	1975 C.3241
Pella	Central College	II/P/18	1982 B.5
Pella	Central College	I/4 KO	1982 B.8
Sioux Center	Dordt College	II/7	1974 C.3258
Sioux Center	Dordt College	III/37	1978 C.3360

Kansas

Lawrence	University of Kansas	II/7	1975 C.3296

Maine

Falmouth	Church of Saint Mary the Virgin	II/20	1978 C.3384

Michigan

Ann Arbor	Marilyn Mason	I/4 KO	1988 B.33
Kalamazoo	Zion Lutheran Church	III/31	1978 C.3386
Rochester	Oakland University	II/21	1975 C.3265

Minnesota

Bloomington	Lutheran Church of the Redemption	II/9	1980 C.3479
Mabel	First Lutheran Church	II/10	1977 C.3363

Mankato	Bethany Lutheran College	II/7	1974 C.3247
St. Paul	Blessed Virgin Church	II/18	1976 C.3302
St. Paul	College of Saint Thomas	II/7	1978 C.3402

Missouri

St. Louis	Fergusson Presbyterian Church	II/17	1977 C.3340

Nebraska

Omaha	Saints Peter and Paul Church	II/16	1977 C.3335
Wayne	Grace Lutheran Church	III/30	1979 C.3406

New Hampshire

North Conway	Christ Church	II/12	1978 C.3388

New Jersey

Bay Head	All Saints Episcopal Church	II/13	1974 C.3214
Princeton	Trinity Church	IV/42	1978 C.3364
Princeton	Westminster Choir College	I/4	1978 C.3377
Princeton	Trinity Church	I/4	1978 C.3395
Princeton	Susan Grainger residence	II/7	1979 C.3430

New York

New York	Community of the Holy Spirit	II/7	1974 C.3191
New York	Church of Saint Luke in the Fields	I/4	1981 C.3376
New York	Church of Saint Luke in the Fields	II/23	1979 C.3412

New York	William Humphries residence	II/p/8½	1987 B.29
Stony Brook	State University of New York	I/4	1978 C.3397

North Carolina

Charlotte	Central Steele Creek Presbyterian	II/17	1980 C.3422
Charlotte	Saint John's Episcopal Church	II/P/25	1988 B.28
Raleigh	Brock Downward residence	II/4	1978 C.3390

Ohio

Akron	Hans Zbinden residence	II/p/8½	1985 B.24
Bowling Green	State University	II/7	1979 C.3438
Solon	George Hoffman residence	II/P/9½	1987 B.30

Pennsylvania

Annville	Lebanon Valley College	I/4 KO	1985 B.18
Bethlehem	Bach Choir	I/4 KO	1987 B.21
Bryn Mawr	Bryn Mawr Presbyterian Church	I/4 KO	1989 B.34
Philadelphia	Michael Korn residence	I/4	1985 C.3425
Scranton	Saint Peter's Cathedral	III/37	1979 C.3414
White Marsh	Saint Thomas Episcopal Church	I/4	1978 C.3396
Wyoming	Saint Joseph's Church	II/11	1979 C.3436

South Carolina

Columbia	Columbia College	III/22	1981 C.3460

Tennessee

| Nashville | First Presbyterian Church | I/4 | 1980 C.3424 |
| Sewanee | School of Theology | I/4 KO | 1984 B.16 |

Texas

| San Antonio | Saint Luke's Episcopal Church | I/4 KO | 1983 B.14 |

Utah

Provo	Brigham Young University	I/6	1979 C.3459
Salt Lake City	Westminster College	I/4	1977 C.3345
Salt Lake City	Church of Jesus Christ of Latter-Day Saints	II/8	1979 C.3437

Vermont

| Burlington | Cathedral of the Immaculate Conception | II/10 | 1977 C.3361 |

Virginia

| Williamsburg | Presbyterian Church | II/17 | 1975 C.3275 |

Washington

| Kenmore | Saint John Vianney Church | I/6 | 1978 C.3370 |

Wisconsin

Kenosha	Carthage College	II/8	1974 C.3233
Kenosha	Carthage College	IV/41	1975 C.3276
Madison	University of Wisconsin	I/4	1977 C.3347
Menomonie	Our Savior's Lutheran Church	II/18	1980 C.3433

| Milwaukee | Fox Point Evangelical Lutheran Church | II/15 | 1976 C.3306 |
| Stoughton | Covenant Lutheran Church | II/9 | 1980 C.3462 |

Wyoming

| Casper | First United Methodist Church | III/30 | 1976 C.3316 |

Appendix H

The Organs by Size

This list is organized by the number of manual keyboards and stops. Organs of the same size are listed in order of opus number. In the first column, the abbreviations used for countries, states, and provinces are:

A	=	Austria
AA	=	Australia
B	=	Belgium
G	=	Germany
GB	=	Great Britain
J	=	Japan
NL	=	Netherlands
PH	=	Philippines
SoK	=	South Korea

Canada

AB	=	Alberta
MB	=	Manitoba
NB	=	New Brunswick
NF	=	Newfoundland
NS	=	Nova Scotia
ON	=	Ontario
PQ	=	Québec
SK	=	Saskatchewan

United States

CA	=	California	MI	=	Michigan
CO	=	Colorado	MN	=	Minnesota
CT	=	Connecticut	MO	=	Missouri
IL	=	Illinois	NE	=	Nebraska
IN	=	Indiana	NH	=	New Hampshire
IA	=	Iowa	NJ	=	New Jersey
KS	=	Kansas	NY	=	New York
ME	=	Maine	NC	=	North Carolina

OH	=	Ohio	VT	=	Vermont
PA	=	Pennsylvania	VA	=	Virginia
TN	=	Tennessee	WA	=	Washington
TX	=	Texas	WI	=	Wisconsin
UT	=	Utah	WY	=	Wyoming

In the third column, the following abbreviations are used:

i	=	interim organ
KO	=	Kisten Orgel ("Box" organ)
KP	=	Kniepositiv ("Knee" positive)
p	=	"pulldown" pedal
Pos	=	Positive organ
R	=	Regal
TO	=	Truhenorgel ("Cabinet" organ)

The fourth column lists the year, workshop, and opus number.
The following abbreviations are used for the workshops:

AB	=	Ahrend & Brunzema: new organs only, 1954–1971
C	=	Casavant Frères: mechanical-action organs only, 1973–1981
B	=	Brunzema Organs: all organs, 1980–1992

I/1

Vienna A	Concentus Musicus	KP	1959 AB.17
Bath, Somerset GB	Residence	KP	1959 AB.21
Munich G	Studio für frühe Musik	KP	1963 AB.33
Berkeley CA	University of California	R	1968 AB.53
Vienna A	Concentus Musicus	R	1968 AB.54
Amsterdam NL	Private residence	KP	1968 AB.55
Berkeley CA	University of California	KP	1968 AB.56
Bremen G	St. Martini	R	1969 AB.61
Brussels B	Residence organ		1985 B.22

I/3

Hohenlimburg G	Reformierte Friedhofskapelle		1955 AB.3
Münster G	Landesverband der Mission	Pos	1956 AB.7

| Montréal PQ | McGill University | | 1980 B.1 |
| Kitchener ON | Saint Peter's Lutheran Church | | 1981 B.2 |

1/4

Iserlohn G	Gemeindehaus In der Grüne	Pos	1956 AB.6
Aurich G	St. Lamberti	Pos, i	1956 AB.8
Ennepetal-Milspe G	Evangelische Kirche	Pos	1958 AB.12
Leer-Heisfelde G	Reformierte Kirche	Pos	1958 AB.13
Grimersum G	Reformierte Kirche	Pos, i	1958 AB.14
Bant NL	Hervormde Kerk	Pos	1959 AB.19
RuttenN	Hervormde Kerk	Pos	1959 AB.20
Bath, Zeeland NL	Hervormde Kerk	Pos	1960 AB.24
Berkeley CA	University of California	TO	1968 AB.52
Bremen G	St. Martini	TO	1969 AB.60
Rock Island IL	Augustana College		1976 C.3242
Denver CO	Saint John's Catholic Church		1976 C.3298
Iowa City IA	Sven Hansell residence		1976 C.3299
St. Catharines ON	Brock University		1976 C.3305
Decorah IA	Good Shepherd Lutheran Church		1974 C.3333
Salt Lake City UT	Westminster College		1977 C.3345
Toronto ON	Festival Singers of Canada		1977 C.3346
Madison WI	University of Wisconsin		1977 C.3347
Edmonton AB	University of Alberta		1977 C.3375
New York NY	Church of Saint Luke in the Fields		1981 C.3376
Princeton NJ	Westminster Choir College		1978 C.3377
Princeton NJ	Trinity Church		1978 C.3395
White Marsh PA	Saint Thomas Episcopal Church		1978 C.3396
Stony Brook NY	State University of New York		1978 C.3397
Sackville NB	Mount Allison University		1978 C.3398
Rockford IL	Our Savior's Lutheran Church		1979 C.3423

Nashville TN	First Presbyterian Church		1980 C.3424
Philadelphia PA	Michael Korn residence		1985 C.3425
Mistassini PQ	Les Pères Trappistes		1980 C.3426
LaGrange IL	First Presbyterian Church	KO	1981 B.3
Guelph ON	University of Guelph	KO	1981 B.4
Waterloo ON	Conrad Graebel Institute	KO	1982 B.6
Waterloo ON	Saint John's Lutheran Church	KO	1982 B.7
Pella IA	Central College	KO	1982 B.8
Regina SK	Luther College	KO	1982 B.9
San Antonio TX	Saint Luke's Episcopal Church	KO	1983 B.14
Waterloo ON	Wilfrid Laurier University	KO	1984 B.15
Sewanee TN	School of Theology	KO	1984 B.16
Manila PH	Chapel	KO	1985 B.17
Annville PA	Lebanon Valley College	KO	1985 B.18
Bloomington IN	Indiana University	KO	1985 B.19
Brantford ON	Mohawk Chapel	KO	1986 B.20
Bethlehem PA	Bach Choir	KO	1987 B.21
Fergus ON	Residence organ		1985 B.23
Toronto ON	Chinese Methodist Church	KO	1987 B.31
Evansville IN	First Presbyterian Church	KO	1987 B.32
Ann Arbor MI	Marilyn Mason	KO	1988 B.33
Bryn Mawr PA	Bryn Mawr Presbyterian Church	KO	1989 B.34
Ottawa ON	Karen Holmes	KO	1989 B.35
Winnipeg MB	Peter Letkemann	KO	1989 B.36
Springfield IL	First Presbyterian Church	KO	1990 B.37
London ON	University of Western Ontario	KO	1991 B.39
Bielefeld G	Daniel Brunzema	KO	1992 B.40
Fergus ON	Brunzema family	KO	1992 B.41

I/5

Leer G	Kirchsaal Hohe Ellern		1962 AB.28
Davenport IA	Saint Ambrose College		1977 C.3385

Toyohashi J	Toyohashi Takasagoden		1979 C.3468
Nagoya J	Nagoya Takasagoden		1979 C.3469
Takamatsu J	Takamatsu Church		1979 C.3470
West Hartford CT	Edward Wagner residence	p	1986 B.26

I/6

Veldhausen G	Altreformierte Kirche	p	1957 AB.10
Groningen NL	Gereformeerd Kerk		1960 AB.22
Wybelsum G	Reformierte Kirche	p	1965 AB.38
Bremerhaven G	Reformierte Kirche		1967 AB.50
Sydney NS	Westminster Presbyterian Church		1975 C.3291
Kenmore WA	Saint John Vianney Church		1978 C.3370
Provo UT	Brigham Young University		1979 C.3459

I/7

Espel NL	Hervormde Kerk	p	1962 AB.29
Hatzum G	Reformierte Kirche	p	1964 AB.35
Carlinville IL	Zion Lutheran Church		1978 C.3373
Edmundston NB	Cathédrale de la Immaculée Conception		1979 C.3441
Los Altos CA	Saint Nicholas Church		1980 C.3475

I/8

Grimersum G	Reformierte Kirche	p	1958 AB.15
Hinte G	Reformierte Kirche	p	1958 AB.16
Freren G	Reformierte Kirche	p	1960 AB.23

I/9

Leer-Loga G	Reformierte Kirche		1969 AB.63

I/10

Winnipeg MB	Saint James Lutheran Church		1982 B.10

I/11

| Wolfville NS | Saint Andrew's United Church | 1983 B.13 |

II/4

Raleigh NC	Brock Downward residence	1978 C.3390
Kumamoto J	Junior College of Music	1979 C.3417
Urawa J	Kita-Urawa Catholic Church	1979 C.3471
Tokyo J	Nippon Gakki Company	1979 C.3472

II/6

| Edmonton AB | University of Alberta | 1982 B.11 |

II/7

New York NY	Community of the Holy Spirit	1973 C.3191
London ON	First Saint Andrew's United Church	1974 C.3235
New Haven CT	Yale University	1974 C.3238
Mankato MN	Bethany Lutheran College	1974 C.3247
Sioux Center IA	Dordt College	1974 C.3258
Montréal PQ	McGill University	1974 C.3259
Hamilton ON	McMaster University	1975 C.3286
Rockford IL	Ronald Burmeister residence	1975 C.3295
Lawrence KS	University of Kansas	1975 C.3296
Saint John's NF	Memorial University	1977 C.3351
Kobe J	Kobe College of Music	1978 C.3399
Edmonton AB	Carol Otto residence	1978 C.3400
Kobe J	Kobe Women's College	1978 C.3401
St. Paul MN	College of Saint Thomas	1978 C.3402
Cedar Falls IA	University of Northern Iowa	1978 C.3403
Nagaro J	Nagaro Prefecture's Cultural Hall	1979 C.3427

Osaka J	Soai College	1979 C.3428
Edmonton AB	Karl Heinz Rose residence	1979 C.3429
Princeton NJ	Susan Grainger residence	1979 C.3430
Bowling Green OH	State University	1979 C.3438
Trois-Rivières PQ	Conservatoire de Musique	1979 C.3478

II/8

Kenosha WI	Carthage College	1974 C.3233
Springfield IL	Our Savior's Lutheran Church	1976 C.3297
Montréal PQ	Saint John's Estonian Lutheran Church	1976 C.3315
Iowa City IA	Our Redeemer Lutheran Church	1976 C.3327
Salt Lake City UT	Church of Jesus Christ of Latter-Day Saints	1979 C.3437
Osaka J	Pool College	1979 C.3439

II/8½

| Akron OH | Hans Zbinden residence p | 1985 B.24 |
| New York NY | William Humphries residence p | 1987 B.29 |

II/9

Minden G	Altsprachliches Gymnasium	1956 AB.5
Bösperde G	Evangelische Kirche	1966 AB.46
Nishinomiya J	Kwansei Gakuin University	1979 C.3450
Stoughton WI	Covenant Lutheran Church	1980 C.3462
Bloomington MN	Lutheran Church of the Redemption	1980 C.3479

II/9½

| Solon OH | George Hoffman residence | 1987 B.30 |

II/10

Burlington VT	Cathedral,	1977 C.3361
	Immaculate Conception	
Mabel MN	First Lutheran Church	1977 C.3363
Setagaya J	Holy Ecclesia of Jesus	1979 C.3419
Gifu City J	Holy Spirit Church	1979 C.3420

II/11

Bremen-Farge G	Reformierte Kirche	1958 AB.11
Emden G	Schweizer Kirche	1962 AB.31
Los Angeles CA	Residence organ	1967 AB.48
Wyoming PA	Saint Joseph's Church	1979 C.3436

II/12

Berkeley CA	University of California	1975 AB.87
Weston CT	Norfield	1973 C.3205
	Congregational Church	
North Conway NH	Christ Church	1978 C.3388

II/13

Leer-Loga G	Friedenskirche		1964 AB.36
Groningen NL	Magnaliakerk	p	1965 AB.40
Leer-Bingum G	St. Matthäi		1969 AB.59
Hamburg-Altona G	Reformierte Kirche		1969 AB.62
Bay Head NJ	All Saints		1974 C.3214
	Episcopal Church		
Cedar Rapids IA	Saint Mark's		1975 C.3262
	Lutheran Church		
Kitchener ON	Blessed Sacrament		1983/1991
	Parish		B.12

II/14

The Hague NL	Johanneskapel	1965 AB.42
Waterloo ON	Wilfrid Laurier University	1975 C.3256

II/15

Gildehaus G	Reformierte Kirche	1965 AB.39

Rockford IL	Our Savior's Lutheran Church	1975 C.3245
Milwaukee WI	Fox Point Evangelical Lutheran Church	1976 C.3306
Ottawa ON	Saint Peter's Lutheran Church	1976 C.3328

II/16

Aalten NL	Gereformeerd Zuiderkerk	1968 AB.51
Kingston ON	Queen's University	1974 C.3223
Champaign IL	Grace Lutheran Church	1975 C.3246
Omaha NE	Saints Peter and Paul Church	1977 C.3335
Seoul SoK	Dong Presbyterian Church	1990 B.38

II/17

Amsterdam NL	Oude Kerk	1965 AB.41
Newton IA	United Presbyterian Church	1975 C.3241
Williamsburg VA	Presbyterian Church	1975 C.3275
Saint Louis MO	Fergusson Presbyterian Church	1977 C.3340
Charlotte NC	Central Steele Creek Presbyterian	1980 C.3422

II/18

St. Paul MN	Blessed Virgin Church	1976 C.3302
Menomonie WI	Our Savior's Lutheran Church	1980 C.3433
Pella IA	Central College	1982 B.5

II/19

| Québec PQ | Conservatoire de Musique | 1974 C.3210 |

318   Appendix H

| Nagoya J | Kinjo Gakuin Church | 1980 C.3457 |

II/20

Gütersloh G	Evangeliumskirche	1968 AB.57
Uelsen G	Reformierte Kirche	1970 AB.69
Falmouth ME	Church of Saint Mary the Virgin	1978 C.3384
Toronto ON	Holy Family Church	1987 B.27

II/21

| Wassenaar NL | Kievitkerk | 1963 AB.34 |
| Rochester MI | Oakland University | 1975 C.3265 |

II/22

| Bremen-Oberneuland G | Evangelische Kirche | 1966 AB.45 |
| Glace Bay NS | Saint Anne's Church | 1986 B.25 |

II/23

| Westerstede G | St. Peter | 1971 AB.72 |
| New York NY | Church of Saint Luke in the Fields | 1979 C.3412 |

II/25

Aurich G	St. Lamberti	1961 AB.27
Toronto ON	University of Toronto	1973 C.3185
Decorah IA	First Lutheran Church	1973 C.3190
Evanston IL	Saint Matthew's Episcopal Church	1977 C.3354
Charlotte NC	Saint John's Episcopal Church	1988 B.28

III/22

| Columbia SC | Columbia College | 1981 C.3460 |

III/24

| Haarlem NL | Doopsgezinde Kerk | 1968 AB.58 |

III/26

| Scheveningen NL | Zorgvlietkerk | 1959 AB.18 |

III/27

| Castrop-Rauxel G | Kirche Schwerin-Frolinde | 1967 AB.49 |

III/30

| Casper WY | First United Methodist Church | 1976 C.3316 |
| Wayne NE | Grace Lutheran Church | 1979 C.3406 |

III/31

| Boulder CO | First Presbyterian Church | 1978 C.3372 |
| Kalamazoo MI | Zion Lutheran Church | 1978 C.3386 |

III/32

| Frankfurt/Main G | Cantate Domino | 1970 AB.68 |
| Moline IL | Trinity Lutheran Church | 1973 C.3200 |

III/33

| Bremen G | St. Martini | 1962 AB.30 |

III/36

Edmonton AB	University of Alberta	1978 C.3358
Adelaide AA	University of Adelaide	1978 C.3405
Kyoto J	Doshisha Women's College	1980 C.3456

III/37

Sioux Center IA	Dordt College	1978 C.3360
Scranton PA	Saint Peter's Cathedral	1979 C.3414

IV/41

Kenosha WI	Carthage College	1975 C.3276

IV/42

Princeton NJ	Trinity Church	1978 C.3364

IV/60

Melbourne AA	Victoria Arts Centre	1980 C.3434

Bibliography

Beckerath, Rudolf von. "Designing a Two-Manual Organ." *The Diapason* 54 (September 1963): 14.

Blanton, Joseph Edwin. *The Revival of the Organ Case*. Albany, Texas: Venture Press, 1965.

Brunzema, Gerhard. "The Covering of Organ Pipes with Pure Tin Foil by Using Epoxy Resin Cement." *ISO Information* 1 (February 1969): 55-56.

————. "Unit Organs?" (letter to the editor). *The American Organist* 19 (January 1985): 12.

————. "Karl Schuke: A Tribute." *The Diapason* 78 (November 1987): 2.

Cramer, Craig. "An Interview with Gerhard Brunzema." *The American Organist* 23 (July 1989): 46-49.

————. "Bedient Company Celebrates 20 Years. An Interview." *The American Organist* 24 (April 1990): 75-80.

D'Aigle, Jeanne. *L'Histoire de Casavant Frères, 1880-1980*. Saint-Hyacinthe, Québec: Les Editions D'Aigle, 1988.

"Formation of Brunzema Organs, Inc., Fergus, Ontario." *The Diapason* 71 (January 1980): 2.

"Gerhard Brunzema, 1927-1992." *Journal of American Organbuilding* 7 (June 1992): 16.

"Gerhard Brunzema Appointed Tonal Director of Casavant Frères." *The Diapason* 63 (June 1972): 1.

Gough, Hugh. "Towards a Theory of the Design and Construction of Musical Instruments, with Special Reference to Those of the Past." *The Brussels Museum of Musical Instruments Bulletin* 7 (1977): 72-76.

Hanson, Carroll; Ringerwole, Joan; Donahue, Thomas; and Folkerts, Davis. "In Memoriam Gerhard Brunzema." *The Diapason* 83 (August 1992): 12.

Harris, John. "Organ Builder Takes Skills around World." *The Globe and Mail* (Toronto, Ontario, Canada, January 19, 1981): 25.

Hradetzky, Gerhard. "Organ-Building in Austria." *ISO Information* 10 (November 1973): 691-720.

Hubbard, Frank. "Reconstructing the Harpsichord." In Schott, Howard, ed., *The Historical Harpsichord*, vol. 1. Stuyvesant, New York: Pendragon Press, 1984.

Jongepier, Jan. "Het orgel in de Doopsgezinde kerk te Haarlem." *Het Orgel* 70 (1974): 331-339.

————. "Orgel Doopsgezinde kerk Haarlem verfraaid." *Het Orgel* 84 (1988): 488-490.

————. "Het orgel in de Ev.-luth. Marienkirche te Marienhafe." *Het Orgel* 85 (1989): 203-207.

Krauss, Egon. "The Baldachin Chamber Organ at Schloss Churburg, Schluderns, Italy." *The Organ Yearbook* 2 (1971): 77-79.

Lade, Günter. *40 Jahre Orgelbau Jürgen Ahrend 1954-1994*. Bremen: H. M. Hauschild GmbH, 1994.

Litton, James. "A New Organ in Princeton." *Music* 12 (October 1978): 44-45.

New Organs. Blessed Sacrament Parish, Kitchener, Ontario. *The American Organist* 18 (March 1984): 54; *The Diapason* 75 (January 1984): 12.

————. Carthage College, Kenosha, Wisconsin. *The Diapason* 65 (May 1974): 8; *Music* 10 (June 1976): 3.

————. Central College, Pella, Iowa. *The American Organist* 16 (October 1982): 65; *The Diapason* 73 (October 1982): 14.

————. Dordt College, Sioux Center, Iowa. *The American Organist* 14 (February 1980): 53; *The Diapason* 70 (November 1979): 1, 3.

————. Edward Wagner residence, West Hartford, Connecticut. *The American Organist* 22 (June 1988): 60; *The Diapason* 79 (June 1988): 14.

————. Fergusson Presbyterian Church, Saint Louis, Missouri. *The Diapason* 69 (December 1977): 20.

————. First Lutheran Church, Mabel, Minnesota. *The American Organist* 13 (July 1979): 42; *The Diapason* 70 (December 1979): 16.

————. Grace Lutheran Church, Champaign, Illinois. *The Diapason* 67 (January 1976): 15.

————. Hans Zbinden residence, Akron, Ohio. *The American Organist* 19 (November 1985): 88; *The Diapason* 76 (November 1985): 1, 15.

————. McMaster University, Hamilton, Ontario. *The American Organist* 23 (May 1989): 127.

————. Oakland University, Rochester, Michigan. *Music* 9 (October 1975): 12.

————. Queen's University, Kingston, Ontario. *The Diapason* 66 (December 1974): 9; *Music* 9 (January 1975): 14.

————. Saint Andrew's United Church, Wolfville, Nova Scotia. *The American Organist* 19 (January 1985): 52; *The Diapason* 75 (February 1984): 11.

————. Saint Anne's Church, Glace Bay, Nova Scotia. *The American Organist* 21 (April 1987): 85; *The Diapason* 77 (November 1986): 13.

————. Saint James Lutheran Church, Winnipeg, Manitoba. *The Diapason* 73 (November 1982): 3.

————. Saint John's Episcopal Church, Charlotte, North Carolina. *The American Organist* 24 (February 1990): 78; *The Diapason* 80 (June 1989): 11.

————. Saint Lamberti, Aurich, Germany. *The Diapason* 53 (September 1962): 29.

————. Saint Peter's Cathedral, Scranton, Pennsylvania. *The Diapason* 69 (October 1978): 16.

————. University of Alberta, Edmonton, Alberta (Brunzema Organs). *The American Organist* 17 (June 1983): 47; *The Diapason* 74 (February 1983): 11.

————. University of Alberta, Edmonton, Alberta (Casavant). *The American Organist* 13 (January 1979): 48; *The Diapason* 70 (December 1978): 14.

————. Wilfrid Laurier University, Waterloo, Ontario. *Music* 9 (April 1975): 8.

————. William A. Humphries residence, New York, New York. *The American Organist* 22 (August 1988): 53; *The Diapason* 79 (November 1988): 11.

————. Zion Lutheran Church, Kalamazoo, Michigan. *The Diapason* 71 (September 1980): 20.

————. Zorgvlietkerk, Scheveningen, Netherlands. *The Diapason* 53 (February 1962): 35.

Noack, Fritz. "Jürgen Ahrend: An Appreciation." In Wallmann, James L., and Moe, Lawrence H., eds., *Jürgen Ahrend, Organbuilder: Celebrating Forty Years of His Career (1954-1994).* Oakland, California: The American Organ Academy, 1995.

Nunc Dimittis. *The Diapason* 83 (June 1992): 4.

Obituaries. *The American Organist* 26 (October 1992): 54.

Os, J. F. van. "Het orgel in de Gereformeerd Zuiderkerk te Aalten." *Het Orgel* 70 (1974): 329-331.

Overduin, Jan. "Brunzema Organs, Incorporated." *The Organ Yearbook* 15 (1984): 124-29.

Pape, Uwe. "Jürgen Ahrend and Gerhard Brunzema." Translated by Peter Williams. *The Organ Yearbook* 3 (1972): 24-35.

————. *The Tracker Organ Revival in America,* Berlin: Pape Verlag, 1978.

Redsell, Matthew James. "Gerhard Brunzema: Instrument Builder and Businessman." *Continuo* 5 (July/August 1982): 9-13.

Reed, Douglas. "An Interview with Harald Vogel." *The Diapason* 77 (March 1986): 10-13.

Royal Canadian College of Organists National Convention. *The American Organist* 17 (May 1983): 68.

Salmen, Walter. *Orgel und Orgelspiel im 16. Jahrhundert.* Innsbruck: Edition Helbling, 1978.

Visser, Piet. "Organs in Amsterdam." *The Organ Yearbook* 1 (1970): 54-63.

Waters, Laraine. "An Interview with Lynn A. Dobson." *The American Organist* 18 (January 1984): 42-43.

"Who's Who." *ISO Information* 4 (October 1970): 273.

Williams, Peter. "Apropos New Organs and Restorations." *The Organ Yearbook* 5 (1974): 111-114.

———. *The European Organ, 1450-1850.* London: Batsford, 1966. Reprint. Bloomington: Indiana University Press, 1978.

Williams, Peter, and Owen, Barbara. *The Organ.* The New Grove® Musical Instrument Series. New York: W. W. Norton, 1988.

Worden, William. "Casavant at Oakland University." *The Tracker* 21 (Fall 1976): 13.

Index

About the Editor

Thomas Donahue received the D.D.S. degree from the State University of New York at Buffalo in 1979. He studied piano and organ with Frank Newcomb, organ with George Damp (Ithaca College), organ and harpsichord with Anthony Newman (SUNY Purchase), and harpsichord with Joyce Lindorff (Cornell University). While at one time a church organist, he now concentrates on continuo playing, composing, and arranging. His articles have appeared in both music periodicals and dental journals. He is the author of *The Modern Classical Organ: A Guide to Its Physical and Musical Structure and Performance Implications.* His companion recording to the current work is entitled "Brunzema in Ontario," released by Calcante Recordings. When not performing and writing, he enjoys woodworking, particularly making harpsichords and pipe organs. He lives in New York State with his wife, Jane, and his two daughters, Carolyn and Katie.

ML 424 .B84 G47 1998

Gerhard Brunzema

DATE DUE
